A GOOD BOY

OUTLIVING THE LEGION OF CHRIST

KEVIN O'SULLIVAN

ATELIER BOOKS

ISBN 978-0-6454879–0-9

❀ Created with Vellum

For Ella and Billy

CONTENTS

A NOTE ON TITLES AND NAMES

Catholic priests are usually given the honorific title *Father* as an acknowledgement of their caring role. I have declined to use this style for any of the Legionary priests in this work. From my experience, none of the people I mention does honour to the title and I refer to them by their names only. I use the title *Brother* when referring to the people with whom I shared my religious life. Most of these men were striving to live good lives and be of service to others. They remain my brothers, whether they think so or not.

Where the involvement of my friends in this book is entirely benign, I have used their full names. Where there is a possibility that someone might be embarrassed by being mentioned I have altered their name or used a first name only. I have not altered the name of any Legionary priest.

JUST BEFORE WE START

You were made and set here to give voice to this, your own
astonishment
Annie Dillard, *A Writer in the World*

y clansman, Muiris O'Súilleabháin, wrote a gem of
a book in 1933 called *Fiche Blian ag Fás* or *Twenty
Years a Growing* in its English translation. In it he tells many stories
within the arc of two narratives. One narrative describes the latter
days of the Irish-speaking islanders on Great Blasket Island as the
population diminished, as families moved to the mainland, and
sons and daughters went to America. The last O'Sullivan family
left the island in January 1954, when I was not quite eighteen
months old and living two hundred miles up the road, in Dublin.
The other strand of the book is a personal tale of Maurice's own
growing up, the first stage of his life according to a saying of his
father about the shape of a life. We spend, said his father, *Twenty
years a growing, twenty years in bloom, twenty years a stooping, and*

1

twenty years in decline. As I wrote the present memoir, I realised that I was writing an account of my own *years a growing*, in my case not twenty, but twenty-five. This was not the original purpose of the book, which was to write an account of the life of my mother, to whom I was very attached, not by way of affection, but rather as a dutiful son. Along the way I realised that I could only tell *my* story and so it became the story of the dutiful son.

My mother impressed upon us that we were in exile, a little clan led by her, as she tried to be a '*mother and father to us all*' since my father had died. Our exile was from the rolling green downs of Wiltshire in the West Country of England to a sprawling concrete estate of pebble-dashed houses south of the city of Dublin. I was to reciprocate her care by being a good boy, studying hard or working hard, and by not telling other people '*Our business*'. What *our business* was that was so important to conceal from others was never very clear to me. There didn't seem to be much going on in our house that others couldn't see or guess at. What were the secrets that we should conceal? What were the consequences if they were revealed? These questions were never answered satisfactorily and arguments for openness never prevailed; we maintained our privacy by not dawdling to chat with neighbours after Mass, and by making sure the net curtains were closed.

It wasn't clear that the exile was permanent. Mum always talked about having come to live in Ireland '*for the duration*', a phrase that English people used in both the First and Second World Wars to mean the duration of the war. It was a hopeful phrase and it spoke of an end, even if no one knew when that end would come; it meant that one day we could all go back to normal. Because we were in exile, Ireland didn't feel like a permanent home to me. I didn't know anything about the Irish side of the family, my father's side, other than being acquainted with his father and sister, my grandpa and auntie, whom I saw once a year, and whom I didn't really like. Although the English side, my mum's side, were across the water in England, they seemed much more alive to me. I knew stories of my English uncles, like the fact that my Uncle John had tried to climb the smokestack at the Avon India Rubber works when he was three years old, or that Uncle Charles had designed and made my mum's evening wear, or that Uncle Richard had played the organ in Wells Cathedral. I even knew that Uncle Alan, a mysterious figure who was an 'uncle' but wasn't my mother's brother, had been in the Royal Engineers and had emigrated to Canada.

As a kid I wasn't entirely sure whether I was English or Irish. I went through phases of trying out accents, I barracked for the English rugby team at Lansdowne Road, I attended the Remembrance Day memorial service in Phoenix Park and, much to the indignation of a Catholic nun who knew me, I sold poppies for the British Legion. At home we stood up if God Save the Queen was played on the radio and we listened to the Queen's Speech on Christmas afternoon. I was my English mother's son.

As my brothers and sisters grew up, one by one they went to England, or Australia, or Scotland. The exception was Bid, my oldest sister, who never managed to get away. On the one occasion that she was ready to leave for London, my mum's chronic illness took an unaccountable and sudden turn for the worse. I am happy that I became close to Bid in the last years of her life and grew to love her. But the others all left, and with their leaving the family shrank and changed. Bid once remarked to me how different we kids had all become, despite the fact that we grew up 'in the same family'. It struck me then that although in one way we are all in the same family, the families we grew up in are quite different. The first three children, Bid and Eileen and Dermot (Derry), were born in England before the war, in a prosperous family with a thriving business, a market town pub dating from the twelfth century, that provided a charming home and even maids to do the housework. Margaret and Gerard were born in Ireland after mum's migration during the war, each birth following a period of navy shore leave for my father. Their various rented homes in Ireland initially had some pretension to refinement until the money ran out and the budget shrank as the family grew. Then there were Heidi (Mary), Nora, and me, post war kids, baby boomers, born well below the poverty line, except that there wasn't a poverty line back then, or certainly not one that we knew about. No carpets? Who had carpet? No television? Who had television? Bread and jam for tea? Sure. My mother was an ingenious cook (I have many of her hand-written recipes) and a knitter and seamstress. We got by. In time the UK Ministry of Pensions came to the party and mum could even pay for us younger kids to go to the better schools, Monkstown Park College for me and Dominican Convent in Dun Laoghaire for Heidi and Nora.

Sandy Toksvig, host of the BBC's QI program, once described herself as being afflicted by the unfortunate condition known as 'posh voice, no money'. I related to this at school, having an accent different from my classmates, especially if I was going through one of my 'being English' phases. Irish people would tilt their heads to look at me quizzically and say: *'Are you Irish?'*, lifting the tone on the word 'Irish' to indicate their doubt. Any English people I met would do the same, substituting 'English' for 'Irish'. I felt caught in the middle and not quite belonging to either. Not that this was a hardship for me. On the contrary, I enjoyed straddling two worlds, I just didn't have my feet planted very well in either of them. I have often thought that my origin from an English Protestant mother and an Irish Catholic father has made me comfortable occupying middle ground, seeing both points of view, being able to mediate.

Like the others, I left home after school, on a journey that was at once shorter and more complicated than the bus ride down to the mail boat taken by my brothers and sisters, and the quick jump across the Irish Sea to Holyhead. But it was a leaving nonetheless, that separated me from my family, from my friends, and from my country. My leaving was to join a religious order. The distance of six kilometres from my home in Sallynoggin to the novitiate in Leopardstown could just as well have been six thousand or sixteen thousand, such was the alien world into which I travelled. From Leopardstown my journey took me to Salamanca, to Madrid, and then to Rome, treasure houses all of them, beacons of culture and art, and history. But in each of them I lived in closed communities on the fringes of all that culture and history lest by being 'in the world' I should become 'of the world' and lose my vocation or my faith or both. As if God would prefer me to find beauty distasteful!

Nine years and much soul-searching later I returned briefly to Sallynoggin to rescue my mother from her exile in Ireland and restore her to her English homeland. As I made the final crossing back to England on the mail boat, I threw the front door key of my childhood home into the sea and recited, I really did, Brutus's lines from *Julius Caesar*:

> There is a tide in the affairs of men Which, taken at
> the flood, leads on to fortune; Omitted, all the
> voyage of their life Is bound in shallows and in
> miseries. On such a full sea are we now afloat,
> And we must take the current when it serves, Or
> lose our ventures.

I should confess that rather than having an intimate knowledge of *Julius Caesar*, at the time I had been reading an Agatha Christie novel called *Taken at the flood*, which had the quote on the fly page. Be that as it may, the house key was cast, and the rift was complete. I am not one for dramatic gestures, but it seemed fitting to mark the moment of return from Egypt to the Promised Land. I didn't know it, but I was on a journey that would eventually lead me to settle on the other side of the world.

And then there was sex. As this chapter is by way of an introduction, I won't pre-empt my story, but I should give you fair warning that if you're squeamish about listening to the agonised soul-searching of a teenaged Irish Catholic boy, you should stop reading now and choose another book. If you're still here, I must tell you that there's more. Besides sex, there was sexuality. Growing up in the nineteen fifties and sixties, opinions were rigid and social sanctions were harsh. Homosexuality was not only sinful, it was illegal, but somehow the sinful aspect seemed more important in my world. Legal sanctions would come into force if you were found out, and most people weren't found out most of the time. The sanctions of conscience, on the other hand, were ever present and unrelenting, and homosexuality was presented as the ultimate filth with which to offend God. Masturbation was bad enough and merited the full 'Mortal Sin' category for which the pain was eternal damnation. It was many years before I would hear and laugh at Dorothy Parker's joke about calling her pet canary Onan, because *'he spilled his seed upon the ground'*. In Catholic Ireland it was no laughing matter.

Shortly after I arrived in Sydney to live in 1994, I went to New Zealand with my colleague Michael Edwards. I had been employed by the New South Wales Government to set up a program for violent offenders. As is often the case, our neighbours in New Zealand seemed to be doing a better job than us, so Michael and I went to see. Michael's job was to set up a program for sex offenders, and our trip across the Tasman was all about sex and violence; no room for drugs or rock 'n roll. Our first stop was a residential program in Hamilton, on the North Island, housing a dozen or so young men, all Maori. I was keen to join their community meeting and they were kind enough to let me. To be with these men is to sense, almost to smell, the physicality that has been their safeguard and protection so far in life. Their bodies are tense and alert enough to fight but they have a paradoxical calmness, a comfort within their own skin that comes from their certainty about their worth and who they are, and from being able to defend themselves. Their aggression is a bad idea in the long term, but it has served them in the absence of any other strategy to date. As we went round the group, each man recited his whakapapa in language that was solemn as well as simple, telling where he was from and who his relations were, as all eyes focussed on him. Each man's words rolled out with confidence and certainty about his past. I knew that all eyes would soon focus on me, and when my turn came, I hastily scrabbled together some things about my family, my paternal family that is. Luckily, I had visited Glengarriff, the home of my father's family, before I left for Australia and I knew the names of my paternal forebears back to my great-great-great grandfather: I could truthfully say that I was 'Kevin, Jer, Ned, Jer, a Shéamus, a Sheán', taking me back a hundred and seventy-five years to the first decade of the nineteenth century. Never mind that I knew little or nothing about any of these people, including my father, in fact the only person I had knowingly met was Ned, my surly grandfather. The experience of the group and its ritual sharing stayed with me, partly because it was a little embarrassing having to make up a kind of ersatz whakapapa to which I felt no connection, and because it brought home to me again how little I knew about my family, on either side.

Two years later I discovered Narrative Therapy, that marvellous antipodean invention of David Epston and Michael White, and with my friend Rachael Haggett I took my first steps to towards understanding the role of story in therapy and, more importantly, in life. I began to change the way I worked with clients, collaborating on re-authoring lives, discovering, not inventing, narratives that had lain dormant or been discarded because of what seemed like the weight of evidence that contradicted them, but was in reality a selection bias dictated by the old narrative itself. If you're any kind of decent therapist, you realise that the things that apply to your client apply to you as well, and I began to wonder about the events and people that had shaped my narratives, and especially those that could pick out one overarching narrative and could make it my preferred, default, go-to, storyline.

Then there was Ethan, now a terrific young man and my great nephew. Ethan's mum fled his violent dad when he was not yet six months old, crossing state lines to keep herself and her baby safe; one dad down. Later, when his mum's next marriage broke down, he was two dads down and feeling a bit lost. His middle name is Sullivan, a good move on my niece's part, and it got him thinking about his heritage. When he was in primary school, he had to do a family history project for which I happily provided some material, not least a mug printed with the O'Sullivan coat of arms and the motto '*Lámh foisteneach abú*' – 'Always a steady hand'. I told him about the Eoghanacht and the Kings of Munster and Donal Cam O'Sullivan, Prince of Beare. In his eyes I could see a mixture of joy and pride to think that he belonged to something bigger; he did a great presentation to his classmates, complete with heraldic mug. But I felt that I was telling him things I had been told about rather than things I knew.

Years later I came off my bike and was taken to the Emergency Department at Royal Prince Alfred Hospital in Sydney's Inner West. I lay for hours in my white hospital gown, being pushed backwards and forwards to the imaging department for various scans, and was visited every thirty minutes or so by a nurse who would ask me what my name was and what was the date. My name I could manage with no problem, but the date escaped me; I had no idea. Until, that is, one of the nurses told me that it was the first of February 2013. I remember thinking, 'That's easy to remember – 1,2,3'. The next time a nurse came to ask the standard questions, I was able to say that it was the first of February 2013, but not because I *knew* it, rather because someone had told me, and I *remembered* what they had said. It didn't come from within. I recount this story because it tells the simple reason why I write: I want to find out what comes from within, from the core of me. I'm not sure I can achieve the confident whakapapa of the men in Hamilton, but I write in order to become the author of my story, however it emerges.

THE BEGINNING – MY MOTHER

*T*here is no better place to begin this tale than with the story of my mother, because she is the person for whom I was *a good boy* for many years.

My mother was four years old when the Titanic sank and the Wright brothers made their flight at Kittyhawk, and she was six when the First World War broke out. My favourite book, *The Wind in the Willows*, a book that never fails to console me on down days, was published the year she was born. In London King Edward VII was on the throne, in Rome, Pope Pius X was in the chair of Peter, in Sydney, Tom Roberts was painting his vibrant blue scenes of Coogee, and in Ireland idealist patriots were planning, again, to rebel. Mum was twenty-eight and a prosperous businesswoman when she fell for my father, the year that Edward VIII more spectacularly fell for Wallis Simpson. Another eighteen years passed before I came along, born to a now impoverished family of ten in a rented council house in South County Dublin. My mother was widowed less than two years after I was born, and I grew up without knowing my father or much about my father's family.

By contrast with my father, I knew my mother for thirty-six

years, but the woman I knew was a post-war version, lonely, poor, and depressed. What about the other forty-four years of her life? What about the fascinating woman I hardly knew, who came into a world that was beginning a cycle of change and upheaval that would beggar belief? This woman, she would have said 'lady', remembered seeing men with red warning flags walking in front of the new-fangled 'motor cars'; she walked the ten miles from Melksham to Devizes for a dance, and then walked back again late at night. A little older, she went *'up to Town'* by the evening train in gowns designed for her by her brother, my uncle Charles, an elegant, handsome and most probably gay man in a time of oppressive disguise. I know so little about my mother that I have to eke out remnants by rummaging through a century's odds and ends. I glean for facts, or even for hints, following the furrows after the crop is gone to see if there are any leftovers I can salvage. Sometimes the results are sparse, sometimes surprisingly ample.

All the earliest things I remember are about my mother. Among the snippets I know about her are some that are heart-rending to remember amid the comfort I now enjoy. I am the beneficiary of her scrimp-and-save, make-do-and-mend, cut-and-come-again ingenuity. Thanks to my mother I can make a meal with whatever is in the fridge, I never throw food away, always finding a place for it in a soup or a casserole or a carton. I can turn the collar of a shirt (although it's a long time since I did it) and run up a reasonable pair of curtains. *'We never died a winter yet'* was her quietly defiant response to some new hardship, the loss of a job, the price of coal going up, the widow's pension not going up, or not enough.

I just called her *'quietly defiant'* - it seems I have my first epithet to describe my mum and I wonder whether I inherited any of that. Putting words on paper, whether others read them or not, seems an audacious thing to do and demands a fairness to the person being described, to protect their portrayal from undue prejudice or bias, even if I know that my impressions of my mother are just that – my impressions.

Growing up, I thought my mother looked exactly like Queen Elizabeth the Queen Mother. They were around the same age, my mother a few years younger. Photos show her as a handsome, serene, self-possessed young woman, Chair of the local branch of the Young Conservatives, Tawny Owl, sought after as a piano accompanist, High Anglican: utterly respectable in the sturdiest tradition of the English merchant class of the early twentieth century. That was before her mother died and my father-to-be got her pregnant and hastily married. It was decades before I realised this last fact when I compared the date of my oldest sister's birthday and my parents' wedding anniversary and found some-what less than the regulation nine months. This discovery brought me a whole ocean closer to my mother.

My mother's mother was born in 1878 in India, in Faisabad, or Fyzabad, east of Lucknow in what had been the princely state of Oudh or Awadh. Her father, my maternal great grandfather George Wey, was from Crewkerne in Somerset. He enlisted in Her Majesty's forces in November 1870 at Taunton and by 1877 was soldiering in India. He was nineteen years and ten months old when he signed up to defend the new British Empire, roughly the age of the average American soldier in Vietnam a hundred years later, and of the Australian recruit celebrated in song at Puckapun-yal: *plus ça change.*

Thirteen years previously, when George was seven or so, India had been rocked by the catastrophe of what the British called the Indian Mutiny - and what the Indians called the Uprising. More than 135,000 sepoys rose against their East India Company masters and there was great slaughter of each side by the other. It made a searing impression on Victorian Britain, and I have wondered what little George, my great-grandfather, heard or knew about this in Crewkerne, and whether it prompted him to go to the defence of the Empire. In any event, George signed up for twelve years *'or so long as her Majesty should require my services'* and some years later, in 1877, he married Ellen Prew in Crewkerne. By 1878, a year after the first Delhi Durbar, we find George and Ellen in Fyzabad where the first of their ten children was born. This was my grandmother, Mary Jane Wey, called Jin by her friends.

The family had returned to England by 1889 and on December 26th, 1900, Mary Jane married Arthur Percy England, son of John and Mary, in Crewkerne. In the wedding photo the women seem a great deal more at ease in their finery than the men. The turn of the century gowns are beautifully made, with close-fitting bodices, fitted sleeves, and corsages at the left shoulder. With the exception of my great grandmother, who would have been described as stout, the women have impossibly small waists and impossibly large hats. Among the men, Percy is the only one who looks relaxed in his wing collar, watch chain and buttonhole flower. Is it me or does he have an insolent look? He leans backwards in his seat, his head cocked to one side, with his lips parted and eyebrows raised as if to say: *'I know. I'm a damned fine chap. She's a lucky lady.'*

Sometime between 1900 and 1906 my grandparents Percy and Jin moved to Bath where my mother Nora was born on July 3rd, 1908. She was the third child, after Charles in 1902 and Richard in 1906, and on her birth certificate, Percy's occupation is given as 'Butler'. In the little lives of the poor, it is not given to know for whom he performed this service.

Mum was born Nora Winifred Mary England in number 15 Hanover Terrace, Bath. Without knowing of this address at the time, eighty-one years later I married a woman I was madly in love with, Jane Barnsley, and we moved into her house in Hanover Terrace, Brighton. When I was a child, I remember telling my mother that I would buy her *'a cottage in Kent'* where she could live with her friend Mrs Jennings. As a small child in suburban Dublin, I had little or no idea where 'Kent' was, but when my wife Jane, the new Mrs O'Sullivan, and I moved from Jane's house in Brighton, it was to a cottage in Kent, in Tunbridge Wells: life amuses with coincidence.

My mother told me how she came by her given names. When she was born, my grandmother couldn't breastfeed her, and the lives of both mother and baby were at risk. The family found a local wet nurse, an Irish woman called Nora. Nora managed to feed my mother, my grandmother survived, and in gratitude gave my mother the name of her nurse as well as her own name, Mary. She was also called Winifred, a Prew family name.

My grandparents moved from Bath to run The Red Lion, an Ushers' pub in Melksham, Wiltshire: what could be more English? Coupled with their surname, England, it was all very *'We'm come up from Somerset, where the cider apples grow'*, although it was of course Wiltshire. The license was in my grandmother's name, given that Percy was known to be too fond of the drink to make him a safe pair of hands for the brewery. It was in Melksham that Mary Jane and Percy's youngest son, my uncle John Llewellyn (Jack), was born in 1911.

The building that housed the Red Lion dates from 1220 and boasts that King John slept in the inn after hunting in nearby Melksham Forest – our only royal connection. Melksham Forest was then a Royal Forest and together with the neighbouring Chippenham Forest once covered thirty-three square miles reserved for the hunting pleasure of the King. To this day the building has the quaint address of '1-3, The City, Melksham'. Alas, it's no longer a pub, having been transformed into a childcare centre some years ago. I am not sure whether an Edwardian Lady would have thought it proper to serve behind the bar of a public house in the noughties of the twentieth century, but there again, I am not sure whether my grandmother would have been regarded as an Edwardian 'lady', being in trade. She was certainly a capable woman who ran a business on her own when my grandfather disappeared from the record in circumstances Mum never really explained. My mother always described him as having been *'lost at sea'*, but I never knew whether that was a kind Edwardian euphemism for having done a bunk, being held at Her Majesty's pleasure, or running away with the maid. I now know that he abandoned the family for good sometime after the birth of his son John (Jack) LLewellyn in 1911 and went to sea with the merchant navy. He died in 1918.

Of my mother's life between 1908 and 1935 I know almost nothing apart from mere snippets and what can be gleaned from a few sepia-tinted photographs. I scan these images from ninety or a hundred years ago searching, sometimes with a magnifying glass, for any detail that can add to the story, like silent witnesses in the cold case of my origins. The earliest photo shows mum as a pudgy baby at the age of two on her mother's lap, in a loose-fitting broderie anglaise baby dress with a doll in her hands. The photo is carefully posed, with my grandfather, hands thrust in trouser pockets, polka dot tie showing beneath a stiff collar, standing behind the group, still looking cocky. My grandmother sits looking calm and deceptively fragile, while Richard in his white sailor suit, chest out, smiles broadly, and Charles, looking solemn, is quite simply the most elegant eight-year-old boy one could imagine. In his gravity, Charles's face reminds me of certain images of the Tsarevich Alexei, who was two years younger.

The next photo shows Mum as Queen of the May in 1912 at the age of not quite four. She is again wearing a little broderie anglaise dress, this time with a waist, the traditional crown of May flowers on her head, and a posy in her hand. Her feet, in lace-up white bootees and knee length white socks, are firmly planted on the bearskin rug, and her hand, placed on the arm of the studio chair, is clearly there in a pose and not relying on the chair for support. Her look is a mixture of coyness and pleased-as-punch, since to be crowned as Queen of the May was, I'm sure, a princess dream for many a little girl. On the back of the photograph are the words: *For I'm to be Queen of the May, Mother,* from Tennyson's rather tragic poem.

A later portrait shows her in the uniform of a Tawny Owl, the assistant leader of a unit of the Brownies. She looks out from the photo with a confident smile and it's easy to imagine her helping the Brownies with their knots and handing out badges for orienteering and needlework and whatever else early twentieth century Brownies got up to. Yet another photo shows a pretty, smiling girl of perhaps sixteen or seventeen, with beautiful skin and white, even teeth. She wears a short-sleeved dress of dark stuff with a kind of corsage on the right shoulder. Even allowing for the bias of an admiring son, you'd have to say that she was a strikingly pretty girl who must have been used to the admiring glances of the young men of Melksham and perhaps the not so discreet wolf whistles of the rubber workers at the Avon India Rubber works around the corner from the Red Lion. It's a fair bet to say her presence behind the bar would have boosted takings.

I think my favourite photo is one taken with her oldest brother, my uncle Charles. The couple are standing in the polished doorway of what looks like a hotel lobby or ballroom, or perhaps a theatre. They are in evening dress, my uncle looking the picture of dapper in white tie and tails with his hair pomaded to within an inch of its life. My mother is wearing a beautifully cut dress and jacket in black satin with, again, a corsage that runs almost from shoulder to waist. The most striking thing about this for me is that she looks entirely at home in her surroundings: clearly this is not the first or only time she has spent such a glamorous evening. She often said that Charles designed her evening wear and if this outfit is one of his creations, I'm surprised that there was not a *Charles England* range in 1930s London.

A further addition to the family came in 1921 when Alan was born to my grandmother's sister, Kitty (Florence Katherine Wey). Kitty was engaged to be married to one Angus Tayler, of Melksham, and became pregnant with him, but Angus then decided he didn't want to marry Kitty, so Kitty went to court on February 18th, 1922, and secured maintenance payments of ten shillings a week for her son. My grandmother welcomed Alan into the Red Lion and brought him up as another son, and when my grandmother died, my Mum looked after him. It was my father who told Alan, just before he went off to war, that the woman he called his aunt was his mother, and the woman he called his mother was his aunt. Knowing nothing of all of this, we kids called him Uncle Alan and assumed he was simply a late arrival, my mother's younger brother.

In due course Charles, Richard, and Jack all left home and found work, and by the early 1930s were well placed. Writing in September 1934 to her brother Henry who was living in Vancouver, my grandmother says: '...*I am more than glad to be able to tell you [that] my boys [are] all in good offices. Jack has been home for the weekend. He has just gone back, he has his motor bike. I think I told you he is at Newbury, Alf [Richard] and Charlie in London. Charlie has a fine business in Finchley'*. The 'fine business' is Charles's restaurant, The Wander Inn, in Finchley, which he had decorated and furnished with the art deco pottery ware of his friend Clarice Cliff. But while my uncles had left home and were settled, and Grandmother Jin was proud of them, Mum gets no mention. I wonder whether she was bit taken for granted, staying behind to help out and support her mum because Percy had left his wife and family. It strikes me that twenty-nine was quite old to be single in those days. I wonder why Mum, who was pretty, and accomplished, and had prospects, didn't marry, and whether she stayed behind in the way that her own eldest daughter, my sister Bid, stayed behind to look after her in turn? Mum was thirteen when Alan came into the family in 1921 and it is likely that, as the only daughter of her busy, working, and now single, mother, she helped to look after the new baby and toddler. There is no sign in the face of the pretty young woman looking out from photographs, many with my grandmother and with Alan, that she resented staying at home. She seems ever cheerful, with a striking smile that lights up her face.

In October 1935 my grandmother died at the age of just fifty-seven. The causes of her death are given as *'Toxaemia, Septic Throat and Splenic Anaemia'* and on her death certificate she is confusingly described as the 'wife', not the 'widow', of 'Arthur Percy England, Steward, Merchant Service'. Her funeral, on November 2nd., was a fitting tribute for the lady described by the Wiltshire Times 'the oldest licensed victualler in the town'. The newspaper columnist lists twenty-five mourners by name as well as *'many other old friends'*, and there are no fewer than fifty floral tributes. Some are from family and friends, including one that simply said, *'in loving memory, Magg (Eastbourne)'*, and many are from other pubs in the town like The Bear, The Bell, and The Unicorn, as well as the West Wilts Licensed Victuallers' Association, and the West Wilts Constitutional Association (Women's Branch). Clearly, my grandmother was well and widely liked. I wish I had known her.

My grandmother's death came as an enormous blow to my mother, and she started to drink heavily, up to a bottle of gin a day. Mum said she kept this up for six weeks and then stopped, never to touch gin again. Growing up I remember her always having a bottle of cognac in the house, always Remy Martin, *'for medicinal purposes'*. This and an occasional dry sherry were her only tipples that I recall. In later life she worried enormously when she had a sore throat, fearing the worst.

The question then arose: who would run the pub? And if none of the family did, where would my mother live so that she could continue to look after Alan? The boys had left home by now, so my mother took the brave step of applying for the licence. For a single woman of 27 in 1935 this was quite an enterprise, so she sought character references from the upstanding folk (all of them men) of Melksham: the vicar, the bank manager, the headmaster, the curate. All of them attest in similar words to her good character and capacity to run the house, and in their restrained Edwardian letter-writing prose they note that she has effectively already done this unassisted during the period of her mother's illness. All describe her as capable, reliable, and efficient, rather like a school report might do. Among the testimonials is one that I particularly treasure. It's from a man to whom I owe a debt I will never be able to pay because he told me something personal about my mother. The Headmaster of Lowbourne Melksham School, Mr F. J. H. Watkins, took a moment for a more general comment to give me the only written insight into how others may have seen my mother in her teens and early twenties:

'I have known Miss England for the past ten years during which time she has impressed me as one possessing a kindly nature, a cultured demeanour, a cheerful disposition and a firm and just character.'

Thank you, Mr. Watkins, for such a warm testimonial. I would be very content to be described in such terms.

The licence passed to my mother, and she got on with the business of running the pub. Then came the fateful day in 1935, around Christmas time, when my Uncle John brought home a friend, one Jeremiah (Jerry) O'Sullivan, far from his home and family in Dún Laoghaire, Ireland, to join the Englands for some festive cheer. Apart from providing Christmas lunch 'with all the trimmings', my mother said that she had baked a monumental number of mince pies, something like twelve dozen, and considering there was no frozen pastry, that was a lot of sifting, mixing and rolling!

It seems that the mince pies did the trick because in fairly short order the couple fell for one another and shared more than festive cheer. My parents were married on the 18th of April 1936 (eighty-six years ago yesterday) and my oldest sister, Bridget, was born on November 22nd, 1936. There is no record of my sister's birth being premature. The marriage took place in St. John the Baptist Roman Catholic Church at Trowbridge, presided over by Fr. Hudson who became a life-long friend of my mother, and witnessed by two of my uncles, Charles and John. Perhaps conscious of her pregnancy, my mother didn't wear white but rather *'a brown wool marocain suit with an oyster satin blouse and hat and shoes to tone'* with *'a spray of lilies-of-the-valley and forget-me-nots'*. Mum's bridesmaid, Masie

Hunt, wore *'an oatmeal coloured frock'* and a string of pearls given to her by my father – I have to wonder who paid for them. The Marriage Certificate describes my father as a 'Rubber Worker' and my mother as a 'Licensed Victualler'; I don't imagine he had much to splash out on pearls, even the recently developed cultured ones. It is ironic that my paternal grandfather later described my mother as 'an English barmaid' that his son had picked up, and she felt looked down on by him for the rest of her life. The reality is that my father got much the better bargain: a wife with a home and a prosperous business. From the factory floor of the Avon India Rubber Company to a well-to-do licensee of a picturesque pub with an established status in the community; quite a step up!

The birth of my oldest sister Bridget, whom we always called Bid, came just a year and three weeks after my grandmother had died. What had become of the demure, stay-at-home young woman, helping her mum and raising her cousin? Did getting pregnant and marrying my father serve as a way to break out of the 'dutiful daughter' image, to kick over the traces? Impossible to know. I knew only the post war version of my mother, lonely, depressed, hurt by life. If I had known then about their affair, about her pregnancy, about the necessary marriage, would I have been able to ask her how it was? Maybe, but maybe not. I reflect on these things now as an older man; old people can ask different questions than the young.

When she talked about Bid's birth, my mother was proud to say that she was working in the bar until the contractions began to come. She went upstairs, had her first child with a minimum of fuss and was back serving behind the bar the next day. I don't know if this is strictly true. Mum was perfectly capable of weaving a good story out of a few facts, so it is possible that some embellishment has taken place, but even so, it clearly shows how she saw herself: a no-fuss, stuff-and-nonsense, pull-yourself-together kind of gal who didn't miss a stride for something like childbirth. This was probably just as well, as my second sister, Eileen, followed in

December 1937 and my oldest brother, Edward Dermot Wey, or Derry as we called him, in March 1940.

Then to cap it all along came the war. By now my father had been out of the Royal Navy for six years and belonged to the Royal Fleet Reserve. He was Irish, a citizen of the recently established Irish Republic, and a Licensed Victualler as well, the license having passed from Mum to him after the marriage by some unquestioned patriarchal matrimonial magic. As a Licensee, he was exempt from being called up, and as an Irishman he was a citizen of a neutral country, but he went anyway. I have wondered why? Was land-lubbing already a bit boring? Was the relationship palling? Were three children under four making him depressed? Whatever the reason, he went to war in the Royal Navy and mum was once again in sole charge of the Red Lion. Of course, there were maids to help, one for upstairs, one for downstairs and the one I liked the sound of best: the 'tweeny', which means, if you look it up, *a servant who helped other servants*. But still there was a busy pub to run, three children to mind and a war to worry about.

THE WAR AND THE MOVE TO IRELAND

*T*he war seemed to come a little closer when the Royal Navy moved its warship design department from London to the city of Bath, twelve miles from Melksham along the A365. With my father back in the navy, Mum was running the pub on her own again, with two small children to look after and another on the way. It was a busy and prosperous life. The Avon India Rubber factory, that employed nearly two and a half thousand men and women, was a two-minute walk away from the Red Lion and during the war it worked twenty-four hours a day producing all sorts of tyres, straps, and tubes, and even bonded rubber to the metal tracks of tanks and armoured cars. There would have been no shortage of custom at the bar or in the snug. In nearby Trowbridge, where my parents had been married, production of the Spitfire by Vickers-Supermarine was to commence in October 1940, and there were plans to establish RAF Melksham, also in 1940, to house the Royal Air Force School of Instrument Training.

Business was thriving; but what if the rubber works, or the Vickers factory, or the Admiralty offices, or the air base, proved too tempting a target for the German bombers? It was all a great deal too close to be able to sleep easily at night and know that her children were safe. In the event Mum's fears were realistic. Over seven hundred people died in the 'Bath Blitz', in fact Hanover Terrace, the street where she was born, received a direct hit, and the surrounding towns were not immune from damage, although Melksham escaped the bombing.

I don't know how they weighed the options or whether they talked about it as a couple, but it was a decision that would affect Mum's life and the life of her family for the next thirty-eight years. In 1940 she relinquished the license of the pub, sold up the goods and chattels, bought War Bonds and moved over to Ireland, 'as I thought, for the duration'. I had always thought that 'for the duration' was my mother's phrase, until later, listening to the experiences of other people who lived through the Second World War, I realised that 'for the duration' was a common saying. Children were sent away 'for the duration' and businesses were shuttered 'for the duration'. It spoke of the hope that it would 'all soon be over' and we could return to normal, resuming truncated lives, relationships, jobs, homes. What was particular in Mum's use of the phrase was the addition of the words: 'as I thought'. I hear in these words a deep sense of nostalgia, of loss and separation. The early difficult Irish years of trying to get on with my grandfather were perhaps bearable while she thought they were temporary, that she could one day go home, but when they were sealed with the injury and subsequent death of my father, the cord seemed broken. Her steps could never be retraced and all that was left was to make the best of it, to 'keep on keeping on', she used to say. This is how I remember living, in a state of waiting, of being in transit, of never thinking that the Irish world around me was quite 'real', that reality lay elsewhere, in England probably, the land we had left behind.

My sister Eileen, who was three years old at the time, described the move. 'We were all issued with gas masks, gosh they were strange, but we had to wear them wherever we went. As a little child you felt you were choking. In November 1940 we all packed up trunks and cases and travelled to Holyhead. I remember it being very dark because of the bombs etc. and we travelled at night. The ship was very dark, and the sailors helped us with torches as we climbed the steps so we could see. Our luggage was looked after, and Mummy carried Derry who was only nine months old. We had a sailor who was all dressed in black to help us, but I don't remember much of the crossing. I expect we slept most of the time. Grandpa and Mummy met for the first time, and she was relieved to be safe with her children.'

The move to Ireland marked the beginning of a difficult relationship with my paternal grandfather, a man I remember as stern, distant, and unsmiling. Like many O'Sullivans of the time, my grandfather Edward (Ned) came from west County Cork, from Derryconnery, two miles above the picturesque town of Glengarriff, nestled in the bight of Bantry Bay. He was born there in 1878, the same year that my maternal grandmother was born in faraway Fyzabad, and just ten years after the last Irish convicts had been transported to Western Australia. He started his working life as the boot-shine boy in the Eccles Hotel in Glengarriff, collecting boots and shoes left outside the bedroom doors at night and replacing them, cleaned, before morning. It seems incredible to me that I have known someone who was born a hundred and forty-four years ago. Brahms was still alive, Queen Victoria would have another twenty-three years on the throne, and it was a mere fifty-two years since Thomas Jefferson and Mrs. Cook, widow of Captain James Cook, had died. Even though I felt no strong connection to him, this year of his birth has become a sort of historical marker for me, and I tend to measure events by how long before or after it they occurred.

At some point Ned moved to the relatively big smoke of Dublin and in 1940, at the time he met my mother, we find him as head waiter in the Edwardian grandeur of the Royal Hibernian Hotel in

Dublin. He had married Mary Mulvany and they had three children: my father Jeremiah 'Jerry' in 1906, Gladys in 1909, and Edward 'Eddy' in 1916. Although still of straitened means, he was clearly an industrious man and managed to put some cash aside for a rainy day. At the time, waiters were not paid a salary, in fact they paid the *Maître d'* a fee to be allowed to work a section of the restaurant and they took home whatever tips they earned. It was not uncommon for wait staff to supplement their precarious incomes by a little illegal after-hours gambling on cards. This is how my grandfather met a man who changed his life in the most surprising of ways.

Piaras Béaslaí, born Percy Frederick Beazley in Liverpool in 1881, was a contemporary, acquaintance, and perhaps a friend of my grandfather. Coming to Ireland, he became actively involved in the Republican cause, changed his name to the Irish, Piaras Béaslaí, and fought in the Easter Rising of 1916. He was elected three times as a member of Dáil Éireann, the Irish Parliament, and was an accomplished journalist and writer. Despite his public stature he appears to have had some financial woes. Grandpa told me that Béaslaí had run up considerable debts and had no ready means to pay them. He did however own a property at number 8 Eden Park, Glasthule, just south of Dún Laoghaire, a handsome four-storey late Georgian house with stone-built stables behind. He put the house as surety against a debt to Grandpa of two hundred pounds, an enormous sum in the 1920s. When Béaslaí was unable to pay, the house passed to grandpa in settlement of the debt. Overnight the family moved from a tiny 'two up two down' at the wrong end of town in Cumberland Street, to a grand dwelling in decidedly the right area.

It was to this house that Mum came with her three young children in 1940 to occupy the garden basement flat. The relationship got off to a bad start, and Mum often talked about how Grandpa had referred to her as an 'English barmaid my son picked up', although how she would know that he had said that I am not sure.

24

Perhaps it was creative editing, but in any event, it spoke volumes about how she felt that he viewed her. The other phrase she recalled with great bitterness was when she told him she might need to ask him for assistance given her growing family. With relished contempt she would repeat his phrase, 'I won't see you starve', adding a sneer and a look down the nose to indicate his disdain and grudging. It didn't help that he regularly introduced her as 'the mother of my son's children', as if unwilling to acknowledge a relationship as close as that of father- and daughter-in-law. She was certainly in no doubt that he despised her, an English Protestant intruder, who had snared his son.

In this house in Glasthule my oldest sister, Bid, by now four, had one of the formative experiences of her life on December 20th, 1940. On leaving Melksham she had been told that they were leaving their pretty home with cosy familiar sights and smells because the nasty Germans might come and drop bombs near their town. Ireland was a place with no bombs where they would be safe: that was the reward for all they were leaving behind. Some weeks after they arrived in Grandpa's house, Bid remembered being woken one night by a terrifying thunderous noise, seeing yellow flames leaping upwards as she peered through the shutters, with the smell of burning wood and the panicked shouts of onlookers. A German raider, mistaking the lights of Glasthule railway station, less than a hundred yards away from the house, for the coast of England, had dropped its bombs to devastating effect. My four-year-old sister, hearing the terrifying noise and seeing the fierce fire, believed she had been lied to and vowed that she would never trust a grown-up again.

For Mum, not only was there a disdainful father-in-law to contend with, there were a brother and sister-in-law as well. The brother-in-law, my uncle Eddy, seems to have been liked by all, but about him I know nothing except that he married a woman called Rose Garigan and died in 1958. I never met either Uncle Eddy or Auntie Rose. The sister-in-law, my Auntie Gladys, was a year younger than my mother and the two just never got on: they were different in almost every way that I remember. Gladys was, until her death at the age of 102 in 2011, slight and wiry, single, Irish, Catholic and childless. My mum was of a much more buxom build, married, English, Protestant (in Irish terms) and with a growing family. Later as a child, I experienced our yearly visit to Grandpa and Gladys with some foreboding. Even though we lived perhaps a thirty-minute walk from his grand house, we visited as a family only one day a year, on Boxing Day, to take him his Christmas present, a small black pocket diary for the year ahead. While my father was still alive, in the late forties and early fifties, he would take the kids to Mass each Sunday in Glasthule and then go to visit Grandpa, but after his death the link became much more tenuous. On the yearly visits that I remember, we sat in the front room, its high ceilings and ornate cornices enjoining us to be on our best behaviour, with our legs dangling from high-backed over-stuffed chairs much too large for children, drinking our orangeade and eating our dry cake with due care and politeness, while our elders made stiff conversation and the crystal lustres fascinated me with their sparkling on the grey marble mantelpiece. For many years I saw no other room in the house apart from the sitting room and the downstairs toilet and I didn't feel brave enough to ask to see other parts of the house. As we entered or left, I could glance up the staircase and see the thick red velvet curtain at the top of the first flight of stairs that screened the upper floors from view. It was somehow mysterious, almost magical, like in a fairy tale book, and it was a bit frightening to me as a small child. If something was hidden behind it, was there a reason? There often was in books. Perhaps something bad lurked there, but I wasn't even game to ask my mother, who was never in a very good mood when we finished our visits.

The extent and the consequences of this quietly simmering family feud became apparent to me only many years later in 1993 when I got to meet my then eighty-five-year-old Auntie Gladys.

Sitting in the no longer forbidding parlour, with the lustres still on the mantlepiece, I was able to talk to her heart to heart for the first time. She shared with me the story of her forty-year love affair with a man I had somehow come to dread, her fiancé Gerald Dobson. As children we had called him 'Gerald Slob-son', and I for one had terrible and vivid dreams about him harming my mother with a poker; Freudian analysts could have a field day. It was one opinion we shared with Grandpa who we knew detested Gerald and called him 'That Bloody Man'. The Bloody Man was, horror of horrors, also a Protestant and, we were told, a drinker, and Grandpa could never countenance the marriage of such a man with his only daughter. My father's marriage to my mother, which had already introduced one foreign heathen into the family, would only have hardened Grandpa's resolve in this regard. Perhaps this is why Gladys got on so poorly with Mum. Perhaps she felt that my mother had someone queered the pitch for any success in her own forlorn love affair.

In 1993 Gladys told me that she and Gerald had a boat moored for many years in the Bullock Harbour, a mile or so from Grandpa's house, where they spent many lazy sea-borne days and where, had our relations been more congenial, we might have joined them for childhood adventures and made our own *Swallows and Amazons*. A happy codicil is that Gladys spent the last years of her life in supported accommodation overlooking Bullock Harbour within sight of the little boats bobbing on the calm blue water inside the breakwall. I also learned from Gladys that my father's family still lived in the house in Derryconnery, Pine Cottage, where my grandfather had been born and that there I would eventually find another Kevin O'Sullivan, son of my father's first cousin Éamon and his wife Mary.

It seems that Mum's tenancy of the basement flat became so distasteful to her that she soon moved away from my grandfather to the other end of the town, in fact to the next town along the coast: Monkstown. Here she made a home for her young family in number 5 Vesey Place and, at about the same time, converted to the Roman Catholic Church. My father was at sea, I'm not sure when they had last seen each other, but Mum told me that she decided to become a Catholic and to surprise him with her instruction and reception into the church. The change in rite was probably not that remarkable as her family had been, and remained, decidedly High Church Anglicans. After the Second Vatican Council her brother, my Uncle John, bemoaned the loss of pomp and ritual that came about. He was a great fan of smells and bells and thought the Romish church had gone much too far down market.

Mum took instruction but wrote nothing to my father who was on active service, and in due course she was ready to take Holy Communion. This was around Christmas 1941, and she loved to tell the story of one of those moments of synchronicity that made the occasion unforgettable even into old age and failing memory. At home in Vesey Place, she was preparing for the moment that might bring her a step closer to her Roman Catholic in-laws and might, just might, endear her to them a little more. She wished only that her husband could be there to share it with her, but he was at war, hunting submarines somewhere in the North Atlantic, perhaps in peril or worse. But came the day, came the man. When she answered a knock at the door, there he was. His ship had docked at Belfast and the crew had been given brief shore leave. A couple of hours by train brought him to Dublin and they went to Mass together.

Small though it is, this incident stands out for me because it is the only one my mother ever told me about my father that spoke of any joy in their being together. It seems to me they spent relatively little truly joyous time. He went to war three years after they married, coming home for brief shore leaves long enough only for mum to become pregnant. By the time he came home for good, he returned as an invalid, after long convalescence in a naval hospital, weaving baskets and stitching samplers: a spent man. He returned with tuberculosis, which is what eventually killed him in 1954, two days before my second birthday.

What was it like to have left home and native land, to change religion, to have three young children and a fourth and then a fifth on the way, to have a husband away at war in dangerous seas? And on top of all that to have a disdainful father- and distant sister-in-law, to live in a small rented flat, to eke out an existence on a war allowance, counting coupons, sewing dresses and making do, and all of this overlaid with an accent that set her apart as English, the quincentennial oppressor, whose yoke had lifted only four or five years earlier with the creation of the Irish Republic. I suspect depression was a companion of her days in that time: it certainly remained so in later years. My sister Bid once told me that as a child she had always wanted to be an adult because adults were clearly very clever and could see things even when they were looking the other way. Often, as children do, she would pause in her drawing or painting and say, 'Look Mummy', to be greeted by 'Oh that's lovely dear' from Mum whose gaze and thoughts were clearly far away, perhaps behind the bar of the Red Lion or at afternoon tea for the Young Conservatives.

My father returned and, unable to go to sea again, sat instead in pubs and shouted rounds of drinks to show that he still could. I cannot imagine that they were happy years. The War Bonds were cashed in and spent. The war service gratuity, a reasonably handsome sum of ninety pounds, was also spent. The family moved to cheaper and cheaper accommodation and eventually, at the end of the forties, to a new estate of Corporation houses in the South Dublin suburb of Sallynoggin.

MY FATHER

*T*oday marks sixty-eight years since my father died. If I tell you I am sixty-nine, you will understand that I have no memories of him. I remember his anniversary only because it is two days before my birthday. There is nothing of sight or sound or smell that remains to me of him, at least not consciously. I have one of his possessions, a small portable writing chest made of oak; the shiny wood bears the patina of many years of polishing and of touch. The slanted front leaves open out to show racks inside for envelopes and paper and there is a narrow drawer below for pens and stamps and the paraphernalia of letter-writing. The pen drawer provided the occasion for my first attempt at DIY when I was about twelve years old. The brass handle of the drawer was broken, missing the curved metal piece that hung between two brackets. I fashioned a replacement from an inch and a half of a wire coat hanger and a pair of pliers; it's still in place and working. The writing chest was, if not a treasured possession, at least a valued memento of my father. I remember my mother saying in an irritated tone that he'd bought it at an auction at a time when they were struggling to feed and clothe the family of eight children, let alone buy unnecessary items like a writing chest.

In about 1990, when my marriage was breaking up and my wife and I were living in Tunbridge Wells, I went to see a counsellor in Sevenoaks in Kent. She was a *rara avis*, a GP who had left medicine and retrained as a counsellor. She was very good, probably the best therapist I have seen as a client. Her restrained Georgian house was near The Vine, in the shadow of the one remaining eponymous oak tree, the other six having been toppled by a fierce storm three years earlier. Her consulting room was a small sitting room to the right of the front door, cosy with lamplight and with two large chintz-covered armchairs and a rug in dark red tones.

One day we were talking about my father and the fact that he had been buried on my second birthday. I was telling her that for some reason I never celebrated my birthday. I didn't really tell anyone the date, I wasn't interested in getting cards or presents, and I hadn't had a party since I left home at sixteen. I ended my musings with the words, 'Funny isn't it!' I remember her looking at me calmly and saying simply, 'It's not really funny at all, is it?' As she looked at me, tears welled up into my chest, my shoulders rose involuntarily and fell as I started to sob. I cried for what seemed like ten or fifteen minutes, not caring about or feeling any embarrassment in her presence: I couldn't stop. They were wracking sobs, coming from the pit of my stomach; my body shook and my nose ran messily as I cried. I had found a way to the visceral memory of my two-year-old self. Abandoned? Angry? Sad? Afraid? Lonely? Or perhaps all of the above.

When I got home, I told my wife Jane, a clinical psychologist, what had happened and how I'd had an epiphany about losing my father. 'I told you that six months ago,' she said, so my second insight of the day was that understanding dawns only when the time is right. Many times since then, almost every year in the first weeks of August, I become aware of a lingering malaise, I feel low and a little agitated for no obvious reason. In time, as my birthday approaches, I remember that it's that time of year, and I wait for the sadness to go away.

In 1992 I was going out with a man called Seán and we lived together in Peckham. Seán was in the fashion industry and he travelled a bit to Europe. In August of that year, he had been away for a week or so and we decided to meet in a bar in Soho Square when he got back from the airport. It was lovely to see him, but shortly after he joined me and we were swapping news, I began for no obvious reason to weep uncontrollably, just like in Sevenoaks. I reassured Seán that I was fine and said I just needed to go outside to calm myself. Out in the leafy square I continued to weep. As before, I couldn't stop and I felt conspicuous. I crossed the square to the church on the other side that had a recessed porch where I could sit and not be noticed by passers-by. Eventually my sobs subsided and I went back in, only to start crying again as soon as we started talking. I had to leave again and I don't remember how long it took for my tears to stop. Thankfully, Seán was sensitive as well as unflappable, and easy to talk to about these things. I shared with him that August was sometimes a difficult time for me and that his going away and coming back again, unlike my father, might have triggered some old grief.

Over the years, little pieces emerged without an obvious indication that they were connected to the same puzzle. As I thought about my father, I wondered why he had gone to war in 1939. He didn't have to. He had been married just over two years and he had two young toddlers and a third child on the way. He had a comfortable home, a steady income, and as a publican he was in a reserved occupation. He was also Irish, a citizen of the new state that had decided to remain neutral. There would have been no expectation and no shame. What did it say about the relationship that he preferred to leave so soon? Not ever seeing my parents together, I had no idea how they related to each other, nor was this ever spoken about. I began to think about these things only in retrospect as I tried to figure out what sort of man he was. I was happy as a child, as far as I can remember, but I did feel the lack of a father, of having someone to call dad like all the other kids in my class. The person who might have taken his place as the man in my life, my grandpa Edward O'Sullivan, was a forbidding man whom I never recall smiling. I had no indication that he liked me.

The thing I knew for sure about my father was that he was dead, and that he had died because of what had happened to him in the war. In Mum's account his ship had been torpedoed towards the end of the war, but he was rescued and taken to the naval hospital at Portsmouth where he developed tuberculosis, which is what killed him ten years later. My boyhood imagination conjured up a shipwreck in raging seas with my father being plucked from the waves just in time, dragged over the gunwale of a lifeboat or winched to safety by a passing vessel. I was aware that in my mother's room there was a small cardboard box containing his war medals, but I only saw them once, and it wasn't until after her death that I realised she had his naval war record.

I know now that he joined the Royal Navy in November 1926 at the age of twenty, having disappeared without notice from his job as a government clerk in the elegant Customs House in Dublin, on the north bank of the River Liffey. He signed on as an Able Seaman for seven years and served on various ships until 1933 when his Special Service time expired. All that remains of those years are the one-line entries on the naval record - ship, rating, dates - and four small, dog-eared black-and-white photos, the largest measuring just over five inches by three. In their small way they tell of an adventurous life. Nineteen twenty-eight finds him in Trondheim, in Norway, nineteen twenty-nine in Gibraltar, posing on the deck of HMS Adventure with his companions from 'Seven mess'. Another, undated, shows him in Malta with his companions all decked out in shore-leave whites and clustered around a magnificent old bus with a sign painted on the side showing that it plied the Valletta-Cospicua route. Many years later I got to know Malta by travelling on buses not all that different from this one. Now, the wealth of the European Community has swept away these rickety buses along with much of tumbledown Malta, a boon no doubt for the Maltese, but a loss for romantically inclined tourists like me. The smallest of the photos shows four sailors, again in shore leave whites, riding camels led by turbaned cameleers and with a sloping pile of masonry to the left of the scene. On the back is written simply: 'Cairo Pyramids'. Is one of these men my father? I have no idea but, *faute de mieux*, I take it as a sign that he was there.

The naval record says that in 1933 he 'Declined reengagement abroad' and enrolled in the Royal Fleet Reserve. As a Class B Reservist, he would have been eligible for a retainer worth the princely sum of three shillings and sixpence per week, enough for about seven pints of beer. In 1930 he had trained as a submarine detector operator, (the record describes him as 'Excellent'), and for the previous four years he had been base maintenance staff and 'obtained a sound technical knowledge of general electrics and repairs'. Perhaps he put this knowledge of electrics and repairs to good use in finding a civilian job at the Avon India Rubber Works in Melksham, which is where he was working when he met my mother. In the 'Phoney War' mobilisation of 1938 he re-joined the Royal Navy and shortly after the outbreak of war he was on HMT (His Majesty's Trawler) *Agate* ready to put his submarine detection training into deadly practice. Trawlers were a class of ships that lacked the glamour of the destroyer or the frigate but did the dangerous grunt work of detecting submarines. Hundreds were either built to specification or requisitioned for use by many navies, including the Royal Navy, during the first and second world wars.

Reading the naval record cards from the nineteen twenties, thirties and forties is fraught with difficulty. More than one ship may have the same name and the same vessel may have different names at different times. As an added layer of difficulty, the designation His Majesty's Ship, 'HMS', which might reasonably be thought to indicate a sea-going vessel, sometimes refers to a 'stone ship' or base where sailors may be posted to work or may spend time between leaving one ship and joining another. Being no naval historian, I have not been able to find out with certainty what happened to render my father 'Physically unfit for naval service' some time in 1945. But I can find no evidence that the last of his ships was torpedoed. What is certain is that he spent time in the Royal Naval Auxiliary Hospital in Southport near Liverpool and obtained a Certificate of Discharge from Service on April 10th, 1945. Convalescence and rehabilitation followed, consisting of woodwork, and raffia weaving, and *gros point* needlework, and perhaps other activities. When he died, the scant relics of all this were a small stool with a woven raffia seat, and several *gros point* pictures sewn on unbleached linen. The two pictures I remember were the East Façade of Bath Abbey, and a depiction of Francis Drake's ship, the Golden Hind. The Abbey picture hung in my mother's bedroom and the Golden Hind above the mantlepiece in the tiny sitting room to the right of the front door. It was seen only by the rare visitors for whose use the room was reserved.

I now realise that as a child I didn't yearn for *this* father, about whom I knew nothing, but for *a* father, of whom I imagined I could be proud, someone who would show me how to do things, make things, fix things, how to shave. Instead, I was with my father when he died, but it took me sixty years to realise this. On the fifteenth of August 1954, a Sunday, my mother got up to make a cup of tea, leaving my father in bed. When she came back with the tea, he was dead. I have known this since childhood, but until recently it didn't occur to me that I was in the same room as my father. I may even have been in the same bed. My parents' room in our tiny house was so small that it's hard to see where a cot could have gone.

As I lay there all unawares, what emotions were crowding in on my mother? What did it feel like to stand there on the lino floor, far from her brothers, stranded in a foreign land by a war that had taken away her home, her livelihood and now her husband? How to feed the seven children still sleeping in the other two bedrooms, as well as her little baby boy, not yet two years old? I imagine her holding me close to her breast, calming her shock with a sweet sleepy child. Was my father's death a welcome release for her? Did she mourn him, or was it her own plight that she lamented? Whatever the nature of her grief, a lock of the hair above her forehead turned white overnight and remained so for as long as she lived.

Years later, having moved to Australia, I was in a psychodrama training group where participants use the group members to act out some unresolved issue to gain greater understanding and healing. I was working with the group on what the loss of my father had meant to me, when I had a sudden intense feeling of being held, uncomfortably tightly, and of knowing that the embrace was not to console me, but rather to console the person hugging me. I was aware of being in a room about the size and shape of my parents' bedroom. Perhaps it was the body memory of that morning.

In 1988 my mother died after ten years of declining health and encroaching dementia. My oldest sister Bid had cared for her for those ten years, in fact Bid had never left home, the only one of my siblings not to escape. Bid had had her own distress. She saw a psychiatrist regularly for many years, drank lots of whiskey, and tried on several occasions to kill herself with the medication the psychiatrist prescribed her. While mum and Bid were living in Didcot, Bid had also thrown herself into the Thames one day and been rescued by a police officer. She kept a newspaper cutting about the bravery award this young man had won. Caring for mum left little room to explore or remedy her distress.

I began to do my clinical psychology training just after my mother died and as I looked at my sister I recognised the signs that some trauma had happened to her. Eventually she trusted me enough to tell me that our father had sexually assaulted her when my mother was pregnant with my youngest sister Nora. Her words were chilling, and I can still hear her say them: 'He said, if I can't have your mother I'll have you'. Bid was twelve or thirteen years old. My heart broke; anger and sadness vied for the hurtful places in my chest. The suicide attempts, the sadness, the drinking, and the self-deprecation all fell into place. Part of her own sadness was that she had secretly never liked our sister Nora, seeing her as connected to my father's deviant logic. In time, Bid was able to tell Nora this and to become friends with her. I suggested Bid see someone, and we found a young psychologist in Eastbourne who helped her with her trauma and contributed enormously to the happiness and contentment of the last years of her life. She became free and learned to dance.

Knowing about Bid's trauma upended my nostalgia for my father. In my mind he had been a brave if unknown man who went off to the war and hunted submarines in the North Atlantic, but now he was a sex offender. My anger and sorrow for Bid mingled with disbelief and disgust. Had anyone known about this? What about my mother or the older brothers and sisters? I knew it was not surprising for the victims of sexual abuse to be silent or, if they spoke, not to be believed. I didn't know the answers to these questions, but it occurred to me that it might explain why my father was never ever mentioned by my brothers and sisters. There were no photos on display, and the half dozen or so that existed were in a box under my mother's bed. He was never there as a point of reference in phrases one might expect to hear like, 'When dad was alive...' 'He used to love...' 'Remember how dad used to ...' 'Your dad used to say...'. None of these was ever uttered. Ever. Were some or most of my siblings secretly glad that he was gone? Was my mother relieved? I have a small black and white photo of all my brothers and sisters taken when I was about two, just after my father died. The photo sits beside me on the bookcase in my study. Except for Bid, who looks drawn and haggard, with dark rings under her eyes, everyone is smiling broadly. I have wondered whether there was a collective sigh of relief.

37

. . .

A SILLY DETAIL occurred to me the other day. I remembered a song
we had on a 45rpm record, a 'single', when I was a small child. It's
about a man who comes home from work dejected, finds no joy at
home and decides to kill himself by jumping off the roof. It went
like this, and I am struck that I remember all the words:

Don't jump off the roof dad
You'll make a hole in the yard
Mother's just planted petunias
The weeding and seeding was hard.
If you must end it all dad
Won't you please give us a break.
Just take a walk to the park dad
And there you can jump in the lake.

I still have the writing chest. It's a pretty thing and there's no
compelling reason to throw it out, but it lives in a cupboard in the
garage. I don't want it in the house.

I ARRIVE IN THE WORLD

*I*reland in the late forties and early fifties had all the deprivation of the post-war era without any of the jubilation of having won the war. In what was one of the most deadpan political understatements of the twentieth century, Éamon De Valera and the newly-minted, neutral, Irish Government had used the euphemism 'The Emergency' for what everyone else with eyes in their head knew was a catastrophic World War that would decide the fate of hundreds of millions, including the Irish. In his 2012 book, *Returning Home*, Bernard Kelly traces the response of the Dublin Government and the Irish people to the twelve thousand or so Irish veterans returning from the war. With the exception, and not always, of friends and relatives who were happy to see them back, they were vilified and shunned, and many kept their war service a secret. Such was the parochial hatred of the English oppressors that there was no acknowledgement that Irish men and women had risked their lives to fight a profoundly evil regime which, had it triumphed, would undoubtedly have swallowed Ireland whole, neutrality and all. Some five thousand of these troops who had been members of the Irish armed forces were classified as deserters and remained so for the next sixty-seven years until their official pardon in 2013. With his closeness to Piaras Béaslaí, who had fought in the Easter Rising in 1916 and was a member of the Dáil, I wonder what my grandfather made of his son? Was he a hero or a traitor? Was he to be welcomed back into the family, or had he made his bed and now must lie on it? I suspect it was not a hero's welcome. There are no stories of warmth or joy at his return. The picture I have of the family at this time is of ever more straitened circumstances: more mouths to feed, same War Pension. I think of my mother preparing ten meals three times a day for seven days a week, washing, ironing, cleaning, mending, sewing, knitting. My God, what a life! I'm sure my siblings helped a lot. The older ones looked after the younger and I was told many years later that I called my sister Margaret 'Little mummy', as opposed to 'Big mummy', who had so many other things to do that delegation was necessary.

My father continued his life as an invalid and fathered a further three children, a testament to the increased libido of the consumptive, which is a tale more prettily told in La Bohème's Parisian garret than in the realities of working-class life in Sallynoggin; the singing is certainly better. I don't know that life was particularly happy for the family of ten in a small house, keeping quiet so as not to disturb the invalid. My sister Margaret, at the boisterous age of eight or nine, is reported to have declared to anyone who would listen: 'There's not enough singing in this house!'

Into this quiet house of little song and rationed food I was born on Sunday the 17th of August 1952. According to the popular rhyme, as 'a child who is born on the Sabbath Day' I was destined to grow up bonny and blithe and good and gay: I have managed one of those at least. As a small child, there were two things I remember my mother saying about me constantly to neighbours, friends, acquaintances, indeed to anyone who would listen. In addition to telling people that 'He was two the day his father was buried', she also cheerfully informed all and sundry that 'He nearly

40

killed me when he was born'. I don't think she was attributing matricidal intent, as at first it might appear; more likely she was referring to the fact that I weighed ten and half pounds at birth and was proportionately large. I was also the eighth of eight children and so by the time my mother was forty-four she'd been through a deal of trouble and strife with my siblings that set her up for a parlous experience at my birth. There is no doubt I was a mummy's boy, a burden I bore for many years. Well into my thirties my mother would introduce me as her 'baby' and it was vain for me to protest that rather than the 'baby', I was the 'youngest in the family'.

I begin my own part of the story with these two phrases because over the years I have realised how they have turned into deep, powerful, pervasive beliefs about my identity that have accompanied me through my life. The more I have thought and written about them, the more I understand how important they are. Through my stabs at my own therapy I came to understand that I had grown up with a sense, a fantasy sense, that I could be destructive to those close to me, particularly women. The moment at which I understood this most clearly was the moment of separation from my wife. I vividly remember standing in the hallway of our house in Tunbridge Wells on Valentine's Day 1991 and overcoming the panic that this woman would somehow collapse and wither away if I walked out the door. I am eternally grateful to my strong, resilient ex-wife for showing me that this did not in fact happen. She survived to tell me how very angry she was that I had abandoned her, and I in turn survived the knowledge that I was capable of causing such pain.

I also grew up with a hovering nostalgia for a dad. Other kids at school, talked about 'my dad', 'me da', 'the aul' fella'. They were able to answer questions like 'what does your dad do?' or 'Is your dad coming to the match?'. The role was unclear, and the name didn't matter, I just wanted someone to be there in the space in my life called Dad. The desire for this person wasn't passionate. I heard my mother tell friends that she had to be 'a mother and a father to the eight of them', and sometimes I thought it would be rude to want more, as if wanting a dad would mean she wasn't doing a good enough job.

I grew up in poverty, although I didn't know it at the time, and when I began to realise it as a teenager, it didn't really bother me. The house I was born and brought up in was number 16 O'Rourke Park, Sallynoggin, an area a couple of miles inland from the pretty seaside town of Dún Laoghaire in County Dublin. Some years ago, in a colleague's office in Sydney, I came across a book about architectural trends in post-war Europe. Flicking idly through its pages as I waited for her, I was astonished to find a picture of the Sallynoggin council housing estate with an enthusiastic description of the new model post-war architecture it represented. Who would have guessed we were making urban architectural history with gardens back and front, and indoor privvies! The house was part of a terrace of perhaps twenty houses, double-fronted, two-storied, with three bedrooms. The gardens were about twenty feet square front and back, a pocket handkerchief lawn with some flower beds, hydrangeas in ours, and simple iron railings with Buxus hedges. In front of our house was a park with beautiful old chestnut trees, from which we collected nuts that we peeled and seasoned and threaded with string to play 'conkers'. Not that we were encouraged to play out there: we might meet undesirables from the estate: 'You can't touch pitch without getting dirty'.

Three bedrooms sounds commodious but not if you have ten people living there. The three boys shared one room with one double bed. The girls shared another room with a combination of single and double beds and my parents had the third. Downstairs was an entrance hall, a tiny sitting room, for guests only, and a living room and kitchen.

My first memory is standing in the kitchen one day when my mother was doing the washing. We had an old-fashioned wicker cane laundry basket, a rich warm brown colour with sharp ends of wicker that caught inattentive fingers, and I can clearly remember that I couldn't see into it because it was taller than me. I think I must have been two or three and my father had already died. The kitchen was a little room, they were all little rooms, about eight feet square, and I can see myself standing in the middle, beside the laundry basket. On my left, along the outside wall below the window, there is a large, square, deep ceramic sink with a cold tap over it and sloping wooden draining boards each side. Behind me to the left is the pantry cupboard with a latched door and three concrete slabs for shelves. On my right is the square kitchen table, with the wooden grain deeply furrowed from scrubbing and wear, a daily hazard for splinters under the fingernails. Behind me on the right is the range, set into an alcove and carefully blacked with stove black. I don't recall my mother using this although I'm sure she must have. By the time I came along we had acquired a cast iron gas stove on pedestal feet that stood in the 'back porch', a tiny room off the kitchen that had initially been just that - the porch or hallway inside the back door, giving access to the 'coal house', a sort of inside shed for coal, Wellington boots, brooms, the shoe polishing bag, and spiders. Under the stairs was the cupboard where the gas meter lived, and I loved the day when the gas man came to collect the single shillings that we fed into the slot. He bent down into the cramped space and unlocked the little metal drawer into which the shillings fell, and then he turned and tipped the whole lot noisily out onto the table. Then came the magic part. With the index and middle fingers of his right hand he flicked pairs of shillings into his left hand at lightning speed and piled them up in lots of ten. In no time at all the piles were counted and my mother paid him the part of the balance owing in notes and other coins, keeping some of the single shillings to use again.

My next memory is of my first day at school when I was four years old. I started out, as did all my brothers and sisters, at St. Joseph's Orphanage on Tivoli Road in Dún Laoghaire. St Joseph's had been built in 1860 as an orphanage offering permanent and temporary residential care, including education, for children in need. The school later opened its doors to day pupils but was still called 'St Joseph's Orphanage'. At the age of four I went to the Infants' School. It was a school rather than a 'kindergarten', and we sat in rows of tiny double desks and had lessons from day one. Our first class was called 'Low Babies' from which one graduated to 'High Babies' and then on into the Primary School. I went on my first day with my brother Gerard, almost an adult figure, at seven or eight years older than I was. The classrooms were off to the left of a long corridor, on the wall of which, at about the right height for little arms to reach, was a row of double coat hooks, a small hook for the coat and a big one for the scarf or hat. My enduring memory of the day is standing in the corridor, my back to the wall, arms spread-eagled, my little fists clenched around the hooks and my feet firmly planted against the wall, crying disconsolately not to be made go into the classroom. I don't know who prised my hands off the hooks, it may have been Gerard, but I soon came to realise that those nuns had strong hands too.

The religious who guided my first academic steps were an interesting lot. They were a French order of nuns, which was exotic (not to say incomprehensible) for a four-year-old, and they were called Daughters of the Heart of Mary. They wore plain clothes, which was somewhat confusing in a time of long black or brown habits and wimples. They wore no habit because they had been persecuted in revolutionary France and had discarded their habit to save their lives. They were also called 'Miss' rather than 'Sister' and my recollection of Miss Keating, the head honcho, is of her wearing an elegant, well-cut dress and jacket with a discreet string of beads. In my imagination they are pearls, but I don't know whether the vow of poverty would have stretched to that.

One of the more embarrassing events of my young boyhood happened in that first classroom which, interestingly, didn't at all scar me for life. I think the name of my first teacher was Miss Egan and I must have felt a bit intimidated by her. As a result, I was afraid to ask to go to the toilet when I needed to. This may also have been because of the custom of asking for permission in Irish. Strange though it may seem, there are likely to be millions of Irish men and women around the world whose knowledge of their native Irish tongue extends to the recitation of the *Our Father*, (most of) the words of the National Anthem, *The Soldiers' Song*, and 'Can I please go to the toilet'. I can still remember it: '*An bhuil cead agam dul go di an leithreas, ma sé do thuil e?*' Which sounds something like: '*On will cad a gum dull goodee on leh'ras maw shay dehull eh*'. In any event, although I can say it now, I couldn't say it then and I sat nervously wriggling in my seat while my need grew ever more pressing. Eventually the pressing paid off and a trickle of golden liquid appeared from under my desk to wend its way slowly across the polished floorboards. To this day I can see it and remember the shame and consternation. What should I do? Deny? 'No Miss Egan, it was Jerry, not me'. 'Well, how come it's your pants that are wet then mister?'

As it transpired, this was clearly not an uncommon experience for Miss Egan as she whisked me away, got me to wash and dry myself and provided me with a cute little pair of blue shorts from the spare shorts drawer; I can see them now. Clearly, a supply was kept for these occasions. Mercifully, I don't recall being made fun of by the other kids and I think she just used the event to encourage us to tell her when we wanted to go - my first tiny lesson in assertiveness. For the rest, the first two years passed uneventfully. Mostly I remember coloured chalks on slate boards, plasticene that we called by its Irish name of '*mála*' (rhyming with 'bawla'), and lonely lunches in a cold playground with sandwiches wrapped in grease-proof paper, cheddar cheese, or fish paste, or my favourite, bread and dripping.

My memories of those childhood years are mostly photographic stills, there is almost no video, no sequences of events. At home I remember my father's monochrome *gros point* work hanging on the walls, unbleached linen stretched in thin black frames. The living room sofa with a bright orange loose cover stood against the background of the dark wood-effect wallpaper. For a while there was a gleaming old piano with brass candle holders that my mother played well; Percy Grainger's *English Country Gardens* and *Drink to me Only with Thine Eyes* were favourites. I was fascinated by the inlaid brass name in cursive script above the keyboard: *Rudolf Ibach Sohn*. Later on, there was a glass display cabinet with sundry pieces of Waterford crystal, some sherry glasses salvaged from the Red Lion, a majolica bell that my mother said had come from Cassino after the Allied bombardment of the monastery on Monte Cassino, and two small crystal swans that my father had brought home from the war wrapped up in thick woollen socks. On the wall near the table my mother's Spode plates took pride of place in their coil sprung hanging frames.

The four blue plates had hung on the wall in their clasps for as long as I could remember, all of my six or seven years. Italian Spode. Special. There were two large serving dishes and two dinner plates with scalloped corners. They had a hallowed aura, as if they were holy icons, unlike anything else in the room. They came from another world, another time, hoarded treasures that pointed to an easier past, a prosperous past, a past connected to things that were loved and stable, and solid, and respectable. Now, they're out of fashion, you can buy them for not very much on eBay. Then, they were treasures, relics to be venerated, not touched. We kids knew all that in our bones; we couldn't have said it in words, but the burden of the scant legacy sat heavily on each of us, small children that we were. Or perhaps it was just me; I don't know. I was a child sensitive to my mother's needs and to her sorrow and loss, and to her bereavement, which I had witnessed, unknowing, at first hand.

I don't know what the game was, but I was playing indoors in the living room with my sister Nora. You can imagine us kids whirling around, arms extended, maybe just seeing who could last the longest before falling over. Alas, it wasn't me that fell but one of the plates, with a flash of blue and a crack as it struck the wooden arm of the sofa, then shiny fragments on the dark grey lino. My tiny conscience, already well-schooled in never paining my mother, was aghast at what I had done. These four plates were among the last of the things she had salvaged from her home before making the wartime journey into exile. My fear was not of any punishment to come, but of witnessing her hurt and knowing that I had caused it.

How could I deal with her distress? What better way than to join in? I began to cry, at first out of duty and perhaps strategy, hoping that by seeing me sad she would be less upset and feel sorry for me. Then the tears acquired a life of their own and ran freely. I felt the sadness I had imagined. Attracted by my sobs, my mother came into the room and I told her between gulps and sniffles what had happened. My tears had the desired effect; she cuddled me and said: 'Don't worry, worse things happen at sea'. She should know; her husband had been a sailor.

FIGHT THE GOOD FIGHT

*R*eal school came with my transfer to the junior school of the Christian Brothers College at Monkstown Park. Our Latin motto was *Certa Bonum Certamen* – Fight the Good Fight, which conveniently abbreviated to CBC. The fight in question was against the devil and all his powers and dominions, the fight to be good, and later the fight to be pure in thought and deeds. It will probably not be encouraging for the teachers among my readers when I say that from my six years of primary school, I remember only one class. It was a drawing class and consisted of the teacher, an elderly Christian Brother, drawing a picture of a car in white chalk on the permanently dusty blackboard for us to copy in our exercise books. I remember the outline of the car, a sort of Model T shape with a high cabin and a protruding front part, taking up the entire blackboard, and my admiration of the teacher's talent at being able to draw with such confidence. I was sharing a desk at the back on the right with Gary Keenan, or perhaps Frank Kelly, and most of the time we amused ourselves playing knuckles. There are two ways of playing knuckles. In the first, the contender whose turn it is to be struck, presents his (it was always played by boys) clenched fist, with the back of the hand upwards, and as the striker is about to strike, he can withdraw his proffered fist at the last moment to avoid being struck. If he succeeds in avoiding the blow, he gets to strike. If he is hit, he has to present the fist again. It is a game that rewards deftness and gives a fighting chance to both parties. In the second version, the contenders simply take turns in holding out their fist to be struck on the knuckles by their opponent's knuckles. The person who loses is the person who gives up first. It is a game that rewards endurance and masochism. We played the latter version.

I was good at school, I loved it and I had some great teachers. I was also able to control my bladder by this time, which was an advantage. What I was not able to do was to fight, although this was not a problem as school was mercifully free of bullies and there was only the odd idiot. I can only remember hiding out in the toilets on the one occasion. I think someone had thrown a particularly hard snowball in my face and I wanted to conceal my tears. Apart from this, I am happy to report a school life free from any terrible trauma even if I did struggle with the nine times table.

Brother Keegan was my primary school maths teacher. He was a small, thin man with a wizened face, sparse, short, grey hair and a perpetual dusting of chalk on his black cassock. The grim set of his mouth spoke of discontentment and he seldom if ever smiled, and never with his eyes. His voice was harsh, the sort of querulous tone of someone who doesn't expect to be believed and has always to argue his point of view. He seldom walked about in the class-room, preferring to stand on the dais in front of the blackboard, nervously wiping the left-hand sleeve of his habit with his right hand, and alternating to wipe the right-hand sleeve with his left hand. I didn't like him and I felt on edge in his lessons. One day in class he asked me what four times nine was and I couldn't answer correctly. I now know the trick with the nine times table: for each multiplication you add one to the first number and take away one from the second, so you get zero nine, one eight, two seven, three six, etc. Easy. But at ten years old I didn't know that, and I answered wrongly.

'Wrong!' he thundered, in a voice that the Queen of Hearts would have been proud of. 'Again!' My second attempt at answering was also wrong. His small grey face became visibly red as he said in a trembling Irish brogue, 'Stand up Mr O'Sullivan. Are you trying to make a joke of my class?' I stood up as bidden and answered, truthfully, that I wasn't, but apparently this was also the wrong answer. He stepped out from behind the desk but without stepping off the dais; he was a small man and didn't want to lose the advantage of height. Pointing at me and trembling, he proceeded to tell me in front of the class that the reason for my slackness was my over-indulgent mother, letting me off easy, writing notes to get me out of this and that. His voice rose and fell in sing-song country tones as he went on for quite some time, as if relishing the opportunity of the nine times table to unload on me and my mother. To his chagrin, his rant didn't get to me and I recall standing quietly, buoyed somehow by the knowledge that this wasn't fair. I wondered if the boys in the front row were being hit by his excited spittle. Now, if you're my teacher you can tell me many things, that I'm unruly, that I've misbehaved, that I'm wrong, that I should tuck my shirt in. But never ever tell me that my mother is making a mess of bringing me up. My inside voice wanted to shout at him that he had no idea what it was like to bring up eight kids alone. How would he? Cocooned in his well-fed, all-expenses-paid religious bubble. I didn't say any of this, I just tried to hold his gaze and stay calm, he and I standing up and facing each other across the room, all the rest of the class sitting down, pretending to find objects of enormous interest in the worn wooden grain of their desks. I was a polite boy, thanks to my upbringing by the mother whom he was berating, and my calmness seemed to enrage him even more. His face got redder and his voice got harsher and more contemptuous, and now the boys in the second row were at risk from his spittle. Having exhausted his diatribe, he raised his right arm and pointed at me with his index finger like an umpire sending me back to the pavilion, or an archangel banishing Adam from Eden.

'Get out of my class' he barked, 'and don't come back until you've learned your nine times table'.

'Yes, sir', I said, and I left.

To be honest, I was quite happy to leave and to sit in peace and quiet on the stone steps that looked down the grassy bank and over the rugby pitch. Adults could be very annoying.

At the end of the lesson he appeared with Mr Swords, 'Peadar' (pronounced *Padder*), to his pupils, the teacher who was about to take the class for geography. Mr Swords carried a bit more weight than was good for him and always seemed to be on the point of bursting out of his tweed suit. Pointing to me pityingly, Keegan invited Peadar to contemplate the spectacle of a boy who didn't know nine times four because he was cossetted by his mother, and the two adults exchanged sarcastic smiles, creasing their eyes in mock disbelief.

I continued to struggle with the nine times table until I learned the trick, but Brother Keegan taught me a valuable lesson that day, which I remembered later as a teacher, never to ridicule a child. As my friend John says: 'It's not big and it's not clever'. The taste is unpleasant, and it lasts.

Apart from Brother Keegan I had a good time. I wasn't an outstanding student, as my Leaving Certificate results attest, but I enjoyed learning and I was well-behaved. It was a safer time and almost all of us rode bikes or walked from home to school. We were probably fitter too, thanks to little or no screen time, and thanks to riding home and back for lunch in under an hour. Part of the safety was simply in numbers; there were so many of us going in similar directions that we rode in twos or threes or fours, and there was little motor traffic. The ride to school took me from O'Rourke Park past the coal yard and the piggery where the 'slop man' fattened his animals with the leftover foodstuffs he collected in his donkey cart, then up through St. Kevin's Villas and out on to Glenageary Road. Now the road passes through an estate of endless identical houses, there's a Costa Coffee, and a Tesco Extra. Then, there was a scattering of bungalows on one side and the vast Mounttown Golf Course on the other. The only nod to the golf course nowadays is Fairway Drive, that runs into Fairway Avenue; not a real fairway in sight. Negotiating the roundabout at Mounttown Road called for caution, and then up the hill to the Gothic Revival St John's Anglican church at the crossroads. It seems bizarre to look back and think that we were afraid to go into St John's and have a look. For us Catholics it seemed a forbidden adventure. Was it perhaps even a sin? What if we were caught? The day that we finally faced the fear and crossed the threshold, we found the innocent smells of polished pews, and musty hassocks and beeswax candles. There was no bolt of lightning, just a pleasant English-sounding vicar who said we were welcome to visit, and a little bit of our sectarian world crumbled away.

Not many of my school companions rode all the way to the council estate in Sallynoggin, as we were at the lower end of the socio-economic scale, not that I knew such a term then. But there were one or two who lived on the estate including my friend Barry Sweeney, the first person to whom I ever knowingly taught something. In Barry's case, I taught him to swim. Now this is remarkable because at the time, and for many years afterwards, I couldn't swim myself. Ireland in the 1950s and 1960s was not famous for its swimmers: the sea water was icy and there were very few public swimming pools or 'public baths' as they were called. One day I was down at Seapoint Beach, just along from the sweeping stone mass of the West Pier of Dún Laoghaire harbour. I think I was around eleven or twelve. The day was sunny, and Barry and his mum were there with me. Barry wanted to learn to swim and for some reason I thought I could teach him; in fact I assured his mum that I could. I had seen it done and I knew that one moved one's arms like so, and moved one's head from side to side to breathe, and that one kicked one's feet behind. These were the instructions that Barry needed to hear so I stood on the pebbled beach shouting them at him confidently until suddenly he was moving through the water under his own steam: he was swimming! Both Barry and his mother were delighted with the outcome and his mum showered me with thanks for helping her son. Then she turned to me and said: 'Are ye' not going to have a bit of a swim yerself Kevin?' 'Ah no Mrs Sweeney' I replied, 'I'm not in the mood today'. The experience has stood me in good stead; I have made a career helping people to do things I can't necessarily do myself.

The school was disciplined and, with the exception of one or two teachers, 'messing around' was strictly for break times in the school yard. Our teachers were good and if you wanted to work hard you could. The leather 'strap' was in use, but not arbitrarily or excessively so, and I don't recall any of the sadism I have heard others describe: punishment was strict but not weird. The strap is made from layers of leather about twelve inches long by two and half wide, saddle-sewn on top of each other to a thickness of about half an inch. In our school this was administered on the outstretched hand, palm upwards, the maximum punishment being six strokes. Flinching or withdrawing the hand as the leather strap fell was fraught with danger; the strap could catch your fingers rather than your palm, and that was much more painful. Often the sanctions were more subtle, of the 'I'm not angry I'm just disappointed' variety, appealing to our sense of needing to 'play up, play up, and play the game'.

There was Mr Mullins, square-framed, ex-Jesuit, coach of the rugby teams, teacher of Latin, who discovered that I could run very fast when, for a laugh, my non-sporting friends and I, Dara, Niall, and David, entered the hundred yard heats for school Sports Day; it turned out I could run fast.

'Where have you been hiding Mr O'Sullivan?' said Mr Mullins.

'Nowhere sir'.

'Rugby practice, Monday'.

And there began a brief career as a second centre in the Monkstown Park Junior Rugby XV. My skillset was limited, and what I learned was that I not only had to run fast, which I was good at, but I also had to catch and pass the ball, which I was not good at. However, to my delight, and to Mr Mullins' too, I was good at tackling. Short of stature and light of heft, I nevertheless had no compunction in launching myself at the legs of much bigger boys and toppling them. Who knew? And as our team typically spent a lot more time defending than attacking, my skills were often in demand. I might not be able to score tries, but I could certainly save them or slow down the rate of our opponents' scoring.

Our English teacher, Mr McNeave, was such a smooth walker that he appeared to float or glide along, always looking straight ahead, arms swinging ever so gently and a neatly folded copy of *The Irish Times* in the pocket of his tweed sports jacket with the leather elbow patches. McNeave introduced us to the wonderful, whimsical prose of Flann O'Brien, who wrote a column for the *Times* under the pen name of Myles na Gopaleen (literally, Miles of the Little Horses). Sometimes the column was in Irish, sometimes in English, and always out of left field, wonderfully, creatively, weird. When I met Mr McNeave at the twentieth anniversary reunion for our class in 1989, he told me that he had just retired and was taking creative writing classes; this prospect delighted me. Then there was Brother Mullane, who taught us Chemistry, Maths, and Religious Education; no conflict between God and science there. He was a small man who seemed to run everywhere, an enthusiastic teacher and a fast-paced talker whose mouth sometimes just didn't keep up with his excellent brain. In Religious Education he once asked us earnestly to consider the little known 'Parable of the Prodigal Sheep', and in maths he set us the unusual problem of finding 'the co-ordinates of the missing link'. But no-one made fun of him, well not much anyway. We knew he worked hard, and he always laughed at his own malapropisms once he realised them, sometimes with our help.

Physics was the domain of 'Percy', Percival d'Ardis Corbett, and for many of his students it remained firmly his domain, as he never managed to share it with us. His classes were chaotic, and the physics lab in the basement rippled with whispered conversations, as chocolate bars and crisps were freely if furtively shared. One day, however, we discovered that he was a musician and that he played the violin in a family ensemble, so we asked him to come and give a talk to the Literary and Debating Society on musical appreciation. Some of us were just discovering music and we were earnestly keen to 'understand' classical music, whatever that meant. I had just encountered Mozart courtesy of my sister Nora's Music Appreciation classes. One day on the radio I heard a tune that I liked. 'That's the Eine Kleine Nachtmusik' she said: I was hooked. Percy was magnificent, shedding his Physics chrysalis and emerging as a musical butterfly to give us a very simple message: Don't try to understand music, just enjoy it, and if you like it, listen to it again. Trust your own judgement and your taste will follow. He ended his talk with some Beethoven, whom he described as 'the daddy of them all'. Here was a terrible physics teacher being an approachable and entertaining human being. His exhortation to the enjoyment of personal taste has stayed with me more clearly than the calculation of specific density or the coefficient of linear expansion.

Mr Hurley taught us history. A nice, kind man, but with a boring method of teaching that involved a lot of dictation and memorising and very little thinking. On one occasion he set us homework to write an essay on any subject we chose. I don't know what my topic was, but I know that I scoured the meagre supply of reference books on our shelf at home to look for interesting quotations and impress my audience. Among others, I managed to quote Plato's Republic, which I must have borrowed from the Carnegie Free Library in Dún Laoghaire. Mr Hurley chose my piece to read aloud to the class and, rather than have me read it, he chose to read it himself. When he came to the passage about Plato, what he read out instead was 'Pluto', and I realised as I sat in my desk, that this adult, this teacher, this clever person, who was in charge of my education, didn't seem to know what I was talking about. It is not an exaggeration to say that the veil of the temple was rent in two and I knew I could not entirely depend on adults for knowledge or wisdom.

Then there was Mr O'Neill, my French teacher and a man I liked enormously, mainly because he took me seriously and encouraged me to excel. From him and from the trusty *Cours de Langue et de Civilisation Francaises* I learned to read and write reasonable French, even though actually speaking it with any fluency was often considered a bridge too far in those days of old-fashioned classroom language teaching. He instilled in me a love of languages as great puzzles I could solve, and I won a prize for my performance in French at the Leaving Certificate, the *Complete Works* of *Pierre Corneille*, the most beautiful book I had ever seen, massive, bound in bright red fabric with rich gold block lettering and red ribbon bookmarks. I say that I won the prize, but I have sometimes wondered whether in fact I won it or whether he simply gave it to me as a gift. None of us was aware of competing for a prize and there was no accompanying certificate describing my achievement. In our time together Mr O'Neill and I had only one contretemps, ironically, a word he taught me. He drove a dark grey Volkswagen Beetle which he parked near the entrance to the students' bike shed. The car was often very grimy, the kind of grime that tempts young lads to write 'Wash me!' in the dust. I didn't write 'Wash me!' but instead wrote my initials, KOS, in foot-long letters on every panel of the car. The day after I did this, we were all queueing in front of the bike shed for it to be unlocked when I heard his voice calling me over. In front of perhaps a hundred boys waiting for their bikes, he called out: 'Kevin O'Sullivan, why have I found your initials on my car two days running?

Do you know anything about this?' Like Honest Abe, I could not tell a lie and I confessed that I had done it. When he asked why, I answered limply: 'I don't know sir', and I really didn't.

He huffed and puffed for a while and I offered to wash the car, but he just told me to erase my handiwork: I rubbed the letters off with my navy blue beret. The discerning reader will of course have figured out that I wrote on his car because I wanted his attention, and I think that Mr O'Neill also discerned that. Good relations resumed within days, if a little sheepishly on my part, and no damage was done to the relationship. I often stayed back after class to choose a new reading book from his collection, or to tell him about my attempts at listening to French radio broadcasts on long wave radio. One evening I went with a friend to one of the free concerts given by the RTÉ (Radio Telefís Éireann) Symphony Orchestra in the legendary Francis Xavier Hall on Upper Sherrard Street in Dublin. Waiting in the queue we met Mr O'Neill and we talked about the evening's programme, it was Gluck and Beethoven, and I felt more adult than I had ever felt before. Here I was, talking to a teacher, socially, about something we both liked! I realise now that he was a strand in the dad I was weaving, and would weave for many years, a male adult who would pay me attention and like me.

School for me was just what I needed, an exercise in growing up and learning that this involved sitting at the same table as the teachers, having reasoned opinions and arguing for them, taking responsibility for actions and plans, collaborating in joint enterprises, and creating something new out of my allotted raw materials, something that I might leave behind me when I was no more.

ARS GRATIA ARTIS

I said I had only one memory of primary school, but in fact I have another: going to see the headmaster in his office at the age of ten and asking to be admitted to membership of the Operatic Society the year before I entered the secondary school. Looking back, it sounds a bit like the request of a somewhat precocious child, but at the time it just seemed like such fun to be able to sing and dance and dress up in the annual performance of Gilbert and Sullivan. Born under the sign of Leo and in the lunar year of the Dragon, the Water Dragon to be precise, performance is in my make-up, so to speak.

The headmaster's office smelt of polished wood and leather armchairs. Outside it there was a little lobby with a high-backed wooden bench where one waited to enter the presence. It was as if this quiet space prepared the interviewee for the formality of the occasion, heightening the anxiety of the guilty and calming the nerves of the deserving. The headmaster, seated behind his enormous, meticulously tidy, mahogany desk, with its pristine leather-cornered blotting pad and green goose-neck table lamp, listened gravely to my request. When I had finished, he put his fingertips together slowly, taking some time to line them up exactly, and said that I must wait another year, but I would certainly be able to take part when I was eleven. I was disappointed but I felt I had been heard and I dealt with his refusal very well. My confidence to do that could only have come from my mother saying something like: 'Yes, go and ask the headmaster if you can join'. It was clearly ok to ask for what one wanted.

The following year, having made it to senior school, I realised that far from having to apply to join the Operatic Society, you had to have a pretty good excuse *not* to join, and that being cast in the production was not a mark of distinction but merely an indication that you could hold a note. But this lack of special-ness didn't dampen my enthusiasm. At the age of eleven, I sang in the girls' chorus of *The Pirates of Penzance,* and I appear in the cast photos, with glossy ringlets poking out under my wide-brimmed Victorian bonnet, as a very pretty, if somewhat coy maiden among my equally pretty and coy classmates as the daughters of Major General Stanley. In the same photo, my friends, Peter Costello and John Maloney, look particularly fetching, with dimples and rouge that conjure up a Regency romp by Georgette Heyer. At the time, we didn't have a hall or a gym on the school grounds and our performances were in Dún Laoghaire Town Hall, an imposing granite edifice, in what I now know to be the Lombardo-Romanesque style, which has graced the harbour end of Marine Road and brought a flavour of Italy to this Irish seaside town since 1879.

For the whole year our rehearsal space consisted of three upstairs classrooms whose hinged wooden partition walls were folded back for the occasion. Opera practice was in the evening, with Mr Flood, whom we called Muddy Waters behind his back, teaching us the tunes from the piano. On the evening of November 22nd, 1963, the younger boys of the female chorus were gaily *'climbing over rocky mountains, skipping rivulets and fountains'* when we heard that President John F. Kennedy had been shot and killed in Dallas, Texas. The news was cataclysmic: he was one of our own, an Irish name, a Waterford family, of the Catholic faith, and to our unsophisticated eyes, one of the good guys. I cycled home alone after opera practice, in the dark, my only illumination the old-fashioned front lamp with two enormous cylindrical batteries – only the richer boys had dynamos on their bikes. What an event to intrude into the safe world I lived in at eleven years old! My sisters Heidi and Nora were huddled on the orange-covered sofa in the living room crying together because of the news. I wondered what it was that had touched them so deeply as to cry. I was puzzled and shocked, but not tearful.

Everyone who lived in my little world shared my shock. How could it be that a charming, smiling man, who had said, 'Ask not what your country can do for you. Ask what you can do for your country', could be gunned down, and in the light of day, like a gangster? Only a few months before, for heaven's sake, he had been in Ireland! We had crowded into the houses that had television sets and watched entranced as he told the people of New Ross that his great grandparents had left Ireland with two things: a strong religious faith and a strong desire for liberty. The crowd went wild. The crowd went wild too when he told the people of West Berlin, 'Ich bin ein Berliner'. I was only eleven, but I knew what had happened during the Cuban Missile Crisis; we all did. We learned about mushroom clouds and practised hiding under tables. Who didn't love this man? Who were these people who thought so differently from me that they wanted to kill him? Surely, he was doing good? It was my first conscious taste of trauma, albeit at one remove. Having been born after the war, and not having known my father, who had fought in it, I was unaware of what it felt like at first hand to have people in the world who wanted to kill people that you loved, or wanted to kill you. JFK's death did what any trauma does: it changed the way I thought about the world and made it a less safe place. I realised later that the tears of my sisters and of others were for a certain loss of hope, that something could change and be better. I had a lot to learn about how the world worked.

The show went on and the dress rehearsal seemed to come suddenly, when we took over the Dún Laoghaire Town Hall and swarmed like large, excited ants through the meeting rooms behind the stage, commandeered as dressing rooms. Piles of big flat boxes from Bourke's theatrical costumiers awaited us, each one containing a single costume for a pirate, or a maiden, or the Major General. The boxes were old and used year after year and the clothes wrapped in crisp tissue paper smelt wonderfully of excitement infused with old make-up and mothballs. For the girls' chorus and 'female' soloists the mothers were in attendance, choosing and fitting and pinning the dresses ready to take home and sew to the measurements of their respective sons. It was taken for granted that every mother knew how to sew; it was part of the job. In any event the sewing was basic, mostly accomplished with blanket stitch, 'homeward bounders', that could be quickly removed when the costume had to be returned.

When the big night arrived, we donned our dresses, helping each other with buttons and bows and wigs, and offered our faces like pros to the ministrations of the mothers who now doubled as make-up artists. I want to say that the smell of the greasepaint offered a Proustian moment, but in fact as I recollect it was merely disgusting, thick and caked-on, and made one very hot under the flood lights. Mr Flood nervously gave us a last-minute team talk and then took up his position in front of his scratch orchestra, the first orchestra I ever heard play. Silent behind the thick green satin curtain, we listened to the overture, grinning nervously, and poking each other until the curtain rose to the applause of the assembled family and friends and even some 'Oohs' and 'Aahs' as the glory of the scene-painters' art was revealed. I don't remember us being awkward or shy about the whole affair; we just had fun.

The ladies chorus in *The Pirates of Penzance* are the wards of Major General Stanley, all shy and naïve young ladies, and the men's chorus are dastardly Cornish pirates who will stop at nothing. Later on, there appears a chorus of lugubrious and timorous policeman, hardly preferable to the pirates, who are at least glamorous. The plot of the opera is, of course, entirely ridiculous, making the performance akin to musical pantomime. The wonderful thing about this is that it takes the pressure off needing to present a flawless performance. Any gaffes can be easily turned into entertainment. Maybe this is why G&S has remained a staple of amateur and professional companies alike. To get a flavour of any of the operas, there is no better way than to listen to Anna Russell performing her hilarious one-woman act: *How to write your own Gilbert and Sullivan Opera*, on the stage of the Metropolitan Opera in New York. She captures perfectly the simpering soprano, the pompous bass, the dashing tenor, and the ill-favoured contralto, as well as the stage dances that look like beginners' step classes (without the steps), and the madrigals that Abba would have made into hits. All in all, it's the perfect introduction to being on the stage, and I loved it. Perhaps the lesson was that if you're doing something that's supposed to look silly, you don't look silly if it goes Pete Tong. To this day, almost nothing embarrasses me.

The following year I distinguished myself among the pining Venetian girls of *The Gondoliers* by strapping on castanets and dancing the 'cachucha, fandango, bolero' as the rest of the chorus 'tra la la'd' with gusto. The peak of my operatic career came in my third appearance, still before my voice had broken, as *Pitti Sing*, one of the Three Little Maids from School in *The Mikado*. By the time this production came along we had a brand-new school hall with a proper proscenium arch stage, but it was the beginning of the end. We performed only one opera in the new venue and then the musical and dramatic guard changed. The following year we performed a pageant celebrating the history of Ireland, all grand gestures and historical tableaux, like something out of E. F. Benson's Mapp and Lucia novels. After that I lost interest.

Twenty years later, driving up and down twice a week on the

A22 from Goldsmiths' College in London to St Bede's School in Sussex in a car that had no radio, I entertained myself through the drive by singing through the airs and choruses of these biting and witty satires on late Victorian life and customs.

Somewhere along the way I entered the Father Matthew Feis, a great annual celebration of song and poetry and drama in the Father Matthew Hall in Church Street, Dublin, named in honour of Father Theobald Mathew, a Franciscan Friar who campaigned for abstinence from alcohol, the cause of enormous social harms in Ireland. An Irish *Feis*, or *Feis Ceoil* (pronounced 'fesh kyole'), like in its Welsh equivalent, the *Eisteddfodd*, is where performers compete for prizes in their various arts. The Oscar winning actress Brenda Fricker, and Gay Byrne, the host of the world's second longest running chat show, *The Late Late Show*, both made their first public performances in the Father Mathew Feis. Alas, I did not parlay my small triumph in the English language poetry category into a career in showbiz, as I recited a poem by Colly Cibber called *The Blind Boy*. I stood small but somehow confident on the stage, head held high, declaiming the words to the accompaniment of the hand gestures that someone now forgotten had taught me. The poem tells the story of a blind boy who manages his lot with radical acceptance, telling his listeners not to pity him, and it has stayed with me for nearly sixty years, particularly the last two lines: 'While thus I sing, I am a king, although a poor blind boy'. The idea of making the best of what you had and not wasting time in nostalgia for the unattainable resonated well with me. I think I had somehow caught the trick of both accepting what there is and at the same time aspiring to greater things. If you have only one or the other, you risk the disappointment of what never was or what never can be. If you have both you can be content almost anywhere.

The second artistic triumph of my primary school days came at another *Feis*, this time at the Damer Hall, home of what has been described as 'the golden age of Irish language theatre', although I don't think this included my performance. I played the title role in Pádraig Pearse's play *An Gadaí* (pronounced 'On Goddee'), *The Thief*. My costume was a plaid shirt and dark shorts, I think they were both from my own wardrobe, and the distinguishing mark was a beautiful woven woollen *'crios'* (pronounced 'kris'), a traditional Irish narrow sash that functions as a belt. The play was in Irish, and we performed well enough to win an award and for me to take out the *Best Actor* gong, but for many of us reciting our lines, *as Gaeilge*, was more a feat of memory than of understanding; our command of Irish really wasn't that good, at least mine certainly wasn't. After we had finished our performance, we went to sit in the audience, still in costume and makeup, to watch the next play in the competition. I was greeted warmly by the family I sat next to, all craning their necks to look along the row towards me, nodding and smiling their congratulations on our performance. They were Irish speakers and I assume that they were whispering nice things, but thankfully the hush in the theatre precluded any conversation and spared me the embarrassment of failing to reply. The dad offered me boiled sweets from a little white paper bag and initially I was happy to accept, saying thank you, *'Go raibh maith agat'*, in my best stage accent; that much I could manage. After a while I didn't really want any more sweets but I couldn't for the life of me think how to say 'No thank you' in Irish. I had to flee, smiling and gesturing with my head towards the exit while the dad insisted on giving me one for the road. Thankfully, when the medals were awarded, no gracious acceptance speech was required.

It will be clear by now that I was more artistic than sporting, and I have related how for many years I managed to avoid the rugby team. For most of my school years my contribution to its physical culture was nothing more strenuous than the Swedish Drill exercises in the annual school sports day. This drill was a sight to behold. Almost the entire school, about six hundred boys, all in white shirts, long white pants and whitened canvas shoes, ranged in a great serried square across the playing fields. Some of us carried two small pennants like semaphore flags, others had canes about a metre long and painted, as were the flags, in broad stripes with the colours of the school: black, gold, and red. We marched onto the field four abreast and then, by a routine of turning left or right, spread out into a great white matrix of roughly twenty-four by twenty-four boys. Once in position, we marched on the spot until the brass band fell silent, and in the hush we looked attentively at the distant conductor standing on a makeshift podium. At his signal the band struck up again, *The Skater's Waltz* by Waldteufel, I can hear the music now, and the great mass came to life as one, raising this arm or that, twisting to the right or to the left, flags up, flags out, flags down, canes above our heads, down to the right, down to the left. To catch the rhythm of our movements, just say to yourself: 'one two three, one two three, one two three' as if you were waltzing, and make one movement for every three beats, repeated endlessly, hypnotically while, without a hat in sight, we all got sunburned faces and heads for the glory of the school.

If I couldn't defeat the school's opponents on the rugby field, I could defeat them on the debating stage. It is a mystery to me how I became good at this or where I got the self-assuredness to speak on virtually any topic under the sun, but I had that utter confidence in the worth of my own opinion that only teenagers ever really achieve. Perhaps one of the purposes of the teenage years is to try out narcissism and, hopefully, get it out of one's system. The Vietnam War, Russian communism, the introduction of the driving test in Ireland, artificial contraception - the topic didn't matter. Just propose a motion and I was equally at home in defending it or opposing it. When I entered fifth year in 1967 the debating society, or to give it its full name, The Literary and Debating Society, had languished through lack of interest. It was usually run by the sixth years, but perhaps they had finished their narcissism run somewhat earlier than usual. Their lack of interest created a leadership vacuum, but they didn't mind if the earnest fifth years took it over, so at the age of fifteen I found myself elected as Auditor of the Society, possibly the grandest title I have ever had. I cringe more than slightly when I think how smug and opinionated I must have been in those years, but it was fun constructing arguments, especially tongue in cheek ones, and even more fun if we carried the votes of the adjudicators against Blackrock College or St Mary's Dominican Convent in Dún Laoghaire. We succeeded in reviving the Society and we organised regular debates, filling the school hall, and debating either among ourselves or competitively with other schools. I prepared speeches, often using an astonishing book we had at home called *Enquire Within Upon Everything*, no internet in 1968, and managed to quote Greek philosophers, noted politicians and historical figures, and even to appeal to the new analytic philosophy to defend or oppose the motion at hand. I can't say for sure which side of any motion I was on, the sides were decided by the toss of a coin, and speakers came to the topic with equal vehemence whether they believed in their cause or not, which was a terrific training in the art of being able to lie convincingly.

I remember only one evening with clarity. We won a debate on Russian communism, and I was awarded ninety-nine points out of a hundred. The adjudicator took one point off because I flicked my hair back in the style of Miss Piggy from *The Muppets*; he must have mistaken my nervousness for affectation. I can no longer flick my hair back as I no longer have hair, but I don't think this means I would earn a full one hundred points today. My knowledge of my own ignorance, while not crippling, acts as a useful brake on my capacity to pontificate.

AN AWKWARD TEEN

*A*ll through my youth I thought that being in Ireland was a transitory thing. It was not a definitive place to be, but rather a place where one waited for the *real thing*. Whatever that was it would inevitably involve leaving Ireland, probably for England, where someone would turn the sound up and real things would happen. Knowing that this was a phase, I was eager for it to pass and I developed a knack of looking beyond the present, to the possibilities of the future. I was impatient, but I knew that certain things had to be got through, to be endured, so that I could get to the good stuff. I taught myself to delay gratification, a talent I still have. I realised that this was my secret: that one day I would be in a place that was more real, one that made more sense, and had greater value. I also realised that no one else in my class, which was pretty much everyone I knew, had this secret knowledge, nor did they need it because, unlike me, they *belonged* in Monkstown, in Dún Laoghaire, in Dalkey, in Ireland. I never spoke about it to anyone but was utterly confident in my insight. Curiously, I didn't need to know what the *real* thing was going to be, just that it was going to be something different than Ireland. It would be ten more years before Abba told me that if I had 'a dream, a song to sing' it would help me 'cope with anything': I already knew.

The swinging psychedelic sixties arrived; I was ten years old when the Beatles had their first hit, *Love Me Do*. Across the Irish Sea lay London's Carnaby Street, miniskirts, Mary Quant, and a whole cultural revolution. My sisters bought the latest records, singles and LPs, 45s and 33s. The brittle 78s of *Mario Lanza* and *Salad Days* and the serene *Meditation* from *Thaïs* were relegated to the back of the record cabinet with its moulded veneer doors and brass casters. By then we had a record player that you plugged in to the socket rather than one you had to wind up. Further afield there was Haight-Ashbury and San Franciscans wearing flowers in their hair. The mantra of the time, courtesy of Timothy Leary, was to turn on, tune in, and drop out. A time of free love and experimentation, of anything goes, of doing 'your thing'. A time of wearing your hair and dressing as you pleased. Dylan had already told those in power not to stand in the doorway or block up the hall but, as always, they ignored his words: the old guard thought it was a phase that would pass and order would be restored. I read *The Republic* for a homework essay and discovered that Plato had criticised the hairstyles and the music of young people in his time. It was my first inkling of *plus ça change*, the realisation that history was just one thing after another, and that each generation misunderstood and criticised the next. We were not just of the sixties, we were firmly in a millennial tradition.

At home in Sallynoggin the stirrings were perhaps not so profound, but there were certainly frissons of change. My sisters wore miniskirts and screamed at the Beatles. I bought a garish shirt with huge paisley swirls, and flared trousers that flapped, but the exhilaration of the time was tempered for me by the need to go to school and achieve. Others might be rebelling but I never quite relinquished the need to be a good boy, the need not to disappoint my mother, or add to the burden that I couldn't define but I knew she bore. I was a year younger than most of my classmates. A quirk of birth date meant that while most of my companions did their Intermediate Certificate aged 15 or 16, I did mine aged 14. The following year, while some others were exploring sex, drugs and rock 'n roll, I was choosing which religious order to join.

It is Christmas time as I write, and I heard the carol *Once in Royal David's City* on the car radio the other day. There is something about the way in which an English boy soprano clips the syllables of *Ma-ry* and rolls the r of *Christ* that still echoes in my now agnostic soul. But the line that caught my attention as I navigated a tricky roundabout was: *'Christian children all must be, mild, obedient, good as he'*. *'Must* be', nothing less, no ifs, no buts: mild, obedient, good. Of the millions of people who have sung this carol socially at Christmas time, or heard it in school concerts, or shopping centres, or lifts, somehow, from the time I was a kid, I came to buy it, to believe it, and to think that I should practise it. And not only must I *be* good, I must *do* good. Martin Luther knew the power of a good rhyme when he spread the Reformation in the lyrics of singable German hymns. My head is full of lines from songs and poems, many laden with moral significance, that have stayed with me all my life: Thomas Gray's *Elegy*, Rudyard Kipling's *If*, Padraig Pearse, William Butler Yeats, Abba. Are they there because I grasped the significance of them, or do I think them significant because they're there?

It's a bit of a mystery to me how my social conscience got to be quite so strong. Perhaps the usually evanescent enthusiasm of teen age absorbed the light of my mother's little kindnesses and exhortations to think of others, and changed from an annual into a hardy perennial. There were certainly no great political or social discussions at home; we were not a family that solved the world's problems at the dinner table. In fact, I don't remember any issues at all being discussed. Perhaps I acquired my social awareness by osmosis from my teachers, religious and secular, none of whom, I am glad to say, tried to sexually abuse me, and all of whom encouraged me to make a difference, true to the school motto of fighting the good fight. Or perhaps I was simply an opinionated git who had some natural talent for speaking and liked the sound of his own voice, and who, having risen to dizzying heights in the Literary and Debating Society, got used to having an opinion on every issue of the day and speaking about it with the dangerous confidence born of little knowledge and many hormones.

My fifteenth birthday came about a month after the end of the riots in Paris that started in May 1968. We all knew the name Dany le Rouge, the red-headed 'red' who was often the face and voice of the rage and the chaos. With piercing, smiling eyes under a shock of orange hair, and an upward tilt of his head that welcomed all questions, his strong voice told the world confidently where it had gone wrong and how he and his companions were putting it right. If a kid seven years older than me could bring France to a standstill and be on the news in Ireland every night, what of me? What could I do? What should I do? At school we debated furiously the injustices of capitalism, the legitimacy or otherwise of the Vietnam war and the threat of nuclear weapons. I have a newspaper photo of myself on a sit-down protest for some forgotten cause involving hunger. I am sitting on the ground among four other students, all from university, our backs against a white caravan, all rugged up against the Dublin cold in duffle coats and scarves. How did I meet these people? How did I get involved? They were all from university; how did I even know them? What was the cause? I can't remember. Somehow it mattered less what the cause was than that one protested, that one obtained credentials for having an opinion, for speaking out, for not buckling to what the system wanted. Like other schools around us, we formed a secondary school union. Again, I'm not sure what we achieved or even what we wanted to achieve, but the important thing was to have taken the step of forming the union. Not sure what to do - there were no Greta Thunbergs among us - we just wanted to put the system on notice that if we wanted to do something at some stage, then we were organised to do it.

Mao's *Little Red Book* had appeared in 1964 and the Cultural Revolution had kicked off in 1966. God help us, we had no idea of the carnage and massacre obscured by this suave name: with the word 'cultural' in the title, it couldn't be that bad, could it? The possession of a *Little Red Book* would certainly be a credential, so I sent off for one. In fact, I sent off for a whole package of goodies: in for a penny... Besides the *Book*, I asked for an English-Chinese dictionary and some magazines in English about the exciting events happening in China. But I was cautious. Someone had warned me about kids who had made contact with the Chinese Communist Party and then been pursued by them with endless attempts to engage them and involve them more; I just wanted my book. I wrote my initial letter in English, but gave my name and address in Irish, a thin veneer. When my parcel arrived, I wrote back to thank them, still with my Irish name, and told them that I was leaving my bourgeois home (a bourgeois home - I should be so lucky!) and would be emigrating to the England of the dark satanic mills, where the revolutionary protest was more advanced. No address yet, but they should definitely contact me via the Poste Restante, High Street, Oxford. It appears to have worked as I haven't heard back yet. Then again, I'm not at all sure that there is a post office in High Street Oxford, in fact at the time I wasn't sure there was even a High Street in Oxford: I just made it up.

During the holidays of the Northern Summer of 1968, I went off to join a work camp, organised by an association called Concordia, founded in 1943 in Brighton, England, to support peace and reconciliation. Under its international volunteering program, groups get together to carry out community projects in a given location, often to do with conservation or reconstruction. I couldn't afford to travel abroad, so I chose a project in Ireland, in the little town of Askeaton in County Limerick. Askeaton is a living object lesson in the adage that *sic transit gloria mundi*. Today it has just over a thousand souls, but for two hundred years the Fitzgerald Earls of Desmond ruled over Munster, a quarter of the island of Ireland, from Askeaton's Desmond Castle on its rocky island in the river Deel. The town also boasts the ruins of the magnificent Askeaton Abbey, burned to the ground along with most of its inhabitants in 1579. So much history for such a little town.

But of the twenty-one students, seven from the host country and fourteen from overseas, none of us knew any of this tragic, gruesome history. We cared about the future, and we meant *The Future* in the abstract sense as the future of humanity - would there be one? - rather than what awaited any of us in our individual lives. As with my fellow protesters leaning up against our caravan earlier in the year, almost all were at university or about to go there having finished school. Only three of us were in secondary school, myself and two teenage girls from a convent school in Cork who were dedicated Maoists. 'Convent school Maoist' seemed a faintly ridiculous concept to me, and I don't think they liked me very much; I was much too conventional for them. If they had led a cultural revolution in Munster, I'm sure I would have been sent to a re-education camp in the first tranche. Muriel Spark could have written them beautifully into a 1960s Irish version of *The Prime of Miss Jean Brodie*. Of all twenty-one of my fellow volunteers, I remember only one by name, Vibeke Madsen, one of two students from Denmark, a Scandinavian vision with truly flaxen plaited hair.

Our main task was to construct a dry stone wall along part of the southern embankment of the river Deel, with some access steps down to the water to enable townsfolk to board small craft. None of us knew how to build dry stone wall, but somehow we quickly learned. The trick is to have a big selection of stones of various sizes and to combine large and small ones so that they lock into one another. Simple. You can see the results on satellite photos of the town: look for the ruins of the Franciscan Friary on the east bank of the river Deel near the N69 and you will see the wall and the steps on the opposite side of the river. Our secondary task was to dig some test holes on the site of a proposed swimming pool near the river. I didn't get involved with that part of our work, and I wasn't aware that we made much progress, but it turns out that Askeaton now has an excellent pool and leisure centre, the only public pool in County Limerick, on the site of our digging efforts. Job done.

With twenty-one young men and women in their late teens and early twenties, there was bound to be sex. As a schoolboy in 1960s Ireland, my most adventurous experience of sex was wanking in a tent with other boy scouts in my patrol, the Eagle patrol of the 52nd Dun Laoghaire Troop, Catholic Boy Scouts of Ireland. Whereas this seemed to be something my companions enjoyed with no moral hesitation or complications, for me it was fraught with guilt. Masturbation was a mortal sin, that was a big deal, you could go to hell if you did it and died before you had a chance to confess. Touching yourself, such a genteel euphemism, was a venial sin, but as soon as semen was involved, bam! - you were done for. I had never seen a man and a woman having sex until, stumbling to bed one night in Askeaton, I tripped over two bodies entwined under a blanket. They weren't at all fazed, I think we even chatted for a few moments, before I said good night, vaguely aware that I had crossed into a world where people had sex. So, I thought, I'd better get on and look for someone to have sex with.

One evening we put on a kind of cultural evening for the amusement both of the locals and ourselves, where each nationality sang a song or did a dance representing their culture. The French girls wanted to sing some Edith Piaf but didn't know the words. I knew some of the words to *Milord* and for the words I didn't know, I knew the approximate sounds without knowing which words they represented. It sounds bizarre, but by dint of my singing the words I knew and them guessing which actual words were supposed to be in the gaps, we worked out all the lyrics. My personal contribution to the evening was to read a short story by Seán O'Faoláin; aptly enough it was a story called *Innocence*, where a young boy recounts his first confession. Because O'Faoláin was from Cork, I undertook to render the story in my best Cork accent, only to be told afterwards by the locals that I had done a pretty good job, but in a distinctly Kerry accent!

One of the people who came to our evening's entertainment was a young woman from the town. I call her a young woman and not a girl because she seemed so much older than I was, at least twenty. We hit it off and one evening I walked her home. Possessing the expertise but none of the desire, I stopped to kiss her near her gate. At the interval of more than fifty years I remember the moment of the kiss as being frankly disappointing. What was all the fuss about? We did tongues and everything, and to be honest not only was it a fizzer, but it was even a bit distasteful and left me with no desire to explore further. I really couldn't see what people were going on about. And let's be clear, it wasn't that I was secretly drooling over the handsome blond eighteen-year-old boys whose muscular arms carted stones for the dry stone walling by the river. I had no clear idea of such a thing as being gay, I just knew the French kissing lark was not all it was cracked up to be.

At a distance of over fifty years, it's not really clear to me what I thought about sex or sexuality or how I thought it would play out for me. Mostly I think I was scared; scared of sin but also scared of girls, physical, actual girls of my age, that is, not the romantic idea of girls. I could write poetry with the best of them and did so on one occasion to Maria, a classmate of my sister Nora, who must have been three or four years older than I was and whom I found incomparably beautiful. Mercifully I don't remember the poem, I'm sure it was teenage awful, but I do remember that it contained particular praise of her breasts, ironically a female body part that I had never seen and was destined not to see until over twenty years later, when I met my wife.

There are little moments that seem insignificant but that stay in memory and hold a message. Although they're fleeting, they are sometimes pivotal points in the creation of the narrative, and they're often the stuff of therapy. One such moment comes to mind when I was about thirteen. We sometimes stopped at a little shop on Lower Mounttown Road to buy sweets on the way home from school. We leaned our bikes against the wall and bought gobstoppers or Mars bars or Tayto crisps and ate them in little groups outside the shop, on the forecourt. Among our group this day was Tom, the older brother of my classmate Michael, about two or three years older than us. The conversation was smutty, as our schoolboy conversations often were, and I tried to join in, which didn't come naturally and was always a bit of an effort to me. At one point I remember Tom leaning over to me as he got on his bike to ride off, and saying to me something like: 'Oh no, we don't just want to wank anymore, we want girls'. 'Gosh' I thought, 'I'm not sure I want to progress to that'. The prospect of 'girls' (Tom had substituted another word for 'girls' in a coarse synecdoche that took the part for the whole) seemed fraught, and I knew there and then I wasn't going to be joining in, at least not for the time being. It made sense that this was what the mainstream of boys wanted, but somehow that didn't include me. Sex, any sex, seemed to be fraught with difficulty as far as religion went, let alone trying to get my head around the taboo thought that if I didn't like girls, was it perhaps that I liked boys? On no account could I let myself think that! Maybe better to sidestep it altogether?

Around the same time, filled with zeal to do something useful for those less fortunate than me, I helped to found a chapter of the St Vincent de Paul Society at our school and became its president. Again, I knew little about what I was doing but I sensed it was worth doing and that if I didn't do it, then possibly no one else would. We visited the poor and sick of our neighbourhoods, drinking unhygienic cups of tea with elderly, lonely widows and widowers. On one occasion I was visiting an elderly lady in Blackrock with a fellow chapter member, Fiacre Long, who went on to become a Christian Brother. Our task was to help her clean the house which, by the look and the musty smell of it, the lady hadn't been able to clean for a very long time. Every surface was sticky and clammy to the touch, the kind of stickiness built up in layers, that stays on your fingers and instinctively makes you want to wash your hands as soon as possible. The kindly lady offered us a cup of tea and a piece of fruit cake for our labours, which we both accepted, making sure to wash the cups and saucers first. As we drank our tea, Fiacre looked at me and said we needed to go straight away or we would be 'late'; for what, he didn't say. I got the message, and we took our leave as politely as possible. Once outside, Fiacre leaned over the wall and threw up. It was to his credit that we went back the following week to scour some more.

In my last summer at school, I got a job in the bathing pavilion in Bray, a seaside town south of Dublin in County Wicklow. The pavilion offered changing rooms for swimmers, a café and a small souvenir shop. I tended the souvenir shop where we sold tat of all descriptions as long as it said *A Present from Bray* on it: tiny plaques, tiny urns, tiny cups and saucers, tiny jugs. A design principle of our entire stock was clearly that nothing should be remotely useful for anything other than as a memento of Bray. I was also in charge of opening up the public changing rooms that took up most of the building and locking them up at the end of the day, as well as periodically emptying the penny slots on the toilet doors. People really did 'spend a penny'. They also left copious messages on the walls and doors of the cubicles, setting up assignations for sex, a fact that was titillating for sure, but also somehow terrifying.

Mum was unwell at the time and one evening I needed to leave a bit early to go and visit her in Baggot Street Hospital, which meant a long bus ride all the way from Bray to Dublin, a journey of over an hour. There were separate men's and ladies' change rooms, and I did the lock-up on my own. On the men's side I could march all the way in and check whether anyone was inside and warn them we were closing. On the women's side I had to be much more circumspect, so I would stand at the door and call out in my best loud but polite voice that we were about to close and could they please finish dressing and leave the building. On the evening in question, I called out as usual and, getting no reply, I locked up. The next morning the boss greeted me with the news that I had locked two ladies in the change rooms but, amazingly, he took my side and didn't blame me for locking them in. He believed me when I said I had done my usual routine of calling out and blamed the customers for not letting me know they were there.

His lenience and favouritism were explained a few evenings later when he offered me a lift home in his van. On the way began to tease me and then to poke me playfully. I responded as if it were a game, batting away his hand but halfway home he stopped the car and decided he wanted to tweak my nipples, painfully, as I remember. It was a bit scary, but I was strong enough to stop him and never accepted a lift home again. I got my own back in a small way later on. My pay was five pounds a week plus a meagre commission on sales. It was pretty boring until one of the sales reps who supplied us with the merchandise suggested I have a sale to improve turnover. His rationale was simple: if I sold more stuff I got more commission, and he got more stock to supply. It was a resounding success, my commission soared, and I didn't feel I needed to explain the improved sales to the manager. His income wasn't my concern. Years later I learned about the Laffer Curve, the method of calculating the optimal price to balance adequate turnover and adequate profit. Thanks to my friend the sales rep, I had found it in 1968.

JOINING THE LEGION

*I*t's Friday morning, the bell has gone for lessons, and we sixth-years have assembled in our white-walled classroom. Our blazers are black, our shirts are white, and our ties are striped with the school colours of gold, red, and black. We're lounging against the windowsills along the wall opposite the door, or standing in knots, or sitting at desks and chatting to each other. The studious ones are swapping homework answers, the less studious ones swapping plans for the weekend, the edgy ones swapping dirty jokes and gravelly laughs, and all of us looking relaxed, almost as if the weekend has already come. The long, dusty green chalkboard on the front wall is empty of French irregular verbs or applied maths formulae, and there's no teacher in the room. Soon after nine the door on the right opens from the corridor and a middle-aged man enters, dressed in black. He looks a bit flustered and red faced, as if he doesn't know what to expect but doesn't hold out much hope of a good outcome. He coughs and introduces himself as Brother A or Father B, and tells us he belongs to the *Order of the Holy Something-or-other*. Most of us look up with that 'interested' look that schoolboys are particularly skilled at using when they want you to think they're paying careful attention, when in reality they haven't the least interest in what you're saying.

I'm describing the ritual known as *'The vocations talk'*. A priest or brother from a religious order or diocese comes and speaks to us, pitching a life of prayer and ministry, to which some would be called and fewer chosen. Few in the class pay any attention to these talks, we would never see these people again, and the occasion is welcomed as a free period. Mostly my recollection is of badly dressed, corpulent, red-faced men who wheezed (that may be my imagination), looked remarkably unfit, and spoke earnestly and somewhat coarsely. Often the talk is tinged with a sense of almost whining desperation, 'vocations are falling', 'religious communities are shrinking', we must step into the breach to prevent the decline and save *Holy Mother Church*.

The striking exception to that playbook came one Friday midway through the year, when not one but two figures entered stage right. They were not red-faced, nor wheezy, nor unfit, nor even middle aged. In fact, briefly put, they were dapper, the last adjective you would apply to most of our Friday morning guests. From their well-coiffed hair to their shiny shoes, via their well-tailored suits, free of snuff or gravy stains, they were, well, *stylish*, in a way that no other speaker had been. The smaller and slightly older man introduced himself softly, gently, in the way you would if you were entering a sick-room and didn't want to disturb: 'I am Father Christopher Fernández and I am from Mexico', he said in careful, clipped English. He extended his right hand as if presenting his colleague who took the cue and said, 'Hi, I'm Walter Barnicki, and I'm from Boston, USA'. That's pretty much all I remember from their talk, that and the fact that they belonged to a strange-sounding order called the *Legionaries of Christ*, which had been founded in Mexico less than thirty years before. There were probably boys in the class who still yawned, internally if not externally, but for many the confected looks of attention were replaced by genuine interest, caught up for a while in the passion of these two intriguing foreigners.

At the end of each vocations talk we would fill in a sort of customer feedback card, ticking a box to say whether or not we were interested in knowing more. Most Fridays there would be one or two or none who said yes; the Legionaries got five *Yeses* from my class, including some unlikely specimens. Over the following months we *Yeses* were invited multiple times to the Legionaries' college in Leopardstown for 'seminars' about Latin America and the missions. There might be the screening of a film and there was always lots to eat. Sometimes there was a private chat. If you've ever been to a time-share sales seminar, it wasn't quite as pushy as that, but it came from the same stable.

As well as the Legion, I explored other religious options too. One of my teachers heard that I was interested in the religious life and urged me to think of entering an English-speaking order (the Legionaries worked in Spanish-speaking countries) on the grounds that I had a gift for English, 'a flair' was what he called it, and sure wouldn't it be great to use it to preach in my native tongue? I had obviously impressed him in the Debating Society. Somehow, I came into contact with the Conventual Franciscan order and spent a week with them at their Gothic Revival monastery in Anglesey in North Wales, where one of the novices showed me a place behind the Friary that he had found to go and sunbathe naked without being seen – sunbathing naked in North Wales with an unrelenting stiff breeze off the Irish Sea! Equal parts naughty and brave, I thought. On another occasion I made my way to County Roscommon in the West of Ireland to yet another religious house. Donamon Castle on the banks of the River Suck would make a perfect setting for a Bronte Sisters novel, with its gaunt grey stone façade and square crenelated towers – just add swirling mist and haunting violins. When I visited it was a seminary for the Missionaries of the Divine Word about whom I remember nothing. From my sojourn with the Missionaries all I can see in my mind's eye are the acres of fluttering wild yellow bog iris streaming past as I rode on the back of a motor bike through the Roscommon countryside on the way to or from the seminary, or perhaps to somewhere else; only the irises and the wind remain.

I'm not really sure how I got to be interested in becoming a priest. At the beginning of fifth year, perhaps riding a wave of Captain W.E. Johns and English-ness, I wanted to be a pilot, and not just any old pilot, but a pilot in the RAF. *Wing Commander O'Sullivan* had a nice ring to it. *Sully* to his comrades-in-arms and his men. *Good old Sully* – he wouldn't let you down. *Air Vice Marshal O'Sullivan* sounded even better; no point in aiming low. To increase my chances of entry to the RAF I loaded up my curriculum choices with heavy-hitting science: physics, chemistry, maths, applied maths, and I threw in French and English as a nod to the *Arts* with a capital A. As well as this I made Airfix models and collected *Flight* magazine: *Four easy-to-use binders to store your Flight magazine week by week!*

But somewhere along the way I lost the passion for flying and pale blue uniforms with braid, and a new planet swam into my ken: what if I were to become a priest? Perhaps it was Father Madden, our curate in Sallynoggin, an intelligent man who took me seriously, and spoke to me like an adult, and from whom I wove another strand of my missing father. Or perhaps it was just a logical extension of *Per Ardua ad Astra*, the motto of the RAF, substituting moral *'Ardua'* for physical ones. Or perhaps it was the perfect way of side-stepping the whole sex thing that frightened and puzzled me so much: if I chose to be celibate, that took the matter right out of my hands, and I didn't have to wonder how to negotiate my feelings and my urges.

In my haste to beef up my scientific expertise for the RAF I had dropped the study of Latin which would be necessary if I wanted to be a priest, but help was at hand in the person of my chemistry teacher Brother Mullane. He was a kind man and gave me hours of his free time to coach me individually.

The decision to become a priest evolved gradually. There wasn't a single moment of decision, at least that I remember, not a Road to Damascus moment when the scales fell from my eyes, and I realised this was to be my future. On the contrary, it crept up on me almost without me noticing, so that if someone had said to me halfway through Sixth year, my last year in High School: 'So Kevin, do you want to become a priest?" I would have said something like: 'D'you know, I think I do!', and it would have been a kind of revelation to me. Once that was clear, or clear-ish, the task was then to decide which path to take to get there. All the orders I looked at had pros and cons, but in the end it came down to a choice between two, the Legionaries and the Franciscans, and I couldn't make up my mind. At some point I happened on a technique I have sometimes used since if I have a difficult choice to make between two options: the toss of a coin – with a twist. How it works is that you tell yourself you'll accept the result, and you assign heads to one option and tails to the other. You toss the coin and if the result sits well, you know to go with it. But sometimes you feel a reluctance to follow the coin, and that tells you that you favour the other path. There's no scientific basis whatever to this method, but it works, sometimes. The coin toss said the Franciscans, but I winced at the prospect and decided to join the Legionaries of Christ.

By now, hundreds of thousands of words, mostly in Spanish, have been written about the Legionaries. Many of these are about the spectacular implosion of their founder and first Superior General, Marcial Maciel Degollado, who was finally removed from the congregation by Pope Benedict XVI in 2006 after decades of allegations of appalling conduct, some of it improper, some of it criminal, none of it prosecuted. It includes the sexual abuse of his young seminarians, of having mistresses and fathering children, of years of addiction to narcotics, and allegations of laundering substantial funds through the multi-billion-dollar asset base of the organisation. Books, articles, and websites now document widespread sexual abuse by Maciel and other Legionary priests and their cover-ups of wrongdoing and abuse. There are some memoirs, like *Our Father who art in bed*, or *Driving Straight on Crooked Lines*, or *Moi, Ancien Légionnaire du Christ*, that tell pieces of the story. None is as brutal as the account by Francisco González Parga, *Yo acuso al Padre Maciel*, that gives an account of the sexual abuse suffered at the hands of the sociopathic founder of this crazy, mind-controlling organisation. In a 2015 interview with a Mexican Televisa journalist, Pope Francis described Maciel as 'a very sick man'. Of this wrongdoing and lawlessness, nothing was known to me or to the others who entered the congregation with me. We were keen and earnest with the zeal of recruits to a cause. We were young, sixteen, seventeen or eighteen years old, with the idealism of our years. On my application to join the Legion, under a question asking why I wanted to join, I wrote: 'I have read, *Be perfect as your heavenly father is also perfect*', and that's simply what I wanted to do. God help me, what an innocent I was.

At home, when I talked out loud about perhaps wanting to become a priest, my mother had always said piously, 'If the Lord wants you'll he'll take you'. When the time came to tell her I was leaving home and entering a religious order on the 13th of July 1969, the refrain changed completely. Now it was a lament that I was 'the last child of a widowed mother on a fixed pension', and the grief of imminent separation: 'Who's to look after me?'.

My mother was implacably opposed to my choice. There was every prospect that I could go to University, a first in the family, and her heart was set on me becoming something clever and important and supporting and consoling her in her old age. I didn't know what to do. I had never really quarrelled with my mother before, which seems amazing when I write it, but it's true. Perhaps because she doted on me, she had never opposed anything I had wanted to do, and because I was such a good boy, I had never wanted to do anything that she would oppose.

This was different, and I remember the terrible atmosphere

between us, so much so that for several weeks I couldn't bear to stay in the house in the evenings. I would get home from school, have some tea, and then go out immediately. For some reason that I don't understand, I found refuge in the home of one of my sister's friends, Cora Walby, who lived about half a mile away at the top of Sallynoggin Hill. Each evening I went to her little house, where she lived with her mother, and did my homework. I'm not sure whether I even spoke very much to the family, or watched TV, or did anything else. I mostly just remember the impossibility of being at home.

I enlisted the help of one of the Legionaries, a particularly charming Irishman called Desmond Coates, to come and charm my mother. I somehow persuaded her to ask Brother Desmond down to have a cup of tea and a bit of a chat. After tea I went upstairs and lay on the floor of my sisters' bedroom listening through the floorboards with an upturned glass - a tip I acquired from some detective novel - to their muffled conversation below. Desmond's charm worked, my mother relented and soon was preparing the clothing list of *white singlets (2), white underpants (2) socks, black (4 pairs)* and the other paraphernalia that would soon be concealed beneath the black cassock of the novice. In preparation for leaving home, I gave away all my possessions, which were not plentiful. There were some records and books and some clothes. Giving away my things was a signal of my certainty that this was what I wanted, a complete break with earthly goods and a new life following Christ. Rather than doing exactly what Jesus had said, selling the goods and giving the proceeds to the poor, I gave stuff away to my friends. In 1969 second-hand clothes, records and books wouldn't raise much revenue – better to cut out the middleman.

Leopardstown, where the Legionaries of Christ had their novitiate, could not have been further removed socially from Sallynoggin. The Legionaries had bought a large tract of land adjacent to the residence of the British Ambassador - they certainly weren't about to slum it on my side of the tracks. I remember very little about arriving there to live. I had already visited numerous times and the house was familiar to me. I say house, but it was more of a college, something between a large boarding school and my idea of a luxury hotel. You can see it on Google Earth at the beginning of Leopardstown Road. At the time that I write it has become a German language teaching centre. The building was impressive, long and low in four stories. It was covered in glazed green tiles, with clean lines and halls paved with gleaming Italian marble. Oh, I thought, so that's the marble halls they dream about dwelling in. We each had our own room with an ensuite bathroom (although I don't think I knew that word then). It was a level of luxury I had never known before, and it wasn't too long before the irony struck me that here I had come to profess poverty and leave the world of ease, and my living standards had jumped remarkably. I had a lot to learn.

The building was in the shape of an 'E' but without the middle of the letter. This, we were told, was where the chapel would be built when some more benefactors stumped up some more cash. When I moved later to study in Salamanca and then in Rome, I found that the Dublin 'Front' was built on the same model as these.

To talk about the Legionaries I need first to go through some background and some vocabulary. You may have gathered from their name that a military theme runs through the organisation. The name is a kind of copy-cat version of the Jesuits' *Society of Jesus* or *Compañia de Jesús* in Spanish. In the Spain of the seventeenth century, *Compañia* meant a military unit as in the present day 'company' in a platoon. Ignatius Loyola was a soldier before he turned his hand to religious life, and he remained imbued with the sense of being combative for Christ, thus bearing out Artistotle's insight that 'Men create gods after their own image, not only with regard to their form but with regard to their mode of life'.

With a name like Marcial and a helping of nominative determinism, one could be forgiven for thinking that Marcial Maciel was always going to be military-minded. In 1941 he founded the Legionaries of Christ in Mexico. At first, he called the congregation *The Missionaries of the Sacred Heart and of Our Lady of Sorrows*, with *Legionaries of Christ* as a kind of strapline. Later he would claim that in a private audience with Pope Pius XII, the pontiff told him that the organisation should be *sicut acies ordinata*, like an army drawn up for battle. The great advantage of a private audience is that no-one can contradict your version of what happened. It is quite possible that Pius XII, terrified of the Communist menace to the Church, would use such a military metaphor taken from the Song of Songs, but as with so much of the narrative about Maciel, it is impossible to tell where fact ends and convenient fantasy takes over. It seems more likely to me that there is a chilling parallel with the name of the Spanish Legion led by fervent Catholic Francisco Franco, whom Maciel admired, and which Franco used to lethal effect against the 'godless', leftist Republican forces in the Spanish Civil War. It would be many years before the darker sides of Maciel's life became known, and eventually they would lead to his ignominious removal and his forced retirement to do penance. In the event, the 'penance' was not onerous: he simply retired to one of the estates he had bought for his use and the use of his mistresses. Regrettably, none of the allegations led to criminal prosecution.

The imagery and the vocabulary of the Legionaries, all linked to the idea of fighting for the Kingdom of Christ, occupy the same ideological space as other institutions where religious and military imagery have merged in a toxic swirl. Think for example of the SS, or of the military orders of chivalry on which they partly modelled themselves, such as the Knights Templar. The Taliban and Al Qaeda are not far away. If the comparison seems extreme, remember that these organisations, and indeed many modern religious terrorists, use the aura of sanctity to justify being a law unto themselves and to excuse what appears to the rest of us to be egregious wrongdoing. Members of the Legion wear 'uniforms' not 'habits', they have a flag, an anthem and a salute. Our salute was none other than the raised extended right arm used by the Nazis. You can experience this action for yourself by standing in front of a mirror and raising your right arm in the gesture you have seen a hundred times on documentaries about World War Two: doesn't feel good, does it? This was my first experience of 'cognitive dissonance' a great many years before I knew the term and understood the theory. Briefly, the experience goes something like this: you raise your arm in a Nazi-style salute and you think: *Oh my God, does this mean I'm subscribing to some sort of mind-control freakish, fascist, arrogant ideology bent on dominance and using deceit?* Then you say: *Surely not – this is a good, decent Christian organisation; they're nice, it must be ok.* Bingo, the trap closes, and it becomes possible to believe almost anything.

Consistent with military metaphors, Legionaries live in 'Fronts', used as in the military and political sense of the word, like 'Liberation Front' or 'Western Front'. In July 1969, I went to live in the 'Dublin Front', the *Frente de Dublín*. The lingua franca of the congregation is Spanish, and many terms are borrowed from this language, often transliterated rather than translated.

The community lives in silence of two kinds: relative and absolute. Relative silence prevails during the day and means that if something needs to be said, like 'pass the salt please' or 'that's my toe you're stepping on', it can be said in a low voice, practically a whisper. The exceptions during the day are the two half hour rest periods called '*Quiete*' in Spanish, after lunch and the evening meal, when conversation is allowed, typically *paseando*, walking up and down in the gardens or the corridors.

Absolute silence prevails from after night prayers until after morning meditation. This *magnum silentium* (things always sounded more solemn in Latin), is not to be broken unless in the direst of need, which usually means serious illness.

At the times that Legionaries are allowed to speak, they are still bound by the strictest of rules about what they can say, how they

87

can say it, and to whom they can say it. Conversations must be entirely positive, never voicing any discontent or any misgivings or any differences of opinion, especially if the opinion diverges in any way from that of the superior. Xavier Léger, in his memoir *Moi – Ancien legionnaire du Christ*, tells how one day after watching a movie, carefully chosen and censored as 'fit' for Legionary consumption, he was chatting about it in his small group at *'quiete'*. He thought the movie was dreadful, and said so, only to be called the next day to his superior's office and excoriated for criticising the film. As the film had been chosen and approved by his superior, he was punished for having broken his vow never to criticise a superior: what perfect strangulation of thought.

Legionaries are only allowed to speak to their brothers in the same community or to their superiors. 'Community' is strictly defined and means those who share the same purpose in the same location. For example, in a *Frente* like Rome, there are routinely two or more 'communities': one made up of those studying philosophy, one made up of those studying theology, and one made up of staff who may work at the Vatican or in the parish of Our Lady of Guadalupe. The philosophers may speak only to the philosophers, the theologians only to the theologians, and no one may speak to those outside. Those outside include other students at the University and indeed lecturers and professors on the faculty.

Legionaries took two private vows in addition to the customary three of poverty, chastity and obedience. The extra two were called the 'private' vows of 'humility' and 'charity'. The vow of 'humility' meant never to seek office in the Legion and, going on the adage that 'those who most want to, shouldn't be allowed to', the vow might seem to provide a useful brake on the ambitions of those who would seek office for personal prestige. The second vow however, disingenuously called the vow of 'charity' was the cornerstone of Maciel's deception and self-protection from the exposure of his crimes and wrongdoing for decades. The Legionary vowed before God never to criticise a superior and to inform on any religious who did. Criticisms of Maciel could never be valid, he was a saint, and they were always dismissed as malicious calumnies spread by those who wanted to destroy the work of God. The vow was abolished by Benedict XVI but too late to prevent the cover ups of Maciel's serial offending.

The Legionaries are a congregation of priests, there are no lay brothers. Those who are not yet ordained use the title 'Brother' with their own given names rather than taking a new religious name, usually the name of a saint, as some nuns and monks do. For the next seven years I was to be Brother Kevin.

THE NOVITIATE

*A*t this point in my story, the narrative splits in two as clearly as a railway line at a junction. But rather than diverging, the tracks run in parallel for the next seven years. One track is for the story I sat down to write with hindsight, forty-six years after the Legionary façade caved in, exposing a puzzled and callow Irishman, aged twenty-four, blinking as he emerged though the dust and rubble into the daylight. The other track is laid through the letters, ninety-nine of them, that I wrote to my mother from the various stations and halts along the way. The first track is narrated in a voice that is critical and perceptive of bumps on the line, of signal failures and points that stuck, a voice that is clever enough ultimately to see through deception. It is sometimes angry, sometimes indignant, sometimes scathing, but mostly calm, philosophical even, not strident or resentful. The second voice has a naiveté that makes me cringe, so much so that it has taken me over thirty years to read the letters since I discovered them in a large brown envelope in my mother's wardrobe after her death. They are pompous, and silly, and sanctimonious, and vacuous, and betray a gullible young man on a religious sugar hit. I thought I was so much more sophisticated with my debating, and reading Plato, and listening to classical music, and affecting a pipe, but it turns out I was a kid after all, naively excited by a new life that I had discovered, a life of ideals and spirituality, and changing the world, and Meaning with a capital M. Or perhaps the letters were, at least in part, a façade, designed to shield my mother from what was actually happening behind a screen of pious ranting and constant requests for prayers. They are quite possibly the output of a son who continued the imperative to be a good boy long after he had left home, to look after his mother's feelings, to reassure her, never to worry her. In the ninety-nine letters there is one allusion only, one, to my having any difficulties in my chosen life. It's also the case that I was explicitly forbidden from saying anything negative about my life or about the Legion, first at the direction of the Novice Master and then by a vow.

This dual narrative poses a problem for me. It is tempting, as I dislike the letter-writer so much, to simply ignore the letters and carry on with the more clear-sighted young man whose doubts and scepticism, faint and embryonic as they were, were vindicated by events, chiefly by the fall of Maciel and the investigation of multiple Legionary priests for sexual assault. But this would not be an honest account. The reality is that both narratives go to make a bigger story and show a young man wrestling with himself, his future, his soul, but also with his fear, a genuinely primal fear, of somehow distressing or even harming his mother.

If you ran for elected office in Ancient Rome you wore a white tunic, a *tunica candida*, and you were called a '*candidatus*', a wearer of white. For the first three months or so of our stay in Leopardstown, the Irish Summer, we were also called candidates, meaning that we were putting ourselves forward to be allowed to take the Legionary uniform and become novices. For the status-conscious among us there was the instant opportunity to use the honorific 'cLC', meaning *Candidate of the Legion of Christ*, when we signed our names. *Kevin O'Sullivan cLC*. Sixteen years old and already letters after my name - a promising start. We wore our own clothes, worked around the house and grounds, and generally got used to the routine of prayer and work that would characterise our days. In the *Frente*, there was a community of novices, the stage we were aspiring to next, but of course we were forbidden from speaking to them, even in the Spanish we had begun to learn.

It was 1969 and terrible things were happening in Northern Ireland where people were dying in the increasing sectarian violence. There had always been tensions but for kids of my generation, born after the Second World War and long after the brief but bloody Irish Civil War, Northern Ireland was just a place where you could go on school trips by train and buy Maltesers and small fireworks called bangers, neither of which was available in the South. But already the previous year, 1968, violence had erupted on the streets when the protests by the new Northern Ireland Civil Rights Association had been met with police brutality, and the conflict escalated fast. The so-called *Battle of the Bogside* happened a month into our stay in Leopardstown, three days of unchecked violence that followed a loyalist march that the Royal Ulster Constabulary had permitted to pass along the edge of the staunchly Catholic area of Bogside. A number of our fellow candidates were from over the border in the North and told us frightening news of their dads and brothers and uncles. Letters and phone calls brought stories of fear and injuries and death. Eventually the pressures of the struggle were too insistent and one by one the Northern brothers returned home to Ulster, perhaps to paramilitary action. I remember thinking how immensely grateful I was that I had grown up in the peaceful South, but I also remember thinking that if I had been a youngster in the North, I hoped I would be brave enough to play my part, even if I wasn't too clear what that 'part' might be.

A counterpoint to the shocking troubles in the North was provided by some rich Mexican school kids who we were told were on a kind of religious Summer Camp and were learning and practising English, among other things. With well-groomed mops of black hair, beautiful skin, and expensive clothes and watches, they just seemed like rich kids on summer vacation, although why you would have a summer vacation in Ireland if you were from sunny Mexico begs a curious question. I only remember one of these kids, a cute and friendly 12-year-old called Álvaro Corcuera. Corcuera eventually joined the Legion and was ordained priest. He took the reins of the Legion from the venal hands of Maciel when he became Superior General in 2005 but he resigned suddenly in 2012, admitting he had known that his most famous priest, a man called Thomas Williams, whose square jaw, perfect teeth, and confident manner made him a darling of networks like CBS, NBC and Sky News, had fathered a child with the daughter of the American Ambassador to the Holy See. Despite knowing this, Corcuera had let Williams continue to teach moral theology anyway: *Don't do what I do, do what I tell you.*

Once or twice a week our little white minibus would come round to the front door and we would pile in, Mexican rich kids smelling of expensive cologne and candidates smelling of standard issue Palmolive soap, for a day out. The bus filled with an excited babble in a mixture of Spanish and English and we soon broke into song in the great tradition of coach trips: *I love to go a wandering* and *Ten Green Bottles* mixed with *Cielito Lindo* and *La Cucaracha*: all the classics! One day as we drove past the hospital on Rochestown Avenue I realised that we would turn down Sallynoggin Road and pass my home. I said to Álvaro, 'I'll show you where my house is'. 'Can we go there?' he said. 'No, we'll just drive past, and I'll point it out'.

Turning down past The Noggin Inn, I gestured across the park with its fine old chestnut trees to where my modest house stood, a front door and four little square windows set in rough, pebble-dashed white walls, in the middle of a terrace of twenty or so identical council houses, the pride of Dún Laoghaire Corporation. Álvaro raised his right hand, with the palm to his face, and flicked two fingers. 'Hijo le' he said, a Latin American 'Wow' that could be rude but isn't really. 'That's cool! It's so big!' 'Not that big!' I said. 'No it's really big... but Kevin, why does your house have so many front doors?' It took me a while, but I finally clicked: he thought the whole street was my house.

That summer I had my first and last attempt at driving a dumper truck. The college building had recently been finished and all hands were set to work to landscape the approach to it along the driveway. Our landscaping efforts were modest, and consisted of digging, raking and levelling the dirt on either side of the drive, so that grass could be sewn. A gentle, even slope was taking shape with a fine tilth of soil ready to receive the seed, when for some reason that I don't recall, but which must have been a really good idea at the time, I got to drive the dumper truck. I had never sat at the wheel of a car, any car, but I had driven a bumper car in a fairground, and I thought it couldn't really be any different. Now I am not sure whether you have ever driven a dumper truck, but if you have, you'll know that the steering is through the back wheels, which poses some challenges for a novice driver, particularly one who is not aware of this. Enough said. I can still see the anguished face of the Rector, little softly spoken Cristóforo Fernández, as I ploughed, literally, four deep tyre-shaped furrows across the carefully raked earth. He spoke, as I recall, somewhat sharply, and I discovered to my naïve surprise that, under his suave exterior, little softly spoken Cristóforo had a temper. I have not driven a dumper truck since.

At the end of the summer during which we lost many of our initial recruits, I received my uniform, a plain black cassock with a broad black cincture band (a wide cloth belt that looks a bit like a cummerbund with an extra piece that drapes over the belt and hangs down at the front) and became a novice. Four days later I wrote about it to my mum, telling her it was 'a very simple ceremony but very moving' and that Maciel had given us our uniforms. I also quoted to her a sermon with what would become a well-worn trope for the consumption of parents, about 'how much Christ appreciates it when parents are willing to surrender their children to him in the religious life; His gratitude is immense and his rewards are great'. At the time, it obviously didn't occur to me to ask how anyone knew this, or who had checked with Christ about the immensity of his gratitude and the extent of the rewards, especially considering that there hadn't been any religious orders in his time. I now know that when one caste reserves to itself the privilege of speaking on behalf of the deity, the result can only be deception, but at the time, I was being inducted into the caste and could only see out from the inside.

The novitiate was a much more austere version of the candidacy. We rose to pray early, worked at household chores, learned Spanish, studied Gregorian Chant, and above all we learned the precious art of reflecting on our own inadequacies. To the mortal sins (destination Hell) and venial sins (destination Purgatory) of mere human beings were added the myriad imperfections that beset the seeker after perfection. We learned to examine our consciences interminably, to become the hypochondriacs of spiritual well-being. It was a world of eggshells where any step in any direction might destroy, and where if you did well there was still a trap: you might be proud of doing well and so fall into sin. The full implications of this Catch-22 spirituality only became clear to me many years later, at the moment when I remember taking responsibility for my own actions and decisions, and ultimately the decision to leave religious life, but that was far in the distance. For now, there was the novitiate to get through, Spanish lessons, soccer, and fifty-seven varieties of religious observance: meditation, mass, evening prayer, spiritual reading, the rosary, benediction, visits to the Blessed Sacrament. You name it, we prayed it.

The other thing we did was to change rooms every week. We would pack up our singlets (two items), socks (four pairs), tee shirts (you get the picture) and decamp to another room, perhaps even the one next door. This was an extraordinarily simple and effective way of teaching us not to become attached to any aspect of material life, not a bed, not a room, not a view, not an aspect, not proximity to the stairs or the chapel: nothing. Everything is interchangeable and no particular specimen matters; be attached to nothing except God. All our civilian clothes were put into storage against the day, *God forbid!*, that we might leave and need them. Not being attached applied to relatives and friends too, and family visits were formal affairs, with relatives received in one of the reception rooms on the ground floor to make polite conversation about how wonderful it was to be following one's vocation.

It seems that friends could visit too. Declan de Paor was my classmate and friend. He was an Irish-speaker and usually styled himself Deaglán, which sounds something like 'Day-glawn'. His surname is translated to English as Power and he was powerfully intelligent and passionate to go with it. One day in the autumn I was called downstairs to the reception area as Deaglán had arrived to see me. We met in a small glass-walled sitting room and sat formally on prim sofas across a coffee table where promotional materials about the Legionaries' pride and joy, the Anahuac University, were displayed. There was no question of going for a spontaneous ramble with my friend under the ash and birch and alder trees in the grounds, their leaves now russet and red with hints of gold, or showing him the joint and saying cheery hellos to my companions: visits, like everything else, were choreographed. His opening salvo got straight to the point.

'What the hell are you doing here? What's that get-up?'

'I'm in the novitiate now. It's my uniform'.

'Uniform! God help us, they've got you wearing a uniform'.

'Look, it's what I want. I'm following my vocation'.

'Vocation my arse. This is a con. Would you look at this place! There's a pretty penny here. What's this got to do with Christianity or with the poor?'

I had a go at explaining how poverty didn't have to equate to misery, the trusty Legionary spin, but Deaglán wasn't having a bar of it. We went backwards and forwards for half an hour or more, me defending my corner and Deaglán insisting seriously that I should come away with him, now!

'Jesus man, I'm rescuing you from this shit. Come away with me – I'm serious!'

I blush to remember the sense of superiority and pity I felt in our argument. Just like the Legionaries said, here was a poor benighted soul who didn't see the beauty of the work and wanted to tear it down. As he left to go, he looked at me from the door with disappointment and sadness in his eyes:

'Well if you want to waste your life with these con merchants, good luck to ye!'

I didn't see Deaglán again but I did sometimes wonder later what life would have been like if he had won and I had waded back into the world. He became an internationally respected geophysicist and held a chair at Old Dominion University in Virginia until his retirement in 2017. He died in 2018.

The paradoxes of the novitiate struck me quite quickly. On the one hand there was the long round of highly structured prayer, work, study, recreation and meals, with daily Spanish lessons a priority. A simple life, with simple food, manual work, dedicated study, unquestioning obedience, and a striving to restrain and tame all desire. On the other hand, there was my ensuite bathroom, the state-of-the-art language laboratory installed on the ground floor, and above all, the glittering Waterford crystal and silver cutlery in the guest dining room when benefactors visited. These were usually Mexican or Spanish businessmen, with expensive ties and salesmen's smiles, and they had endowed various building projects in the Legion's growing real estate portfolio, like the Irish Institute, the Cumbres Institute in Mexico City, and the new Universidad Anahuac, then its fifth year. No expense was spared to wine and dine and entertain these guests. I sometimes served in the dining room, maybe my good manners had been noticed (thank you Mum), and there was a certain fawning, deferential quality to the way in which these men were treated by the priests who entertained them, a quality never seen when these same priests were directing our steps to the religious life as our strict superiors. Each major benefactor would have had a personal relationship with Maciel and the local lieutenants didn't want a bad report back to the godfather. In stark contrast to the Waterford crystal and the silver service was the dismissive treatment of some of our relatives. There was Mrs K, for example, mother of a beautiful, gentle, self-effacing brother with a ready smile and a strong brogue that indicated his rural origin. Arriving one day to see her son, she was placed unceremoniously in one of the small rooms by the front door, not quite inside the building, perched uncomfortably and expectantly on the edge of an ornate chair with faux-gilt curlicues, probably the most expensive piece of furniture she had ever sat on. She had travelled a long way to see her only son, but it seemed no one was going to provide some tea for her until I suggested that I should do it, and perhaps find some biscuits. Permission was grudgingly given, as if the visit was a nuisance, not to be encouraged: Mrs K had clearly not endowed any real estate. I wish I had seen these events at the time for what they were – signs of blatant hypocrisy – but I didn't, not yet. I saw them, yet I didn't see them. Idealism, like love, can be blind.

Each novice had a timetable even for the 'free times' during the day, written out neatly on a white index card small enough to be carried around in the pocket of the cassock. This timetable of the five or ten minute 'free' slots had to be approved by one's superior and featured things like *Visit to the Blessed Sacrament*, *Clean shoes*, *Tidy drawers* and other worthy pursuits. Adding in things like *Put feet up* or *Have a quick snooze* wasn't really an option. After lunch and dinner, we were allowed to walk up and down in the gardens, or the inside corridors if it were wet. This promenade, our *'quiete'*, could be done in groups of three or four, never in a group of two, and never in a group of five because this might break into a group of two and a group of three: a group of two was verboten. There are shades of the Holy Hand Grenade in *Monty Python and the Holy Grail*. The prohibition of twosomes was part of avoiding *amistades particulares*, which we transliterated badly as *particular friendships* and really just meant personal friendships. It's quite ironic, in view of the many accusations of sexual misconduct against Father Maciel and other priests and religious in the Legion, that such measures were thought necessary. One of the many Legionaries against whom accusations of sexual abuse were upheld, although not in court, was my novice master, Father Guillermo Izquierdo[1]. He was one of identical twins from the Canary Islands, both Legionary priests. In appearance he was quite a gentle man with a smile-creased face and a sense of humour, but he had a darker side that few suspected who were not the subjects of his sexual attentions.

When I entered the novitiate I had just turned 17 and, not unusually, sex occupied quite a lot of my thinking time, as I am sure it did for my fellow novices although we never spoke about it, or at least I never did. Not only had I grown up in a Catholic family – almost everybody in Ireland did that – but I actually believed the things I was told, mostly about sin and hell. I was comfortable around girls and women – I grew up with five sisters – but I wasn't attracted to girls in the way that I heard other boys talking about them, so I came to the conclusion that somehow I wasn't normal: maybe I was a late starter? At the time, masturbation was regarded as a mortal sin, one for which you could literally go to hell, and long before I was 17 and a religious novice, I had been terrified into believing that my eternal salvation could depend on several moments of pleasure and some ejaculate. Such, we were taught, was God's obsession: that every sperm is indeed sacred. I struggled with this all through my novitiate, trying desperately never to come, taking myself off to odd corners of the building that were unoccupied so as not to attract attention and probably succeeding in doing just that. As time went by, the desire didn't go away and staying 'pure' didn't get any easier. In the second year of the novitiate, I knew that by year's end I would have to take a vow of chastity and I knew that I wouldn't be able to keep such a vow. I went to the novice master and told him my problems, or as much about them as I could bear to. Looking back, my moral struggle was clearly greater than his. As far as I can remember, which is not exactly, I told him I needed to leave because chastity was a hopeless ideal for me. He suggested I go home temporarily, an extraordinary measure to take in the Legion and one I have not heard any other novice describe. The cover story was that my mother was ill, she was in Baggot Street Hospital in Dublin again, and I was going home as a dutiful son. The deal was that I should wear my clerical garb any time I went out of the house but I could wear civvies at home.

During my childhood my mother had often been ill and in and out of hospital, so it was no great novelty to be visiting her in Baggot Street. The problem was how to tell her that I wanted to leave the congregation. Anyone who knows the concept of the 'spoiled priest' prevalent in the Irish Catholic Church until recently, and maybe still today for all I know, will understand the burden of this decision. Leaving the seminary led to ruin, social ostracism and quite probably eternal damnation: 'He who puts his hand to the plough and turns back is not fit for the Kingdom of Heaven'.

Stepping outside the Legionary door didn't mean stepping outside my conscience or escaping from my fear of sinning. I kept my actions in check but freed from the routine of the novitiate, my thoughts turned more frequently to sex, and women didn't feature in the erotic thoughts that made it past the gatekeeper whether waking or sleeping. I barely allowed myself to think about the implications of this. In my tortured mind there was no moral, religious, or even social space where I could contemplate an alternative to being heterosexual, but neither could I contemplate a life of chastity; better to leave the congregation and work it out, somehow, in the world, however friendless the world seemed just then.

I vividly remember my conversation with my mother. The hospital ward was long and hushed under high Victorian ceilings and my mother was in a bed at the end on the left, propped up against pillows. Nurses glided around in close fitting blue uniforms and brilliant white starched aprons and veils, tucking in bed corners, checking pulses on their upside-down watches, and closing curtains to offer enamel bedpans. Those were the days when, unlike now, patients were actively discouraged from getting out of bed or doing anything for themselves. I sat nervously on the tubular metal chair beside the bed and asked Mum how she was feeling. I don't really remember what she said because my mind was racing with my mission: it was a day that might change my life. I prepared the ground by telling her how very unhappy I was and then letting her know that I wanted out. I watched her face carefully, a skill acquired over seventeen years of being a good boy. I expected that she might be happy to have her son back with the prospect of university, a career, and care in her old age. Instead, she looked at me from the hospital bed with an angry face and said: 'I haven't made all the sacrifices I've made so that you can leave that place!'. They were not the words I had expected to hear, and they shocked me so much that I can hear them still. Fifty-one years later, when I finally brought myself to read the letter that I sent to Mum after my return to the novitiate, I found the same words verbatim, and also found that I thanked her for saying them, and for her 'example of how to be generous'. In the hospital ward, sitting beside her bed, I was shocked, but I had nothing to counter her view. I'm not a selfish person and I thought she was right. I knew how hard it had been for her to bring up a large family on straitened means in a foreign land. I went home and arranged to return to Leopardstown.

The first night I spent back in the novitiate was terrifying. I went to bed at the appointed time, but I couldn't sleep. It was one of the most frightening nights I can remember in my entire life. As a clinical psychologist, I have come to understand quite a lot about anxiety and panic and the nearest I can get to describing my night is as if I was having a panic attack that lasted for hours and simply wouldn't go away: perhaps I was. Perhaps part of me knew that I had walked back into something toxic that would not end well. For some reason I awoke the next day with a strong sense, I'm not sure why, that not only was I trapped but that despite my desperate desire not to be, I was homosexual. This realisation was the opposite of a joyful, liberating coming out. It meant being prone to sin, being tarnished in some way, being incomplete, being 'less than', being at risk of committing acts much more repulsive to God than the generality of man- or womankind. I had to redouble my guard.

I certainly didn't share this experience with my novice master, but I did let him know that my concerns about sex weren't abating. We had the conversation in his office at one end of the long corridor on the first floor, sitting across from each other at his desk. He had a two-room suite with an office at the front and a door connecting to his bedroom behind. It was an awkward and embarrassing exchange; what teenager wants to talk about sex with an adult? I stumbled through vague references to my 'improper thoughts', searching for prim words like 'touching myself' and 'impure desires', while hastening to add that I had never 'ejaculated'. What teenager would talk like that! After listening for a while to my painful narrative with his bald head bowed, he looked up calmly and, holding my gaze with his pale eyes, he said he had a suggestion about how to help my situation. He said that as my impure thoughts and desires clearly hurt Christ, my Saviour, very much, penance needed to be done to make reparation. He suggested that as my spiritual guide and advisor he would do this penance for me, and he would do this by having me whip him with a small set of knotted cords called a *Disciplina*, a penitential practice that had gone out of use in the Legionary house in Dublin after it had been banned by the Archbishop of Dublin, John Charles McQuaid. I was to do the whipping and he would endure the pain, 'offering it up' to the Lord to ask forgiveness. The whipping was to take place in Izquierdo's bedroom, situated behind his office, a room I had never entered. I was to go to his office at a certain time and would find the door through to the bedroom unlocked. Perhaps the most bizarre part of all of this is that I was able to believe that the encounter was to be a spiritual, holy act of penance and not a perverted piece of ephebophilia perpetrated on a trusting, confused, and vulnerable youngster by someone who was in charge of his spiritual wellbeing: good old cognitive dissonance strikes again.

Obediently, I went to the novice master's room at the appointed time. My knock was greeted by Izquierdo's voice from within.

'Quién es?'

'El hermano Kevin', I answered.

'Adelante', came the reply and I entered the dimly lit room. The door opened at an angle that hid the bed behind it, and I was well inside the room before I realised the scene that awaited me. Izquierdo was lying stark naked on his bed with the discipline whip in his hands. Initially I froze, looking but not looking at the shocking scene. I can't remember the precise words he said, but he told me that as we had discussed, I should whip him and be aware of how much pain I was giving Our Lord by my sin. Somehow this sexual scene was to make amends for my sexual desires. I'm glad to say for the sake of my own sanity that at this point something clicked in my head that said, *This is crazy – get out of here!* and that I had enough good sense to heed the voice. I fled without a word and hurried back to my room wondering what the hell had just happened. Izquierdo never spoke of the incident again and I never mentioned it to anyone. Even at the time, his silence meant to me that he realised he had gone beyond the pale, but my credulous, ill-shapen moral world somehow found room to accommodate this appalling behaviour. This is the first time, fifty-one years later, that I have written down what happened in Izquierdo's room.

Perhaps to engage me further in the community and to distract me from my preoccupation with sex, not to say from my indictable encounter with my novice master, I was made bursar of the house and tasked with working with the Rector, little Father Fernández of the occasional temper tantrum, in administering the finances. I had no qualification for this other than being able to do basic arithmetic, file stuff in alphabetical order, and type a clearly phrased letter, but this was enough to get me the keys to the safe and a small office on the ground floor of the college: I had a responsible role in the community. Perhaps Izquierdo was banking on increasing my involvement in the management of the house so I might feel less inclined to tell what had happened.

The house received a *mensualidad*, a monthly payment to cover expenditure, mostly food and utility bills. I knew that it came from Mexico, from the funds contributed by the benefactors that we wined and dined with Waterford crystal, but what surprised me was that it came in the form of a money order drawn monthly on the Chase Manhattan Bank in New York. Despite my sheltered upbringing on a council estate in Dublin, I recognised this as major financial institution. What I didn't know at the time was that the bank had been involved in helpful transactions with Nazi Germany during the Second World War and in unhelpful transactions with Jewish people in Nazi-occupied Paris. Learning much later that the government of Falangist dictator Francisco Franco had wanted the Legionaries in Spain to ingratiate his fascist regime with the Holy See, I began to join the dots. Ignorant as I was of these things at the time, I still had the distinct impression that behind the charming simplicity and humility of my Legionary confrères there was a well-oiled financial machine. It turns out I was right[2]. Last time I checked, and that was some time ago, the Legion had assets of around forty-three billion US dollars[3].

Someone must have told Mr Norris, our gardener, that I held the day-to-day purse strings. Early in my tenure Mr Norris came to the window of my office - he didn't want to come into the house in his Wellingtons - and asked if I could purchase a supply of 'triply ingins' for him to plant. I had no idea what he was referring to or what 'ingins' were, triply or otherwise, but he seemed confident, and the cost was low so I said yes. Later I found out to my relief that the mysterious things he wanted to buy were a type of onions called 'triples' because of their growth habit. I have never again encountered 'triply ingins' but I have often worked on the principle that if someone knows more than you do about the matter in hand, and the stakes aren't high, it's probably ok to let them make the decisions.

A less business-like engagement with the community came in the form of music. On some of my visits to Leopardstown before joining up, I had met a boy around my age called Michael, also doing his Leaving Certificate, and a talented clarinettist. We became friends and I visited Michael's house many times that Spring, sharing a love of music. Michael introduced me to the Mozart clarinet concerto, the recording by Gervase de Peyer, the *Leonora* overture number three by Beethoven, and to *Fingal's Cave* by Mendelsohn, all of which he was studying for his Leaving Certificate music exam. In the middle of the Leonora there is a trumpet fanfare that was the introductory music for the evening news on Radio Telefís Éirinn. This was one of many bits of musical trivia that Michael taught me. Michael's sister Mary played the cello and introduced me to the Bach solo cello suites, his brother John played the violin, and another brother also played professionally, perhaps the viola. His dad, a big, hearty, loving man with a great chortling belly laugh, had wanted to be a concert pianist but, recognising the vagaries of artistic income, had opted for a desk career in the Irish transport company, Córas Iompair Éireann. After dinner, Michael's dad made the piano sing and strut to Albéniz and Granados and Manuel de Falla with a gusto that made me fear for the poor innocent keyboard. His undeniably chubby fingers fell on the keys like so many crazed tap dancers rapping and stamping though the intoxicating Spanish rhythms. When Michael and I joined up together we were allowed to use our talents for music, (he was the musician, I could just sing), to teach our fellow recruits the new English language hymns that were being written to accompany the liturgy in English, a result of the changes that followed the Second Vatican Council. We had lots of silly fun together, he was a terrific young man and, despite the prohibition of *amistades particulares*, I thought of him as my friend. I think that, like some others, he had a hard time in the Legion. I don't know what became of him; I'm sad that we lost touch.

From time-to-time Maciel would visit our community and the world for a while revolved around his presence. It was never very clear what he was doing but we assumed it was some arcane, sacred, and important business that occupied him. His was the first personality cult I witnessed close up, although I didn't know what I was seeing. He was surrounded by an aura of mystery and people hung on his every word. We were encouraged to write to him regularly and letters from him were treasured. Little did we know that these were not written by him but written for him by one or other of a stable of trusted Legionaries and simply signed by him. The letters were collected and bound into volumes and had the force of Holy Writ. They were among the books read to us in the dining room during meals. Even at this early stage, I couldn't help noticing anomalies in his life, discrepancies between what he did and what he said, but there was an explanation for everything. The fact that he didn't say mass very often was explained by saying that he felt the spiritual connection to God too intensely to do this. His use of after-shave cologne, a no-no for us mere mortals, was because he had a peculiar skin condition. The fact that Cesare, the chef from the Roman *Frente*, would come to cook in Dublin when Maciel was there was explained as being necessitated by his digestive problems. Bolts of cloth from Dormeuil in London were necessary for his handmade suits because of his sensitive skin. We were told all of these things and we swallowed the explanations whole, never pausing to chew on their implausibility. In my letters I refer to him breathlessly as a 'genius' and a 'misunderstood saint'. What we didn't know at the time was that he would also explain his need to have sex as being the result of a urinary problem that meant he needed to ejaculate frequently so as to avoid infection, and that he needed the help of another person to come. Or perhaps some of my companions in Dublin *did* know this. Perhaps some of them were invited to the inner sanctum of his first-floor suite to help with his urinary tract condition. Who would know? I don't think Maciel would ever have read Orwell, but Doublespeak was alive and well in the Legion. Other books have provided fuller descriptions of his crazily disordered personality[4] and I won't attempt to analyse it here, but the term 'toxic narcissism', popularised during the presidency of Donald Trump, is as good a shorthand description as any. Did I mention that he was never called Father Maciel, but always *Nuestro Padre* (Spanish for *Our Father*) or *Mon Père* (French for *My Father*)? In the immortal words of Australian comedy character Kath Day-Night of *Kath and Kim* fame: 'Tickets!'

There were funny moments too, as when one of my companions, Pádraic, keen to practise his Spanish, asked Maciel whether he'd had a good journey from Mexico to Dublin. Unfortunately, Pádraic interchanged the vowels in the word for journey, *el viaje*, and instead asked Maciel if he 'had enjoyed the old woman', *la vieja*. Much laughter all round. When it later emerged that Maciel had fathered children with several women, I thought how prophetic Pádraic's question had been. Not such a laugh after all.

The day arrived for me to take my vows and become a religious. One of only two or three photos I have from my time as a Legionary shows me on that day as I waited to make my commitment, and a more supercilious, holier-than-thou, expression is hard to imagine. I'm seated in the front row of the chapel in my black cassock, my hands folded modestly in my lap, perfectly groomed hair, horn-rimmed spectacles, head inclined slightly to the right, and an expression on my face as if I was the Deputy Headmaster asking a particularly unruly student to tell me why I shouldn't expel him. What was I thinking! I think my mother and my sisters Bridget and Nora were there, but in true *forsaking-mother-and-father-and-cleaving-to-the-Lord* style, I'm not sure that I was more than polite to them. Among all the other consequences, good and bad, my experience of religious life alienated me drastically and intentionally from most of my family in a way that only ever partly healed.

SALAMANCA

*G*reat sopranos are given glowing sobriquets by adoring fans: *La Divina* for Maria Callas, *La Stupenda* for Joan Sutherland. Salamanca is lovingly called *La Dorada* because of the golden glow the sun coaxes from its honey-coloured sandstone. Leaving Dublin to go there with my little band of brothers, no longer novices but fully professed religious, must have been exciting. It was my first time in a plane, my first time to Europe, my first time using my passport. But I remember nothing about the trip, nothing at all. Thankfully, the historical record is saved by an excited letter I wrote to my mother just a few hours after I arrived in Salamanca. In it I wax lyrical about the view from the air on the first leg from Dublin to London, and recount how I saw the White Horse of Uffington as we flew over Oxfordshire, and then St Paul's Cathedral and the Houses of Parliament as we made our descent into Heathrow. I strike a whimsical note in recounting how we were placed in a holding pattern over Watford - I put it in capitals with an exclamation mark: *WATFORD!* I sound like such a jaded habitué of jet travel. I tell how I met the Archbishop of Agra in the restaurant at

Heathrow and only realised who he was as he was about to leave, and he said: 'Well, it was nice talking to you. I'm the Archbishop of Agra in India. If you're ever there you're welcome to come and see me'. On the BEA flight from London to Madrid – I make an air-spotter's point of saying the aircraft was a Trident – I itemise each of the courses of our meal, from the orange juice to the Cointreau, via the beef salad and prawns with cucumber: perhaps that's where I got my enduring love of airline food!

After a night in Madrid, we left 'at eight thirty exactly', my letter home says, for the four-hour coach trip to Salamanca via the old route through Arévalo. If you make the trip now it's two hours by motorway, but in the early seventies rural Spain had only just begun to modernise and to build four-lane roads. The country was still putting itself back together uneasily after the devastation of the Civil War and some of the scars were still visible. Unlike in the rest of Europe, there was no broad consensus that the good guys had won the war, and everyone could move on. A good tranche of the populace still knew they were on the losing side and many in the country were fearful and secretive about their political views. But that was something I would realise later; for now I was, literally, an innocent abroad.

During the novitiate in Dublin, we were told what an important, historic city Salamanca was. A city of the Celts (I was a Celt and had some fellow-feeling), it had been captured by Hannibal and then, as Helmantica, it became a Roman, Renaissance, Baroque jewel. The postcard money shot is the golden stone of the cathedrals that rise from the northern bank of the river Tormes as it winds around the city on its way to the Duero, then on into Portugal and to the Atlantic Ocean.

In Salamanca, this great city of learning, we were told we would meet brothers from Spain, Mexico, and the USA. The university was founded in 1134 and was the third oldest in the world. It counted among its illustrious alumni Lope de Vega, Fray Luis de León, and Miguel de Unamuno. Christopher Columbus gave lectures there about his voyages. It was the Oxford of Castile and León with an Irish College dating from the 16th century, which Donal Cam O'Sullivan Beare, the last prince of our O'Sullivan line, had visited. It was almost fantastical to think we would go there and be part of this tradition and culture. What an unbelievably exciting prospect for a working-class nerdy kid from Sallynoggin! Cue the majestic theme music, something by John Williams perhaps, strings rising in arpeggios, a cello obbligato, kettle drums foreshadowing a grand denouement, trumpets calling in the distance... But then the intro reel comes to a grinding, discordant halt: someone shut off the projector in mid-frame.

In reality our existence was to be entirely suburban. The *Frente*, the college where we spent almost all the days and nights of the next year was four kilometres from the sandstone centre of the city. I recall only one visit to the city centre, to go to a forgettable lecture in one of the university buildings where I sat stiffly on hard, uncomfortable benches, polished to a high sheen by hundreds of years of clerical bottoms. And that trip was a bus ride door to door; there was no wandering allowed. Did I spend a year in the magnificent city they call *La Dorada*? Did I ever visit the *Casa de las Conchas* with its carved seashells, or the venerable university, or the dual cathedrals, old and new whose walls, windows and arches are a catalogue of European architecture from the severe, rounded Romanesque to the ornate posturing Baroque of the Plateresque? Although I told my mother enthusiastically that our college was 'five hundred yards (it's more like a kilometre) from the city proper, which begins as soon as you get to the bull ring!', did I ever stroll around the splendid expanse of the Plaza Mayor or sit for a coffee? Did I ever do more than catch a fleeting glimpse of the bull ring or climb to the top of the Clerecía Towers for a glorious bird's eye view of the city? No, I saw none of these places. I spent a year in Avenida de la Merced 108, hidden behind a high tree-lined fence and an electric gate. I would have to wait over thirty years to stroll around the city with my husband, to touch the honey-coloured sandstone of grand buildings and stand silent in front of the house where a plaque, since removed, told the visitor that *Here Francisco Franco was proclaimed Generalísimo of the Nationalist Forces* in the Spanish Civil War.

I can hear as I write that this is all said in the voice of the angry young man and his after-the-fact indignation. As far as I can tell, the earnest teenager objected to nothing of this separated, contrived existence. For him, or at least for the official version of the letters, the people were all great, the studies were all interesting, and all were dedicated to the only fight worth fighting: the advent of the Kingdom of Christ: *Please keep praying for me as I do for you.* The landscape and the city? Well, after an initial description that could have been gleaned from a postcard, the teenage letter-writer describes them as 'brown and yellow'. Hindsight has reversed this picture. The city is golden and full of treasures, and the landscape is imbued with a wild beauty that sometimes swelters and sometimes freezes but is never taken for granted. The people, on the other hand, or some of them, are vile.

The college was built in the traditional Legionary format, an E shape with the long side as the front and the chapel in the middle prong: four stories of dull, dark red brick. It housed two communities, one of novices and one of juniors, around a hundred people in total. Our accommodation was in small cubicles, just big enough to house a single bed, an upright chair, and a wooden *prie dieu*, with a curtain across the entrance that gave minimal privacy. I remember the *prie dieu* well, because I got housemaid's knee from kneeling on it so frequently for such long periods of time. You may laugh. Housemaid's knee, *prepatellar bursitis*, to give it its posh name, is the only condition that Jerome K. Jerome of *Three men in a Boat* fame finds that he doesn't have after browsing through a medical textbook in the British Library. He was lucky; it's a painful swelling in the kneecap that makes moving around, and even sitting down and standing up quite difficult. Housemaid's Knee would have meant no boating holiday on the Thames, and certainly no cycling holiday *On the Bummel* in Germany: there is no treatment other than rest.

The rows of cubicles were built back-to-back in the centre of the floor plan with a wide corridor around them where the study tables were set side-by side near the windows to take advantage of the light. At night the curtain across the cubicle entrance gave privacy in terms of sight but not of sound. I lay awake at night in my little space waiting for the discreet swish of the curtain that would tell me that the Brother Regulator, a kind of prefect, had checked that I was in bed. The cubicles were open at the top and the space above me seemed cavernous, stretching across the whole floor of the building. As I think back, it reminds me bizarrely of being in a cubicle of a gay sauna in Melbourne some decades later, after much exploration and self-discovery. The American R&B singer Charlene was singing her hit, *I've been to Paradise, but I've never been to me* on the piped music system, which for some reason struck all the customers hidden in their separate little cubicles as hilariously funny. Titters began with a couple in a far corner, others quickly joined, and soon the whole clientele was guffawing and belly laughing together. I'd never heard collective laughter in a sauna before nor did I ever hear it again. Back in Salamanca in 1971 there was no cheesy soundtrack and certainly no laughing.

The first night, after night prayers and lights out, among the breathing and the belching and the farts, I heard a new night sound, like someone flicking a string of beads. This rhythmic clicking came from many of the cubicles around me and lasted only a few minutes. It was something I had been told about but never heard for myself: the sound of the *Disciplina*, the little knotted whip that religious use to flagellate themselves for penance, and that my ephebophile novice master had suggested I use to whip him as he lay naked on his bed. I tried to count the clicking sounds, as counting sometimes helps me assuage anxiety: five, six, seven... ten, but then other clicking sounds started up from different parts of the space and I lost count. The secretness of the disembodied sound was eerily disturbing. It was clearly a common practice, so why did no one speak to us about it? The companion to the *Disciplina* was another physical punishment, the *Cilicio*, a spiked belt of stiff wire typically worn around the thigh, also banned in Dublin by order of Archbishop McQuaid as being inappropriate for young novices in the mid twentieth century. I wondered why, if it wasn't ok to use in Dublin, how come it was ok to use here? In time I would come to use both forms of this medieval, useless, and self-indulgent practice.

The certificates I have accumulated from my studies live in an A3 size folder at the top of the wardrobe. The largest among them is an outsize confection of elaborate calligraphy in reds and blues. The text is contained inside an intricate border with an architectural motif, with scrolls and curls and stylised acanthus leaves, with an excise stamp on the lower left-hand corner to the value of fifty pesetas, and no fewer than three signatures along the bottom, starting with mine. The certificate is so big that it doesn't fit into the plastic sleeve and, if you don't read Spanish, you may easily mistake it for an international treaty, or the award of a peerage. It solemnly proclaims that The Rector of the Complutense University of Madrid awards to Kevin O'Sullivan the title of *Bachiller Superior,* which means that my secondary school studies are recognised, and I can enrol to study in the university.

The purpose of spending time in Salamanca, a period called the 'juniorate', was to bring all of us who had just finished our novitiate up to speed with our studies and to prepare for philosophy studies in Rome. It was a sort of religious finishing school - all that was lacking were lessons in poise. I wish we'd had them - walking gracefully with books on our heads would have been more fun than whipping ourselves. The American and Irish brothers had all finished high school, but the Mexican and Spanish brothers had not necessarily done so. Some of them had come up through junior seminaries and needed to take the *Bachillerato* or high school exam. In the meantime, we English-speakers practised our

Spanish and obtained the glorious certificate of convalidation that I've described above, and when I say we 'obtained' the convalidation, I mean that it was bought for us for fifty pesetas – no personal effort was required.

The atmosphere of the house was unrelentingly austere. The rector, Rafael Arumí, was an enigmatic man who gave nothing away. I don't recall him smiling and I do recall being a bit afraid of him. There seemed to be a lot of penance and not much joy. But then, what had I expected? Wasn't it all about offering it up for the Lord? Our daily life was much like that of the Dublin novitiate only in more dismal surroundings and with more formal studies, but still punctuated by minuscule 'free times' just long enough for a pious visit to the Blessed Sacrament in the chapel - as if God would get lonely without us - or to tidy the socks and singlets in the cubicle drawer. How earnest we were!

On Thursdays we had our weekly *paseo*, a country ramble in groups of three or four, never two and never five, just as in the novitiate. We never engaged as friends and we never touched one of our fellow religious nor any other human being, not a tap on the arm, not a touch on the shoulder, not a handshake. The only exception was an awkward shoulders-only hug when we greeted a new arrival or took our leave to go to another *Frente*. It's not hard to see how sensitive this makes you to physical contact and how much it heightens any risk of a craving for the touch of another person rather than lessening it.

Unlike now, Ciudad Jardin (*Garden City*) in Salamanca was true to its name, perched on the very edge of town, with the countryside just down the street. In my letters home I note without nostalgia the contrast of this hot sunny land to the ever-present green of Ireland. We strolled in our groups through this dry brown country baked by a semi-arid climate with very little rainfall. Olive trees grew in small clumps of five or ten, not the serried kilometres of plantations you see now in the south of Spain. Dry stone walls marked the limits of smallholdings, grey bearded goats on long tethers munched hay that stuck out like extra whiskers from the corners of their mouths. I say we strolled, but sometimes we trudged through temperatures in the mid to high thirties or trotted along to keep warm on below freezing days. Rain or shine, our provisions for the *paseo* were always the same: three enormous *bocadillos* made on long torpedo rolls, baked fresh and crusty. The fillings were unchanging: one had a slice of tortilla Española, another a slab of quince paste at least half an inch thick, and the filling of the third was a slab of pure fresh *manteca*, a soft white cheese with a buttery centre, as thick and solid as the slab of quince. To drink we had two or three lemons and a bag of sugar with which to make lemonade when we found some water for our canteen. Fountains and taps were easy to find in the villages and along the road. I think these rambles were likely the happiest times many of us spent in that decidedly grim year.

The landscape now is dotted with *urbanizaciones*, housing developments, with uniform homes in straight streets. Fifty years ago, besides the towns like Villares de la Reina or Villamayor, there were a handful of tiny villages with a few ramshackle houses and a church, always much better built than the houses. The churches taught me a valuable lesson about art. In college we were studying the history of art under the skilled tutelage of brother Hector Tamayo. I loved the art classes and escaped for a while into times and places much more elegant than our sparsely furnished, cold, red brick home. We viewed hundreds, maybe thousands, of slides of the art of antiquity right through to the impressionists and post-impressionists. Persia, Greece, Rome, Byzantium, Florence, all came to light on the folding screen. Years later when I visited the archaeological museum in Athens, or the Prado in Madrid, it was like meeting relatives I had only known in photographs. But after a while one Raphael or Mantegna masterpiece merged into another and I became habituated to their magnificence. I realised that the little village churches we saw on our walks had been built and decorated around the time of the great Italian and Spanish masters and they tried to mimic their grandeur on a tiny scale. But while the architecture had withstood time and the bell towers and arches were intact, the art, the frescoes and murals, and the paintings, were uniformly dreadful. I began to appreciate that the art on the slides we looked at was the exception rather than the rule.

Some of these churches were tiny, less than eight metres long by three or four wide, a single large room where frescoes, and bas reliefs, and framed paintings jostled with each other to decorate every surface. In one of these small churches, a little *oratorio* that had no village around it, we found a rickety wooden staircase and climbed to the organ loft. Reaching behind the painted pipes we managed to get the organ bellows going and I perched precariously on the wooden stool in front of the keyboard to play the three or four pieces that I knew by heart, some hymns and a sonatina by Bach that my piano teacher in Glenageary had taught me. The bell rope was hanging beside the organ and passed through a hole in the floor of the little balcony. It was around noon, and someone dared me to ring the Angelus, a call to prayer that Catholics observe at six o'clock in the morning, midday, and six o'clock at night. Jean Francois Millet, a French Realist artist of the mid nineteenth century, has left a poignant image of two workers in a field saying this prayer at the end of their day. I clasped the rope and after a few tentative tugs the three times three clangs of the bell rang out over the fields around. No one had told us we could ring the bell and we felt we were living dangerously. As pranks go, our escapade would have to be among the tamest, in fact it might not make the prank cut in any sane world, but we were acutely aware that we were on the edge of what was allowed, perhaps transgressing even, and casting caution to the winds. Imagine for a moment how insipid and compliant my life must have been as a nineteen-year-old for me to think that playing the church organ and ringing the Angelus bell was a prank. I think we were spoken to when word got back to the college, but I don't recall whether any terrible consequences ensued.

117

Wikipedia tells me that Salamanca has on average 76 days with temperatures below freezing. It's not wrong. Winter in Salamanca is extremely cold, and I have no recollection of ever being warm in the college; I acquired chilblains to go with my housemaid's knee. In those days our stretch of the Avenida de la Merced was lined with acacia trees. I have a winter memory of looking out the window along the road to the northeast and seeing the trees covered with frozen droplets picking out each leaf as if the trees had been decorated for Christmas with glinting frost crystals instead of tinsel, or made as sparkling epergnes for the table of some elegant giant. Apart from the little village churches and our art classes, this was one of the few beautiful moments I remember with clarity in my twelve dull months.

Thankfully there was another source of beauty that came to me through the services of Professor José Serrano who, as well as teaching Spanish literature, was our choir master. Serrano, like the ham, was archetypically Spanish, the epitome of a Spanish hidalgo. He was scrupulously courteous with a great deal of bowing and rotating inclinations of his head, on the top of which his hair was pomaded to within an inch of its life, as black and shiny as his black and shiny shoes. He sometimes sported a *capa española* which made him look like a sort of Count Dracula without the teeth. His gift to us was to teach us to sing the glorious a capella Spanish liturgical music of the sixteenth century by Orlando de Lasso and Tomás Luis de Vitoria. As art, the music is intricately beautiful; as part of the liturgy, particularly for one who believes in what is being celebrated, the effect it produces is haunting.

The lights in the chapel are dim, barely reflected in the highly polished marble of the pavement. No heady incense fills the senses, no candles burn, and no red flame is lit in the sanctuary to indicate the divine presence – today there is no divine presence. The doors of the tabernacle, usually locked and draped in costly brocade are flung open in a gesture of desolation. At a signal from Serrano we rise, twenty or so of us, listening for the ping! of his tuning fork rapped on the wood of the pew. His hand is raised, his head dips, rises, and dips again as the second basses commence the drone-like plaint:

Tenebrae factae sunt

The first and second tenors and then the other basses add their sorrow to the slow-moving river of sound that ebbs and flows inexorably, and the listener is in no doubt that we are mourning the bereavement of Good Friday. *Darkness fell on the Earth,* we cry, *while they crucified Jesus.*

Dum crucifixissent Jesum Judaei.

I have long since ceased to believe, but this music stirs in me some instinct towards beauty and to compassion for the sadness of others.

The residue of my twelve months in Salamanca is sparse. My senses remember the cold, and the cheerless atmosphere of the house – it always seemed dimly lit - and being a bit afraid of Arumí, but there was joy in the study of art and of Spanish litera-ture and in the performance of music. My letters home evince an unwavering dedication to *The Cause,* and I was in no doubt that I was in the right place. My sexual difficulties were behind me: I had made a vow of chastity and I took it seriously. Once all sex was put aside, there seemed no need to deal with the issue of sexuality and I felt safe in my choice. I was ready for the next chapter.

In the Legionary formation plan, the juniorate was followed by philosophy studies in Rome, and as the day approached, I became more and more excited about the next move. Rome! Surely I would see more of the Eternal City than I had of Salamanca? With any luck the winter wouldn't be as cold either: no chilblains in Rome. But as we came to the end of our studies, a group of us were told that we would not be going to Rome just yet; Madrid was to be our next destination, to set up a new *Frente* and take part in a whole new project that for now was cloaked in secrecy.

MADRID

These days if you want to buy one of the older, grander houses in the suburb of Aravaca on the edge of Madrid's *Casa de Campo* - and why wouldn't you? - you won't get much change out of three million euros, and the really big ones will cost you four or five million. One of the smaller, newer ones near the shopping centre won't set you back that much but it won't have the cachet of the venerable dwellings in what is grandly called the *diplomatic quarter*. Not even the oversized nouveau riche creations have this, despite their swimming pools. The real estate blurb tells you it's '*Country-style living, only nine kilometres from the Puerta del Sol!*' It's also close to the main motorway to the northeast, the *Carretera de la Coruña*, which is handy if, like Francisco Franco, you're from up there and you like to spend nostalgic weekends in the old village where you can have a well-earned rest from being a Fascist dictator. Friday afternoons in the 1970s would often see the motorway lined both sides with armed men guarding the passage of the *Generalísimo's* motorcade. Whether they were ordinary police, the *Guardia Civil*, or soldiers, we didn't know - it didn't do to look too closely - but the question was academic: a sub-machine gun is a sub-machine gun.

In September 1972, still with no idea what we were about to do, we stepped out of the two cars that had brought us from the city centre onto the concrete driveway that curved around the square three-storey house at number 10 Calle de Bolarque. The House was called Villa Ely, it was solid rather than beautiful, and it was to be our home for the next two years. The house is much bigger than most of its neighbours, with a four-square central structure that looks a bit like a castle keep, and additions on the ground floor that surround it like a skirt. My first impression was of overgrown vegetation that cast a green tinged light and made it look as if the building had been left unoccupied for decades and the forest had encroached, threatening to engulf the structure: we had arrived just in time to save it. Our mission was two-fold: to prune the vegetation and open a new Legionary front in Madrid.

The Colonia de Camarines was a small affair at that time, quiet and private – I don't recall ever seeing the neighbours - a community of substantial houses behind high gates adjoining the vast *Casa de Campo*, Spain's largest park. The *Country House* that gives its name to the park was the country house of the Spanish kings from the middle of the sixteenth century when Philip II moved his Court from Toledo to Madrid. Again, the Legionaries weren't about to slum it. The suburb is unrecognisable now, full of modern, matching houses, with few of the green shady spaces I remember.

There were about twelve of us in the community when we *William* started out, mostly from Spain and Mexico, with three brothers *Eugene* *Keith* from the United States and myself as the lone Irishman. I have *Michael* always liked beginnings and I'm sure my excitement at being chosen made up for the complete absence of any knowledge about what we were going to do. They said jump, we jumped. Octavio Acevedo headed up the new community and Enrique Esquivel was to oversee our studies. One of the reception rooms on the ground floor was set aside to be our chapel, and I suppose the house had at least five bedrooms, one each for Acevedo and Esquivel and three rooms with bunks for the rest of us, but I don't know for sure. As we never went into any room that wasn't our own, I have no clear idea of the layout of the house. Did we have a kitchen? Was there a loft? Where was our washing done? Even knowing the paranoid secrecy that characterised the Legion, I am surprised at how little I remember about the house. This kind of need-to-know, keep-'em-guessing uncertainty was beloved of the Legionaries. The less we foot-soldiers knew the better. Commentary of any kind was not invited, ever, whether to brothers inside the organisation or to family outside. It was quashed as soon as it began; only say positive things about what's happening. *You took a vow of obedience, didn't you? Well, think about that, mister.*

As to the life we were to lead in Madrid, I shake my head in disbelief at the pantomime, *opera buffa*, routine of the following two years. I say we led a life in Madrid, but we didn't. Just like in Salamanca, we were to see nothing of the living, breathing, artistic, sporting, loud, messy city around us, apart from four authorised places. In a kind of reverse *Truman Show* effect, the people who saw us thought we were living in their world, but we weren't: it was a huge hoax. Besides the suburban house in Aravaca, we had an apartment at number 6, Calle del Conde de la Cimera, on the edge of the University City, two apartments, numbers 4 and 5, knocked into one on the seventh floor of a modern apartment building. This was where we spent our city time if we weren't attending lectures down the road at the University of Madrid, *La Complutense*, which was our third authorised place. The fourth base of our lives was a university student residence, The Hispano-Mexican College, a commercial venture belonging to the Legionaries, on the Paseo Juan XXIII, five minutes or so down the hill from Conde de la Cimera. Of this last building, we saw only the dining room and, on a Sunday afternoon, the basketball court at the rear of the building.

Thus, the whole city of Madrid was resolved for us into four places: a house in the suburbs, a flat in the city, a dining room in a student residence, and whatever lecture hall our classes were in at the university. These places and the routes between them were the only experience I had of living surrounded by an exciting European city of three and half million people: any experience of the outside, let alone any human connection, was forbidden. Our view of the world was as simple as that of Orwell's pigs in *Animal Farm* with their chant of *Four legs good, two legs bad!* Our chant was *Inside good, outside bad!* On one side of Aravaca was the Casa de Campo, leisure haunt of millions of Madrileños: we didn't go there. In Conde de la Cimera we were a ten-minute drive from the Santiago Bernabeu stadium and the excitement of Real Madrid: we didn't go there. Fifteen minutes would have taken us to the Prado or to the Parque de Retiro: we didn't go there. Anything apart from our daily routine was taboo: *Outside bad, inside good!*

As well as the geographical restrictions, which after all we'd had in Salamanca, our life was also shrouded in bizarre secrecy. We wore secular clothes unless we were inside the apartment at Conde de la Cimera or inside the house in Aravaca. No one was to know who we were, where we lived or that we were religious brothers. This was especially important for our dealings with the other occupants of the student residence where we ate and played basketball. In a rare frank admission that the organisation prioritised money, we were told it would be bad for business if the other students realised that there were *curas* using the residence. They might feel that it cramped their style, and it would make the residence a less attractive place to live: custom might decline. So on day one we went as a group to *El Corte Inglés*, a popular Spanish department store, to be kitted out with our disguises. Each brother had two pairs of slacks, brown or navy blue or grey, two sweaters, various shades of blue or grey or brown, a tie, and finally each of us was measured for a tailored custom-made suit, the first and only made-to-measure suit I have ever possessed. It didn't escape my attention that I had recently taken a vow of poverty, but the Legion had a ready answer for my qualms.

The wisdom went that being poor didn't mean you had to be scruffy, and the other thing about earthly goods was that they were given to you, not chosen by you, for your use, not for your possession. One of the rituals that symbolised this was held every year, on January 3rd, the anniversary of foundation, and it involved pens. We were allowed to use only one pen and when it ran out, and only then, you handed it in to receive another from your superior. But once a year the community assembled, and each brother or priest placed their pen on a large tray that was carried around to collect them. Then, one by one, we went up to the rector to receive a pen, chosen by him at random, or perhaps not, from the tray. The pen you received might be a Bic biro or it might be a Waterman or a Schaefer. The point was that you had no choice in the matter, and that the next year the Waterman you were using would be placed back on the tray for redistribution. Poverty wasn't about not having access to nice things, it was about not being able to choose them and not being attached to possessing them. The theory is not that bad but the practice, in the case of Maciel and others, fell far short. Thus, the Dormeuil cashmere suits, the expensive cologne, the private chef, the vintage car and chauffeur, the first-class travel, the rooms at the Waldorf Astoria, could all be neatly explained. The begging bowl was made of gold, but the monk said a kind passer-by had given it to him, and it was just a bowl.

The four sites around which our life revolved all had a strict dress code as part of their rules. Starting in the morning in the house at Aravaca, we rose early and dressed in black cassocks to say morning prayer and do an hour's meditation. At the end of this we hung up our cassocks and changed into civvies: slacks, white shirt, sweater (in all weathers), black socks, and black shoes. We bundled into our two cars, a Volkswagen minibus and a Peugeot station wagon, for the twenty-minute drive into the city. We alighted from the cars at a 'safe' distance from the residence so that we wouldn't be seen to be arriving in a group in two cars driven by two priests, Esquivel and Acevedo, wearing clerical suits and collars. We staggered our arrival at the residence, some hurrying on and some hanging back, so as not to arrive as a group. But this disguise was an utter fiction from the first day. We all arrived within five minutes of each other, walking purposefully, speaking in subdued voices, never strolling or larking about as young students might. We all wore the same clothes, give or take a variation in colour of the sweater and slacks, with white shirts, black socks, and black leather shoes. The sweaters alone would have been a giveaway, worn without fail even in twenty-seven degrees on a September day. We all had the same short back and sides haircut, all parted on the left. We all sat together and spoke together, all but three or four had non-Spanish accents, and none of us spoke to other students, nor did we live at the residence. We were clearly a group; and the resident students were immediately fascinated.

Cornered in the queue for coffee, what could be simpler for a fellow student than to strike up friendly conversation? 'You're not Spanish are you? Where are you from?' I knew that the admission, 'I'm Irish', would be enough to ratchet up the interest, but how to not say where you're from? 'Mind your own business', or 'I don't want to talk about it', would be frankly rude and would only succeed in deepening the intrigue. 'So, do you like Madrid? Are you here in a group of some kind?' The dreaded question lobbed early and like a grenade onto my canteen tray. 'No, no we're just all foreigners'. As if 'foreign' explained identical slacks, sweaters, shirts, and shoes. 'But not everyone – there are some Spaniards aren't there?' He had correctly spotted some Spanish accents among our number. No, we weren't a group, no we didn't belong to an organisation, no we certainly weren't religious. Thankfully I had reached the end of the servery and pretended to concentrate on mixing my *café con leche*. With a quick nod and a smile as if to say, 'We're done here', I fled to one of the further tables where I could see Legionary faces.

Try valiantly as we might to follow instructions and avoid conversations and, if questioned, to give evasive answers, it just didn't work. Add to this that all of our behaviour was under observation by two priests breakfasting, lunching or dining together in a corner of the dining room, who always arrived mysteriously just after we did and left just before we did. It was bizarre, and stupid too. To blow our cover, all the students had to do was to follow us when we left the dining room, and this they did one day within the first two weeks, and discovered that we were disappearing into a block of apartments up the hill on Conde de la Cimera. Someone hadn't thought the plan through.

After breakfast those of us who had lectures first thing would walk down, together of course, to the University, still in our sweaters and slacks. Those who had lectures later in the morning walked up to the apartment and discarded the sweater and shirt in favour of a white housecoat called a *guardapolvos*, worn over a white tee shirt. When the time came for us to leave for lectures we changed yet again into our made-to-measure suits, adding a tie to the ensemble. Anything less like a 1970s student at the Complutense University of Madrid could scarcely be imagined. After not many weeks Brother Jose Félix Medina and I were going or coming from a lecture in our sharp suits when we were halted in our tracks with a cheery, 'Good morning brothers! How good to meet you!' We looked at each other and answered with a cautious 'Hello' – who were these people? We became aware in our diffidence of something a little odd about the two young men who greeted us with broad smiles and proffered hands. 'This is such a great surprise. It's so good to meet fellow Mormons - which house are you at?' The white shirts, dark ties and dark slacks looked somehow familiar. The penny dropped. 'Ah I see', said Medina smiling politely, 'No, we're not Mormons, it's just that we're, eh, [pause while Medina thinks on his feet] going to a wedding, after class!'

This was the first of many, many lame excuses, funerals, interviews, and meetings of various kinds that we trotted out to explain our outfits until our fellow students gave up and just accepted that we were weird.

Returning from lectures, we either went straight to the residence for lunch, if we were wearing sweaters and slacks, or called into the apartment to change out of suits and into sweaters and slacks. We weren't allowed to wear our suits in the residence: apparently even our superiors had some vestigial sense of the absurd. After lunch we all returned to the apartment and changed into our white cotton housecoats and tee shirts for an afternoon of philosophy study with Esquivel. We used the Latin textbooks that our confrères were using in Rome and worked our way through primers of logic, epistemology, and cosmology. The idea was that we would study philosophy at the same time as doing our degrees at the *Complutense* so as not to delay our arrival at ordination.

The next costume change came in the late afternoon when we donned black clerical suits and dog collars to say the Rosary, followed by fifteen minutes of spiritual reading and then by the celebration of Mass. Then the black suits were put back behind the sliding doors of the wardrobes where they lived, and we changed back into sweaters and slacks to trickle down to the residence in threes and fours (still never in twos) for dinner. As for breakfast and lunch, we were shadowed in the dining room by Esquivel and Acevedo who imagined that they were discreetly invisible. However, our sign to leave was when they rose from their table to go. They, of course, were our drivers, with the cars parked once again at a safe distance, and as soon as they moved, so did we, clearing the dining room within five minutes or so. Acevedo in particular was not happy to be kept waiting. Arriving back at Aravaca, we performed the two last costume changes of the day, back into our cassocks for night prayers before a very last change into pyjamas and bed. At least seven costume changes a day, and ten if you got to wear your made-to-measure suit! No wonder I have almost no recollection of the Aravaca house: we left before dawn and returned after dinner: it was an expensive dorm room.

After some weeks of being told to lie about who I was, I strongly resented this concealment, and I really didn't understand it. I had given up everything, left my family, given away my possessions and was committed to being who I was: a religious brother preparing for ordination and ministry. I didn't care who knew and would have welcomed the opportunity to dialogue (it was a big word back then) and give an account of myself to anyone who asked. If the Mormon elders could be open and frank about their ministry, why not us? What were we protecting by hiding and lying like this? Certainly not ourselves; more likely the cash flow of the student residence. But surely if it was that simple, we could have devised alternative catering arrangements. There were two kitchens in the apartments at Conde de la Cimera, and there must have been one in the Aravaca house too. And in any case the disguise clearly wasn't working.

Yet with all this cloak and dagger nonsense we were forbidden to comment on the partitioning of our lives. Any comment was interpreted as a questioning of the wisdom behind the scheme, which, after all, was devised by Maciel, and who could question that! For this we had taken a so-called vow of 'charity' which could more properly be described as a 'gag'. I remember once that Acevedo overheard a jovial conversation that several of us were having at Aravaca about our 'other life' in civvies. He stormed up to the group and berated us in the strongest terms for our disloyalty and insubordination. This was never to be spoken of, and it wasn't, ever again.

Acevedo was a rude, short-tempered, and boorish man with a hard face and eyes that never smiled. He wasn't much over five feet tall, and his stature meant that he was always looking upwards from under his eyelids, set in deep sockets. God help us, he had done a master's degree in educational psychology. His Legionary superiors told him he was going to study at Yale, but they lied, and he ended up at the rather less prestigious Southern Connecticut State College. Perhaps this accounted for his permanently disgruntled frowns. He seemed to have missed the empathy classes at Southern Connecticut, and most likely the courtesy ones too. Besides being my superior, he was my spiritual director, a practice prohibited by canon law but universally implemented in the Legion. Spiritual direction is a bit like clinical supervision for a therapist or social worker, an opportunity to explore the challenges that go with the effort to live the religious life. It's supposed to be a supportive and uplifting activity, boosting the morale of the brother or sister. With Acevedo it consisted of sitting across the table from him in his tiny office while he either scowled at me impatiently or read the newspaper, or both, and I poured my heart out. I feel sad when I think of him trapped in a life of duty that held no obvious place for compassion or joy.

Esquivel on the other hand was jolly and cultured, a small roly-poly man with a ready smile and mischievous eyes. He was a priest for fifty years and died believing in the validity of his work. To him I confided that my problems with sexual thoughts had resurfaced, and he tried to be helpful. He at least gave me to understand that my troubles were not unique, and unlike Izquierdo in Dublin he didn't ask me to whip him as he lay naked on his bed. He pointed me to a passage in Plato, about the beauty of bodies meeting bodies, that was supposed to help but didn't really; it was too enigmatic. I recently watched Esquivel's 2020 funeral on Youtube, which included a brief bio about his time in the Legion. It makes no mention of his two years in Madrid. It seems this has been wiped or vaporised in true Orwellian style: it was the policy of the Legion never to acknowledge any mistake. Selective forgetting and denial, along with shunning, were Legionary specialities that we were to experience before too long. Years later, I requested and received all the documents relating to my studies that the

Legionaries still held. Among the papers, I found, to my surprise, a formal certificate signed and sealed by Rafael Arumí, stating that I was enrolled in the Centre for Higher Studies in Salamanca during the academic year of 1972-1973. This fictional document also shows that I achieved exceptional marks, either nine or ten out of ten, for all nine subjects that I studied. These nine subjects just happened to be the same ones that I needed for my enrolment half way through the first year at the Angelicum. Madrid appears to have vanished from the record.

One glorious day dawned, the only time in my almost two years in Madrid, when Acevedo told me I was to go with Brother Medina, a native of Madrid, to lodge an application for some forgotten purpose at an office of the labyrinthine Castillian bureaucracy so wittily lampooned by Mariano José de Larra in *Vuelva usted mañana* (Come back tomorrow). My role in the outing was negligible, to be a sort of chaperone, for who knows what escapades might ensue if we ventured out solo. When walking, we were supposed to maintain what was called a 'modest' gaze in *Handmaid's Tale* style, eyes lowered towards the ground, never catching another's eye, and looking around just enough not to bump into things. But this might be my only expedition ever outside the beaten tracks of my humdrum and bizarre days, so I was determined to drink it all in.

In those days political unrest was emerging in Spain, led by trade unionists and students. In our little religious bubble, we were blissfully unaware of these forces, despite the fact that the *Policía Armada*, the armed police called *Los Grises*, from the grey colour of their uniforms, were often seen on campus with their machine guns and riot shields. If we had walked the streets of the city, we would have seen the protest posters and the graffiti, but even when we saw what was happening at the university – it was hard not to – we didn't question or comment or discuss. These were things of the world, and we were not of the world.

There was a slightly Monty Python's *Life of Brian* feel to the

names of some of the left-wing protest groups. One of the movements was called the *Frente Revolucionario Antifascista y Patriota* or
FRAP for short. Another was the *Federación Universitaria
Democrática de España* or FUDE for short. As we walked along, I
saw some graffiti on a poster that said, '*FRAP y FUDE me la sacude*'.
It was a neat jingle where 'FUDE' (fooday) rhymed with 'sacude'
(sackooday). Words fascinate me so I read it out aloud. Medina
didn't hear it the first time, so I repeated it louder.

'Hey, brother Medina, that's clever: FRAP y FUDE me la
sacude.'

His head snapped around as if stung.

'Don't say that brother!' His voice constricted to a hiss, his face
reddened, and his eyes darted around to see if anyone had heard.

'Why not brother?' I said, smiling uncomprehendingly

'It means… it means… eh… it means when they masturbate
you…'

To his great embarrassment and my great amusement, I had
just proclaimed to any passers-by in earshot that '*FRAP and FUDE
jerk me off*', and to add to the scandal, we were both wearing black
suits and clerical collars. Horrors! This is my sole memory of
Madrid outside the confines of my straitened clerical routine, and
one of only two funny moments I can remember: one humorous
moment a year – not a great average.

Like everything else in our lives, the degree courses that we
attended at the university were chosen for us. Two or three of us
were studying law, some others, physics, some economics, and
Brother Medina and I were studying classics, *la filología clásica*. My
core classes were Latin and Greek, but we also had lectures in
philosophy and in Spanish literature, history and geography. Our
literature teacher was proud of his connection, through his own
teacher, with Federico García Lorca as a student on his travels in
rural Spain collecting folk stories. This was a brave admission
even in 1973. García Lorca had been murdered by the fascists a
long time previously, in 1936, but the fascists were still in power,

even if Franco had already chosen Juan Carlos de Borbón to be the new king.

The pleasure of these classes made up for the bizarre costume drama that we lived outside the university city. I was relatively free, although not free to socialise, and so much nearer to the everyday world that other people lived in than I had been since walking through the doors of the Legion in 1969. For at least a few hours a day we were surrounded by ordinary kids of our own age who laughed and teased each other and flirted. Although on our made-to-measure suit days we would stand out like tits on a bull, on other days, with sweaters and slacks, we could just about pass muster. At worst they might think we were prudish Opus Dei types.

One morning, as we listened to Professor Sánchez rhapsodise about 'el acondicionamiento asfáltico de la red viaria [1]- tarmacadam road building was big in Spain just then - I gazed absent-mindedly at my companions in the crowded lecture room, day-dreaming about what it would be like to talk to them. I was yearning for real company, hating more and more the concealment. The high wooden desks were just wide enough to hold the exercise books that we used to take notes or doodle in, and so close together that you could easily touch the person in front of you. It was the seventies and lots of the students wore tight flared hipsters and wide belts. The girl in front of me was wearing just such a combination, and as she leant forward on her desk the stiff white belt pulled away from her body in a more fashionable version of what in other situations is called 'builder's crack', opening up a kind of crevice between her bum and her pants. Like my neighbour, I was leaning forward with my forearms on the desk and dangling my pen in front of me when it slipped from my hand and fell straight into the perfectly shaped docking area of her buttocks. Panic! My permitted vocabulary didn't extend to swearing, even inside, but whatever words were allowed I used them all. Shit - what to do? Should I tap her on the shoulder and politely ask for my pen back?

Should I keep mum and try to retrieve it by stealth without her noticing? Do nothing and leave it there? Disclaim any responsibility with raised eyebrows and a quizzical look if she turned round? My extreme embarrassment prompted me to go for the second option and I slowly edged my hand down toward the top of her pants. I managed to take the pen gently between my thumb and forefinger and extract it with surgical deftness, as I thought, without her noticing. I was wrong. When the pen was safely back in my hand, she turned around with a mischievous smile and said: *Oye, cuidado donde metes tu bolígrafo!*[2] She was clearly unfazed by the incident and assumed I was flirting with her. As soon as the bell rang, I scarpered *rápido* lest she find me and flirt back.

MONTICCHIO

Vide 'o mare quant'è bello, spira tanto sentimento,
Torna a Surriento, De Curtis

e slept fitfully as the train sped on its eight-hour journey through the north-east of Spain past Zaragoza and Lérida. Awoken by the periodic announcement of the *Próxima Estación* by the guard, we were soon lulled again to sleep by the deep reassuring hum of the electric locomotive and the not unpleasant vibration that we could feel though our feet on the carpeted floor. In the half light of the early morning, before the dawn, the railway met the coast as it crossed the French border and suddenly to our right there was the Med, silvery, shimmering, palest blue in the morning light, laid out against the sky *like a patient etherised upon a table*: the sea at the middle of the Earth. Snaking around the edge of Roussillon and the Languedoc we ate the last of our *bocadillos*; like the most English of tourists, we had taken home-made sandwiches to the French riviera. As we approached Montpellier someone realised that we were out of food.

'Who can speak French, brothers?'

I hesitated before answering. I wasn't that good, but after all Mr O'Neill had presented me with the *Complete Works of Corneille* after my Leaving Cert, so he thought I was ok.

'I can, padre', and before I knew it, I was out of the station and racing through the maze of little streets around the Gare Saint Roch. My white housecoat flapped behind me as I ran, and I marshalled the necessary snatches of French under my breath: *Je voudrai... boulangerie... du pain... c'est combien?* In the floury boulangerie my panting breath and my curious white coat drew all the attention of the early-rising *ménagères* to me: '*S'il vous plaît madame, on va avec le train vers l'Italie, on part immédiatement, on a besoin....*[1] Back on the train with not many seconds to spare I thought that Mr O'Neill would have been proud of my French performance, but afterwards I sometimes let myself wonder what would have happened had I been left behind: perhaps there's an exciting novel there, or maybe a wistful short story.

Our first year in Madrid had been bizarre and exhausting in equal measure, requiring a constant effort of concealment except for the hours of sleep at Aravaca and of study inside the apartment. By the end of the university year, we were all worn out and I think even our dour superior knew it. But then, joy and reprieve, and here we were on our way to Italy for the summer holiday, down the coast near Sorrento to be exact, to rusticate with the community from Rome: a treat. Psychologists call this 'variable reinforcement' and it's what makes us play gaming machines and buy lottery tickets: as long as you give the punters the occasional win, even a *very* occasional win, they put up with all sorts of loss and disappointment in the meantime. We had packed our meagre things the previous day and caught the TALGO train at Atocha Station. Spain does high-speed rail very well, and already in 1973, the *Tren Articulado Ligero Goicoechea Oriol* was more luxurious and faster than anything I had seen before. What I didn't know at the time was that José Luis de Oriol Urigüen was the most important contributor to the Spanish coffers of the Legion. The wealth of the Oriol family was vast, and they facilitated the expansion of the Legion in Spain by providing most of the land on which the Legionaries built their schools and university. They also provided no fewer than four sons who became priests in the Legion and a daughter, Malén, who rose to the top of Regnum Christi. All the siblings left after Maciel was exposed, and the family is now taking action to recover as much of its property as it can. But in 1973 relations were still cordial and I assume our return train tickets were on the house. We travelled in our strange white house coats, looking for all the world like a travelling convention of scientists, who apparently knew a lot of Spanish and Italian songs that they sang in two-part harmony, sometimes even with a descant thrown in.

It's with good reason that Italian is the first language of opera. Try this, our destination, for size: *Monticchio di Massalubrense presso Sant'Agata sui due Golfi*. Melodious, isn't it! Donizetti could have set it to music. It's a huge mouthful for a tiny village that sits high in the hills above the two gulfs of Naples to the north, and Salerno to the south. Closer to home, the village looks down over two smaller gulfs within gulfs, Sorrento to the north and Nerano to the south. The island of Capri, with all its romantic evocations, is about ten kilometres west as the crow flies.

When we arrived in Rome en route to our hilltop destination, the Colleggio Massimo at via Aurelia 677 was already empty; the brothers had decamped south. We spent one night there before piling on to the smaller of the community's two Mercedes buses, a beautiful curvaceous vehicle, straight out of a Miss Marple film, all cream and eau de nil, with a lovingly polished chrome trim and curved window panels along the sides of the roof. For the reader who is a coach enthusiast, I think it may have been a 1948 OP3750 model.

We hit the aptly named Sunshine Highway, the *Autostrada del Sole*, to Naples and then through Castellamare di Stabia and Vico Equense into the hilly country between the two gulfs that give Sant'Agata its name. The Amalfi coast and Positano are to the south and Naples and Pompeii are to the north. This is some of the most iconically beautiful coastline in the Mediterranean, and here we were, far from the deceit and double-dealing of Madrid and free to be ourselves. After a year of concealment and – let's not mince words - lying, the relief was immense, and I have never slept better in my life, before or since, than in those first two weeks of holidays in Monticchio. To my mum I wrote:

I'd love to have a poetic vein so as to be able to describe this region to you. Imagine a sea so postcard-blue you can see the bottom; mountains that sweep down to the shore, covered with olive trees and vines; the Sun toasting you from a sky that looks as if the angels have swept it; the lilting, half-singing accent of these people, and just a little out to sea, Capri with its memories in sentimental Neapolitan songs and Gracie Fields...

Our home was a virtually unused convent, the Monastero del Santissimo Rosario, a foursquare, two-storey edifice from the middle of the eighteenth century built around a leafy courtyard in the middle of the town. It was fifty years ago, and we stayed there about three months, yet I remember so much more about our tumbledown convent than I do about the fine house in Aravaca where we lived for two years. In Madrid, perhaps the fear of discovery dampened my senses and closed off my perception. Living in fear is not conducive to a joyful engagement with the things, or the people, that surround you.

The courtyard was divided into four quarters by wide paved paths making squares of lawn bordered by stone kerbs and planted with blue and pink hydrangeas and roses that straggled upwards in thin, sandy soil. The two or three large cycas looked like spikey horticultural sculptures, placed at random in the squares of grass.

You had to sit on the ground to enjoy the shade of the low-growing lemon trees that provided lemonade for nuns and Legionaries alike. The arches on one side of the cloister were closed in with glass panels and behind them was the domain of the nuns. The other side gave access to all the ramshackle rooms on the ground floor, and in the corner a not-quite-grand staircase rose to the first-floor rooms where we slept. There was another rickety wooden staircase that prompted a pun from one of the plumper priests. He called the wooden stairs his 'Otis', like the lift company, but he translated 'Otis' as meaning: '*O t'espaviles o te caes*' (look sharp or you'll fall): to be honest, it's only mildly funny in Spanish. Most of all I remember the large flat roof where we ate dinner in the still, dry air of the Mediterranean evenings, while the edges of the sky grew pink around us.

The first two weeks of the holidays were called the *vacaciones mayores*, 'the major holidays'. During this time no intellectual effort was permitted, not even reading a book for pleasure. During the rest of the time, the *vacaciones menores* or 'minor holidays' we mixed our walks and swimming with short summer courses, a language perhaps, or the history of art, and we were allowed to read. But for two weeks we went to the beach every day, in our accustomed groups of three or four, with the usual sandwiches filled with hearty slices of Spanish omelette, quince paste, and manteca, the lemons, the sugar, and the canteen for water. Each morning the list of groups was posted on the notice board downstairs, each with a designated leader who was given a watch to keep us on time. We sought out our companions for the day, picked up our supplies and lost no time in setting off. In our identical white tee shirts, ironed beige chinos with a sharp crease, and sandshoes, we must have looked like teams of competitors in some adventure game or treasure hunt, but we didn't care.

My favourite spot was the secluded little bay at Recommone, down past the village of Torca, a stroll of about an hour and a half. There wasn't much there, and certainly there were no other human beings, but there was a gently sloping, south-facing beach and a concrete platform to one side where the brave and the swimmers would jump the two or three metres into the clear teal water. I couldn't swim, and I certainly wasn't going to jump, so I paddled around in the shallows and watched the little fish or sat in the shade and chatted with my new companions. We had some sets of flippers, goggles, and snorkel tubes to share, and one day I was crouched in the shallow water near the beach enjoying the warmth of the sun on my back while I looked though goggles at the sparkling yellows and the cobalt blues of the fish darting through the water. Suddenly I realised that my feet weren't touching the ground: I was floating! At the age of twenty, I was floating for the first time ever, and I felt safe in the water. What a moment! This must be like what Barry Sweeney experienced when I taught him to swim at Seapoint! It wasn't long before I plucked up the courage to jump off the platform, knowing that I could float on my back and paddle myself back into the beach with my flippers. The jump was made easier by one of my companions, a loud, very funny Irish brother from the Rome community; we'll call him Brother Pat. He coordinated what he called *aplauso terapéutico*, 'therapeutic applause', getting everyone to clap and cheer in admiration when anyone jumped in. It certainly helped. Years later this became part of the process – the clapping, not so much the cheering - in the therapeutic jurisprudence model that is used in specialised drug courts, but I don't think Brother Pat claims the credit.

A LONGER *PASEO*, if you felt really energetic and didn't want to linger at your destination, was Positano, a brisk three-hour trek away. No strolling on that walk, but you were rewarded with a picture postcard view of tiers of cream and white houses cascading down the hillside, draped in vibrant purple and red strands of bougainvillea, the whole scene curving gently around a sandy bay set against the turquoise of the water. You could enjoy this exquisite view for about ten minutes while you caught your breath, wolfed down your sandwiches and then set off to race back to Monticchio to be in time for tea: well worth the effort.

When the day has ended, and the *paseo* is finished, we wash the salty sting of the sea off our skin in the shiveringly cold showers that we take in the huge communal concrete trough on the ground floor – always with our swim shorts on - soaping ourselves furiously to distract the senses from the heart-stopping shock of the cold after the warmth of the Sun that has caressed us all day. Some of the more saintly brothers stand impassive under the stream, no doubt *offering up* the experience as penance for their sins. Not me. I jump out as quickly as I can, towelling furiously, and soon the pleasant tiredness of a day well spent creeps into my limbs. The clatter of pans and the smells of onions sizzling with oregano, lentils boiling, and thinly sliced potatoes frying slowly for *tortilla española* all make a homely background to the thirty minutes of prayer before dinner. The mesmerising repetition of the Hail Marys of the rosary doesn't help my tired limbs as I walk up and down in the cloister, and it sets me up for nodding off during my fifteen minutes of spiritual reading. Oh well, God had a holiday on the seventh day of creation – I'm sure he nodded off. I make a mental note that this isn't a thought I could have allowed myself in Madrid!

For dinner, we each take a chair up to the roof terrace and range them all around the parapet. If I take my chair up promptly when the bell goes, I can steal a few precious moments of solitude to look out over the astonishing blue of the Gulf of Salerno and dream whatever dreams are forbidden in the company of others. Huge vats as big as witches' cauldrons are hauled up the steps by willing arms and through the door in the little access block over the apse of the church. The cauldrons are heaved up onto the low stone bench with a dull clang, and lentils, surprisingly tasty, are ladled into bowls, grace is said, and then *Buen provecho a todos* –

igualmente! The buzz of conversation is all about the day, and who went where and did what: Positano, Recommone, swimming, diving, travel chess on the beach. I was proud the day I told the others about learning to float. We sit surrounded by the warmth of companionship, the drone of inconsequential chatter, and the clink and clatter of glass and cutlery; eighty or so tired, fit young men, well-exercised, with healthy appetites and nothing to do except enjoy each other's company and watch the sun go down behind the hills that hide Capri. After dinner, sweet mint tea is brought up by the gallon. 'More tea? More tea?' The cry goes up:

'Cook! More tea please!'

'More tea? Why not mor-ti-fi-cation!' – this in a broad Spanish accent - and laughter all around.

They were rare moments of unguarded fun, simple but spontaneous, and I saw my companions as never before, happy, laughing and joking, with none of the hypervigilance and anxiety that beset us in Madrid. So perhaps it was possible to live this Legionary life and be a kind, warm, friendly man who didn't fret eternally and uselessly about petty imperfections?

Maciel appeared at some point. I'm sure he didn't stay the night with us; I can't imagine that our draughty stone convent rooms at Monticchio could have catered to his refined needs. When he returned to Rome to entertain some visitors, a dozen of us were detailed to go up with him for a few days to prepare a kind of private concert for his guests with some music, some singing, and the recitation of poetry, the kind of event that's called *una academia* in Spanish. The music was provided by a scratch band of my fellow students, which was therefore called an *estudiantina*, and consisted mainly of guitars and mandolins with a marimba and sometimes a psaltery or an accordion. Searching for a theme, we decided on a Roman motif, and I suggested calling the program 'Andante con moto per Roma', my first Italian pun and possibly my last. My artistic contribution to the performance was the opening number, the recitation of a long dramatic blank verse poem that began: '*Paz al atardecer, Roma a lo lejos...*'[2] This show may also have been the time I demonstrated my extraordinarily limited talents on the accordion, but as the only tune I could play was Brahms' Hungarian Dance number 5, that wouldn't fit with the Roman theme. Maybe I'm conflating several musical triumphs in one!

Back in Monticchio we resumed our routine of walks, swimming, and summer studies. We took turns to cook and clean and generally lived a simple life, even meeting the villagers sometimes. Near to the convent some workmen were building a retaining wall with rocks and concrete, mixing the cement and sand and water with shovels on a large tarpaulin on the ground. Having a break for lunch, they sat under an ancient, gnarled olive tree, sprinkling salt on cut tomatoes and rubbing olive oil on crusty bread. Battered hats and neck scarves gave scant protection from the sun, but the weather-beaten faces took it in their friendly stride.

'*Buon appetito a tutti!*'

'*Grazie Padre*' – we were all 'Padre' in the village - and a friendly raising of hands.

The cement they had poured was drying swiftly in the noonday sun.

'*That'll soon be done.*'

'*Beh! Too soon, Padre.*' The friendly faces all shook their heads wisely.

'*Better if it dries more slowly. Better to do when is cold weather. In Italy we say "fabbrica d'inverno, fabbrica d'inferno*' ' - what's built in winter will survive Hell.

Fifty years later I relish this little saying: if you manage to accomplish something despite difficult conditions, there's a good chance it will survive.

Nobody really wanted to go back to Madrid, and I think if we had known the disintegration that was to come, we would have wanted it even less. Inevitably we returned and resumed our secretive lives and our costume changes. In the real world, in comparison to which our charades and dissimulation seemed childish, student unrest was growing bolder in Madrid and the university was frequently visited by the hated riot squad, the *Grises*, who arrived almost daily with their riot shields and their submachine guns at the ready. They emptied classrooms and watched steely-eyed as students literally walked the gauntlet between their ranks, now and then picking out individuals and taking them away for questioning, which was often accompanied by beatings and sometimes by outright torture. I remember one day having to calm an American girl who panicked as she walked between the lines of riot shields. I grabbed her arm and talked to her intently in English, telling her that the calmer she remained the less likely she was to attract attention and therefore questioning. One day a posse of *Grises* came into our classroom, asking the lecturer with faux politeness if he would mind telling them whether a certain student by the name of X was in the room? The lecturer kept his cool, bowed his head over the attendance roll, checking it slowly. He then looked up into the captain's eyes and assured him that no, X was not there today. The *Grises* left and X, who was sitting beside his girlfriend not far along the row from me at the back of the room, breathed a sigh of relief. The lecture continued without further comment.

My studies were interesting, but the concealment was awful, and Acevedo was behaving like a prick. Cracks began to appear during the Autumn. Several brothers disappeared overnight and, in true Legionary style, were never spoken of again. Later we learned that some had gone to Rome, and some had gone home. Their departures were secret, when no one else was around to see, and their absence was never mentioned. No goodbyes, no '*Good luck!*', no explanation, no compassion.

I was increasingly unhappy and unsettled in the crazy pressure cooker life. My difficulties about sex and sexuality began to surface again, and my religious life soon became intolerable. I have never been one to drag out decisions. I talked to Acevedo about leaving the Legion, it was the only thing that would elicit any kind of concerned response from him. He was like a bank manager afraid of losing customers because he doesn't want the regional manager to think badly of him. Acevedo suggested I go to Salamanca to talk to Arumí, who had taken aloofness lessons in the same school as Acevedo but didn't have the same churlish edge. As an alternative to leaving then and there, Arumí suggested I go to Rome, to talk to Maciel before making a decision. By this time our little community had lost four or five brothers, which was unnerving, and there was an anxious atmosphere, helped of course by the complete absence of any discussion about what was happening: the Legionaries made an art form of denial and selective ignoring.

By February, after my visit to Arumí in Salamanca, so many brothers had left Madrid that I was alone in my dorm with only one other person where before there had been four. I'll call my roommate José María. For some weeks, as we studied together in the city apartment, he had been teasing me, poking me, pinching me, play-punching me, nothing very unusual in two ordinary mates joking around, but off-the-scale-out-of-order for a Legionary for whom any touching at all was forbidden. His contact became more and more sexual. Increasingly frequently he would goose me on the bum and say, 'Ya te cogí!' with a laugh. Knowing no Mexican slang, I thought he was saying: 'I just grabbed you'. What I didn't know until later was that 'coger' means both to grab and to fuck. What he was actually saying was 'I just fucked you'.

I thought he was horsing around and although I felt a bit uncomfortable, I wasn't particularly concerned - our life was all a bit weird - so I fended him off good-naturedly. The evening before I was to leave for Rome, the minibus took off back to Aravaca after dinner leaving too many passengers for the station wagon. We all piled in somehow and I ended up having to sit on José María's lap. During the drive I became aware that he was squeezing and stroking my bum slowly and rhythmically. I had never experienced this before; it startled me, and I didn't like it. I moved around a bit but that didn't help at all. I knew for sure that what was happening was sexual - and worse, between two men - and although it horrified me religiously, I knew my breathing was shortening and my body was responding outside my control. We travelled in our customary religious silence and there was no way of covering or distracting from what was happening. I had to remain perfectly silent and still. 'Ache' is word that is often used in erotic writing and when it is, I know what it means. My body desperately wanted to respond but my mind fought equally desperately to tell me this was all kinds of wrong, sinful, an abomination. If I gave in there would be no forgiveness and no turning back. This was absolutely a mortal sin of the worst kind.

We alighted at Aravaca as if nothing had happened, changed into cassocks, said night prayer and prepared for bed. After night prayer, the *magnum silentium* reigned, a deep and solemn silence that can be broken only in extreme circumstances. As we lay in our bunk beds at opposite sides of the room, José María's voice said softly:

'Kevin, are you awake?'

Was I awake? My God was I awake! My head was racing, going over again and again what had just happened and what I was to do. Had I joined in? Was it my sin? How great was my guilt? Could I come back from this? Next day I would fly to Rome. Should I disclose the incident? To whom and in what detail should I speak? Should I tell Maciel? I was so awake that I was quite sure I wouldn't sleep that night. I said: 'Yes, I am'.

'Can I get into your bed?', came José María's voice. It was the gentlest, most tender, invitation to intimacy there could be. I felt faint. How I would have loved to say yes. How could this simple thing be wrong? Surely it was a loving act? But we had taken vows, so I summoned every reluctant ounce of moral strength and that's what I said:

'José María, we can't do that, we've taken vows of chastity. We can't do that.'

He didn't insist, and we went to sleep in our separate beds.

Our encounter should not be numbered with the many abusive acts that were carried out by priests in the Legion, and principally by Maciel, using their power and status to seduce young subordinates. We were two sex-starved twenty-one-year-olds one of whom looked for solace in the other. My refusal came out of my terror of sin and damnation. Had I accepted José María's invitation I might have saved myself many years of confused soul-searching, but right then I couldn't do it. At the time I had no idea, no one did, of the extent of the sexual abuse that had happened in the junior seminaries where young adolescent boys were groomed and preyed on by Maciel. José María was good-looking and fun, and he started in the Legion at a junior seminary. I have often wondered whether he had been a victim of Maciel's or of another priest, if not before we met, then after I had disclosed his actions. The grief of this possibility is with me still.

ROME 1974-1976

*T*he Basilicas of Rome are built to remind you that the Roman Church took over from the Roman Empire. The *Basilica* was the place where the Roman magistrates sat and dispensed justice, and the Christian Basilicas are designed to inspire awe and veneration, and perhaps a little fear. Some, like St John in Lateran and St Peter's at the Vatican are crowded with magnificent larger-than-life superhero statuary with marble hands raised in blessing and eyes that, although they are no more than smooth round stone, manage to stare out sternly over the congregation. The extravagant, flamboyant, Las Vegas-style ceilings, the gilt coffering in St John, the wild frescoes in St Peter's, use Renaissance hacks to hint at celestial worlds out of sight to which the worshipper may certainly aspire, but with no guarantees. They are perfect settings in which to play on religious heart strings, an enormous real life sound stage for the *Days of our Religious Lives* to unfold.

Santa Sabina on the Aventine Hill is in some ways more restrained than other Roman churches, but it manages its awe in a different way. It is a plain, vast rectangular space with a single apse at the northeast end. Once you know that the columns along the nave are repurposed from the Roman temple of Juno that stood on the site, and that the door on the southeast façade is from the fifth century, the building compels by its austerity and by the sheer weight of history. The stones say: *Remember the Roman Empire? Well, it's gone. We're here now.* Santa Sabina was the site of my first experience of the gold-trimmed pageantry of a papal occasion, with its soundtrack of solemn choral works, strong, clear, pure *a cappella* chants and intricately woven polyphony that dazzled the ear. The baritone voices of the men reading from scripture over the loudspeakers were impossibly polished and cultured; I had never heard voices like them. I learned later that they were professional broadcasters, usually from the RAI, the Italian Radio and Television network. The smoke of incense snaked through the air from the hot embers of thuribles swinging on their chains, seducing my nose and my taste buds. The whole performance enveloped me in sensory overload so that my eyes and ears and nose gave up and my mind and heart began to soar. As I revisit this scene, I need poetry and I think of Keats: '*My heart aches and a drowsy numbness fills my sense as though of hemlock I had drunk*'. Years later in dance parties I would recognise and welcome this feeling, but today, as I stood in the church, one week after my arrival in Rome, it cowed me. The magnificence of the pomp was so self-assured, but I felt shaky and uncertain whether I should even be there. Would I be staying in Rome? Were these the last days of my religious life? Would I be sent home? Would I choose to go home? What would this day be like? What would my future be?

I had flown to Rome the previous week, on an Iberia flight from Madrid, trying to look nonchalant and composed in my black clericals. In fact, I was anxious and guilty and ashamed, especially given what had happened with José María the night before. The Madrid experiment was falling apart, and I had no idea what was happening, especially since nothing was ever discussed or explained. My countryman, Oscar Wilde, captive in Reading Gaol, wrote that '*Where there is sorrow there is holy ground*', but I could only see the sorrow. Since four or five brothers had already left Madrid, at least I didn't feel that the collapse of the community was something to do with me personally. But then, as far as I knew, they hadn't almost had sex with one of their companions. Or had they? Soon after take-off I asked the air hostess for a boiled sweet to suck to make my ears pop. Instead, she brought me a Portuguese newspaper and asked whether this one would do? Clearly my Spanish was not quite as good as I had thought.

I was met at the airport and driven to via Aurelia 677 to meet the brothers who were studying philosophy, many of whom I remembered from Monticchio. For the next two years my only permitted conversations would be with them, not with the brothers studying theology, nor with the various priests who worked in the Vatican Curia, nor even, without express permission, with my lecturers at university. In Salamanca, Arumí had told me to come to Rome and speak to Maciel and I assumed that some arrangement had been made for him to see me. This would be arranged without my knowledge or participation: in the Legion, individuals did not expect to have agency. As in each Legionary house, Maciel had a suite of rooms reserved for his use and entry was strictly by appointment only. I know now that his privacy was essential so that he was not caught in flagrante with some poor unfortunate handsome conscript or found in a drug-induced stupor. Such was the cult of his personality that some brothers would find excuses to walk past his rooms in the few free times we had available on the off chance of running into him and just saying hello and perhaps have him sign a prayer book or a volume of his letters for them. This was long before I started studying psychology, but unbeknown to me I was getting practical classes in the behaviour of the corporate narcissist.

It was several days before I saw him. He liked to keep people waiting and call them at unexpected times, sometimes late at night. He eventually called me to speak with him and we walked up and down in the corridor outside his rooms. I have never been inside the private suite and having read the harrowing account by Francisco Gonzalez Parga[1], one of his victims, I'm glad I never made it to the inner sanctum. As we walked up and down, I told him about my difficulties with sexual thoughts that had led to me coming to Rome, and I also told him about what had happened the night before I left. He remained silent for a while, looking straight ahead, and then he said: 'Who initiated the contact?' I am ashamed to say I told him that José María had done so. Many years later, when I got to know the extent of Maciel's predation on young seminarians, it occurred to me that I might have set up José María as a suitable victim for him. I sincerely hope not. I have tried to find José María, but he has a common name, and my search has not succeeded. As far as I can tell, he is no longer a member of the Legion. I hope that he escaped and that he's safe and well.

Maciel was nothing if not charismatic and convincing, he dismissed my difficulties and he reassured me confidently that I should continue in my religious life, and that my problems could be overcome with generosity on my part: increased 'generosity' was the Legionary answer to everything. Curiously, he also told me to have a strong coffee and a brandy and to think about things less. I know this because several months later I wrote to him thanking him for this advice and for his encouragement. I perked up for a few days after the conversation, but I still remained dubious and uncertain about continuing in the Legion.

I had arrived in Rome on Wednesday, February 20th, 1974. The following Wednesday was Ash Wednesday and the whole Legionary community attended the Ash Wednesday liturgy in the Basilica of Santa Sabina presided over by Pope Paul VI. The Legionaries liked to show up to events where the Pope was likely to notice them. Ash Wednesday is about doing penance for your sins, and one of the readings in the liturgy is from the second letter of St Paul to the Corinthians: *'Therefore we are ambassadors for Christ, as though God were making His appeal through us. We implore you on behalf of Christ: Let yourselves be reconciled with God.'* I stood there with my brothers in my black double-breasted Legionary uniform, clutching my beautifully printed memorial booklet, in sensory overload. In my memory, the space around me is dark, I can barely see those at my side, and I am standing alone in a small pool of light, like a stage spotlight. Although I am surrounded by hundreds of others, all I can see is myself, my arms in front of me, my hands holding the small, square order of service, with the light shining on the glossy paper. I can hear the words reverberating through the penumbra around and above me in a voice as rich as molten gold: *'Lasciatevi riconciliare con Dio',* said the glowing, resonating voice. In a moment of exaltation, responding to the occasion, I heard the words as if they were addressed to me personally, calling me, inviting me, right here and right now to take action. I was struck by the phrase: *'Lasciatevi'*– 'Allow yourselves'. I didn't have to *do* something new or different, I just had to *allow* myself to be welcomed and forgiven. It was a moment of epiphany, of revelation as to what I should do: I would stay and work at atoning for my behaviour and strive to do better. I would allow myself to be reconciled with God. Amen! In later years, at such ecstatic moments of clarity I might take off my sweaty tee-shirt and dance with my hands in the air, but not yet.

The next day I was enrolled in the Pontifical University of St Thomas Aquinas, commonly called the Angelicum because Thomas Aquinas was the 'Angelic' doctor. Lectures at the Angelicum meant I had to learn Italian, very quickly! In a departure from custom, I was assigned a theology student as my tutor, a genial Irishman, and my lessons took place on the back seat of the bus as we rode into Rome each morning. Spanish and Italian are obviously very similar, and I also knew Latin, to make up the gaps. The point of our lessons was to help me to understand the philosophy lectures, so we used the university course books as our language teaching texts. I would read from the Latin text, translating into broken Italian to the best of my ability, and learning the pronunciation from my tutor along the way. Basically, I made it up as I went along, and my teacher only corrected me if I was wrong. From memory I had a reasonable grasp, enough to follow lectures, in about three or four weeks.

Slipping into the new routine was simple. After Madrid, anything would have been simple. We had one task and one identity; there were no disguises, no lies to those who met us, and no rushing backstage to change costume. Which is not to say we still didn't stand out as a group. It was ten years after the Second Vatican Council that had worked hard to bring the church up to date – *Aggiornamento* was the catch cry – and clerical garb or a monk's habit were seen on the street less often than before. But not so with the Legionaries. We still wore identical neatly cut double-breasted black suits with clerical collars, black lace-up shoes down below and short back and sides haircuts, with a straight side-parting on the left, up above. Under our suit jackets, which were never ever removed, no matter what the temperature, we didn't wear shirts, but only white tee shirts and detachable nylon shirtsleeves fastened above the elbow with elasticated fabric and with double cuffs protruding from the jacket sleeve to give the appearance of a shirt. Over the tee shirt we wore a clerical stock, a square of black fabric with a collar attached.

As always, we were forbidden to speak to anyone who was not in our immediate community. We could say hello, but nothing else. Clearly, our companions in the university understood this and simply left us alone. We interpreted their puzzlement as evidence of our special-ness and they interpreted our distance, correctly so, as disdain.

The daily routine was unchanging. Morning prayer and mass were followed by breakfast, usually of delicious fresh eggs from the college's chickens. The college had several hundred birds in a barn, tended by the brothers, and the sale of eggs was a handy source of revenue. My memory of the breakfast eggs belongs with those 'good old days' memories when strawberries were sweet and chocolate bars were so much bigger. If you have never tasted an egg laid a couple of hours before you ate it, you are missing a feast. My regular ration was two soft-boiled eggs broken into a small bowl and mixed with torn pieces of crusty roll, with a little pinch of salt to bring out the taste. The effect is like a Sergeant Major shouting at your taste buds: 'No slouching there! Wake up all of you! You're all needed here!' Two eggs every day: no one talked about cholesterol. After breakfast we got aboard the two Mercedes buses of the college fleet, and this was one of the few times that the communities of philosophers and theologians were mixed, although we were still forbidden to speak to each other. One bus went to the Angelicum, on Largo Angelicum behind the Markets of Trajan, and the other to the Gregorian, in Piazza della Pilotta.

My first destination, The Angelicum, is a truly venerable institution, operating continuously since 1222 when it was founded as a house of studies for the Dominican friars who still teach there. In its teaching it was, and probably still is, a bastion of Thomist philosophy and theology: a one-book school with Thomas Aquinas's *Summa Theologica* as the text. It was a conservative place, even by Roman standards, the teachers were all Dominican friars who wore traditional habits, and most textbooks were still in Latin, although teaching was by now largely in Italian. We had been studying these texts in Madrid with Esquivel and I was already familiar with them. Our lecturers were mostly avuncular older men, from a variety of nationalities, who had been doing the job for years and, as Thomist philosophy by and large doesn't change, they had been giving the same lectures year in year out for many decades. The only exception was a young lecturer who daringly wore jeans under his habit and tried valiantly to teach us about Hegel. His attempts were entirely unsuccessful in my case and over time I began to suspect he didn't really understand it himself. The students were a fairly conservative lot too, and we weren't the only ones wearing habits of various kinds, although we were the only ones that called our habit a *uniform*.

Today the Angelicum website shows a group of young people, mostly women – *do the elders know!* – casually dressed and chatting in a circle, sitting on the grass in the sunny courtyard. In 1974 it still felt like a medieval monastery with classrooms, full of earnest looking young men in cassocks and Dominican teachers in their cream habits with black scapular capes, loose leather belts and oversized rosary beads swinging with the gait of the friar. Entering its tree shaded cloister gave deliciously cool respite from the Roman sun, and this green-tinged shade is the only sensory memory I have of my eighteen months as a student there.

Logic, ontology, cosmology, psychology, St Thomas stepped through them all with meticulous order, going from the general to the particular, establishing principles, assembling arguments, and drawing conclusions: *Quod erat demonstrandum.* The formula was applied to any issue at hand. I even remember one Thomist philosophy joke. Did you hear the one about St Thomas writing a thesis on the Crucifixion? He started by examining the nature of wood in general: *De ligno in genere.* Hilarious! Of course, it works better in Latin.

Lectures took up the morning, after which the buses collected us again for the trip home. Any breaks between lectures had to be spent together - we were all spies to each other - and exchanging pleasantries, however trivial, with a non-Legionary was sure to be reported back to superiors in via Aurelia 677. When I finally escaped from this cult, some years later, I found that I had no idea how to be friends with anyone. How could I, schooled as I was in remaining anxiously separate from outsiders, and paranoid about where a 'particular friendship' with one of my associates might go?

Afternoons were given up to study at home in the college and for those who were postgraduate students there were sometimes seminars back at the university, accessed this time by public transport. An afternoon seminar later helped me set up an escape route when it all became too much. There is a decent sports field behind the college in via Aurelia and also a swimming pool, so we played soccer or swam. The pool was deep enough to have a diving board, and one of the brothers, Robert, was a skilled diver. Robert was a charming, softly-spoken American brother with a ready smile and a gentle manner. He and I collected eggs in the barn or got under the house together with torches to fix the plumbing or the electrics (I think my role was to hold the torch). Robert was also significantly good looking, with a muscled diver's physique. In fact, he was so well muscled he found it difficult to swim, but his diving was confident, elegant, and fearless. I noticed at the time that he was a favourite of Maciel's, who would joke with him and tease him and sometimes sent for him to perform little tasks. Now I know to worry for his wellbeing.

The academic year ended in June, and we set out for Monticchio once more, where we had the pleasure of seeing the remnants of the Madrid community again. They had come to Rome, this time for good, and the costume drama had been abandoned. I don't remember whether José María arrived with the group. I don't think he did, and I had no way of finding out. The fate of the community in Madrid, like every other uncertain or questionable aspect of Legionary life, was not a subject we were ever allowed to discuss. We were only to have positive conversations about how wonderful the congregation was, never to voice doubt about any aspect whatever. Those questions were never to be asked, and an absent religious, who wasn't positively known to be in another *Frente*, was never referred to. Pictures were removed from yearbooks, references to the absent brother were deleted, and his memory expunged from the collective. It was some time before I would come across 'vaporization' in George Orwell's *1984*, but when I did, I understood it instantly. I wrote home to my mum that Maciel's mother, affectionately known as Mamá Maurita, had come to spend some time with us in Monticchio. She was a warm and delightful person and she died before she saw the horror of her son's exposure as a sexual offender and a fraud. Monticchio was its glorious self and once again we walked and swam, ate bocadillos, made lemonade, read, and slept.

When we returned to Rome, the routine of our studies was punctuated by more occasions of Papal pageantry at Christmas, Easter and other high holidays. Christmas saw the preparation of expensive presents for all of the influential cardinals or bishops with whom the Legion wished to curry favour. A bottle of Chivas Regal, a bottle of Remy Martin, and a bottle of Chartreuse, say, or Drambuie, were a typical gift. Three bottles for a cardinal or influential bishop, and two for a lesser bishop or monsignor in the Curia. This liquor was brought to Rome illegally as contraband in a hidden compartment in the larger of the two Mercedes buses on trips from Salamanca.

As a firm capable of supplying large numbers of well-groomed, clean-shaven, serious-looking young clones, the Legionaries were in demand as acolytes at Papal and Curial services, usually at St Peter's in the Vatican. The duties were light, chiefly consisting of parading around in a surplice looking solemn, with hands pressed together before one's breast. Extra duties might entail carrying a processional cross, or a baroque silver candlestick, or swinging a thurible perhaps, or lifting a robe, or assisting a cardinal or bishop, or the Pope, to don or doff vestments for mass. By tradition, as a Catholic priest gets ready to say mass the first vestment he puts on is the amice, a square of white fabric with long ribbons like a small apron, which goes across the shoulders. The ribbons of the amice are passed around the chest and then around the back, and depending on the waistline of the subject, might be passed again to the front where they are tied in a bow. One day I was helping an American cardinal, whose name I will withhold for the sake of politeness, to put on the amice, but his girth was frankly outsize, and try as I might, I couldn't get the ribbons to meet to tie them off. I was apologetic and didn't really know what to do: 'Too much Spigadoro!' he cried good naturedly, to cover his embarrassment and mine. We just tucked the ribbons into his sash and hoped they'd stay. Spigadoro is a popular brand of pasta.

The high point of my liturgical performance career came at the funeral of another cardinal, Italian this time, at which I was asked to chant one of the readings in his requiem mass in St Peter's. If 'chanting' a reading sounds strange, it is. Instead of reading the text with an ordinary voice, the cantor sings the words in simple, repeated cadences. The acoustics of St Peter's do wonders for one's voice; it's so much better than singing in the shower!

The year of 1975 had been proclaimed as a Holy Year by Pope Paul VI, in which pilgrims who came to Rome earned certain indulgences. Remarkably, indulgences are still around, despite being one of the triggers for the Reformation led by Martin Luther. My mother and my sister Nora decided to come to Rome, I think more for a sunny holiday than for the indulgences, and we were able to spend some time together. I remember a trip to the Tivoli Gardens and sight-seeing in the city, which ironically, I had never done with my religious brothers. I especially remember our visit to St Peter's Basilica because Nora was wearing a light summer dress with no sleeves. Horrors! The custodians of the Basilica have it on good authority that God abhors the sight of women's arms, certainly anything involving the elbow or above. He has clearly been struck with divine remorse at having created these limbs and joints and so they must be hidden from view. Protecting God's sensibility in this way involves concealing all arms and knees in severely cut plastic overalls resembling garbage bags (they may be actual garbage bags). Now this is strange. If I believed in God, the last thing I would think of him is that he was a bit of a snowdrop, with such delicate feeling that he had to be protected from the sight of elbows and knees. From what I read, he's actually pretty good at smiting people when he wants to and not above sending a deadly plague or flood. Why one would see the need to protect him from hurt feelings is beyond me. But maybe I just don't get it.

On the same visit to St Peter's I was approached by some young Japanese women with souvenir rosary beads they had purchased, asking me to bless them. What to do? Of course, I couldn't give them a priestly blessing, but it seemed pointless, not to say impossible, to explain that to three enthusiastic and pious tourists who didn't speak English or Italian. I looked the part, smartly attired in black suit and clericals. I looked like a duck, why not quack like one? I took the proffered rosaries and piously repeated the Latin blessing: *Benedicat vos omnipotens Deus, Pater et Filius et Spiritus Sanctus.* They left happy, with much bowing, and many repetitions of *arigatou gozaimasu*, and they probably still treasure the rosaries they had blessed in St Peter's Square on that trip to Rome in the Holy Year. My mother of course was glowing with pride. I remember little else about Mum's visit. My sister told me some years ago that we had pizza one evening at the college with Desmond Coates, whom they knew from Dublin, but I have no recollection of that. They returned to Ireland, and it was soon time for the simplicity and solace of Monticchio.

THINGS FALL APART: ROME
1975-1976

Things fall apart; the centre cannot hold;
Mere anarchy is loosed upon the world
William Butler Yeats – *The Second Coming*

*B*y mid-September Rome has lost the oppressive summer heat that drives its well-to-do inhabitants to the hills, the *castelli romani*, or to the coast. Along the city streets the cypress pines begin to lose their coating of grey dust and their hard foliage darkens to a deep rich green. Showers begin to soften the earth of public parks and even the lemon yellow and pale blues of the stucco buildings look refreshed as if someone has dusted them off and spruced them up with a fine mist spray. For me, the new academic year also had different colours. Having finished my bachelor's degree in philosophy I was moved from the stolid, thirteenth century Thomist world of the Angelicum to the shiny marble halls of the Gregorian and enrolled in a post-graduate degree, a *Licentia*, in philosophy. As with every change in my religious life, this wasn't a choice made by me - I wasn't consulted - but I rather liked it. It took me into a wider philosophical world, with a chance to study Gramsci, and Kierkegaard, and Maritain, with smaller classes and seminars and a choice of elective courses. It was a wider human world too, with lecturers who didn't wear religious habits and students who looked like ordinary young men and women.

The Greg, as the *Pontificia Università Gregoriana* is affectionately known, is the successor of the *Collegium Romanum* founded by the Jesuit St Ignatius of Loyola in 1551. In contrast with the warm, red brick, cosy, and ancient Angelicum, the Greg is housed in a rather grand classical style building in Piazza della Pilotta which, belying its renaissance looks, was purpose-built in the late 1920s. The architecture betokens a completely different milieu to the Angelicum. Being at the Angelicum was like living in a monastery anywhere between the thirteenth and nineteenth centuries, a perfect film set for any Italian historical drama of the last 700 years – *Hire it as is, Original cloister, Scenery needs no adjustment - Habits included!* The Greg, in contrast, was bright and quite elegant in its own way. The staff wore ordinary jackets and pants, rarely clerical garb, and the university even had the modern credentials of an Institute of Psychology next door across the Piazza della Pilotta. We also knew that many of those that had gone before us had become bishops, cardinals, and popes: it was clearly the place to be. The Gregorian calendar, which most of us now use, commissioned by Pope Gregory XIII, was devised and calculated by a professor at the Greg. The alumnus most dear to my heart is the former President of the Irish Republic and all-round *femme formidable*, Mary McAleese, who studied there for a doctorate in canon law.

Lectures at the Greg felt important, as if they mattered to how we might think about the world *now*, how we would approach, engage, and make a difference there. Despite teaching classes in metaphysics, Father Johannes Lotz thundered away in the aula magna in his strong German accent about the need for a united Europe, *Europa Unita*, so that the continent wouldn't tear itself apart again. Father Joseph de Finance had been a permanent professor at the Greg since I was two years old and by the time I knew him he was an Emeritus Professor. Although he was over seventy when I met him, he was sprightly and energetic, with sparkling eyes and acrobatic hands. He supervised my thesis on Jacques Maritain and was an expert on Marx. He taught me to distinguish fine communist writing from the bastardised and destructive state-capitalist experiments claiming it as their inspiration. He also gave me my first inkling of the crucial importance of controlling the narrative. In some assignment or other I had written about the 'collapse of the Second Internationale' (*il crollo del Secondo Internazionale*). In the margin, de Finance wrote the two words *Dizione marxista* (Marxist terminology) meaning that I had fallen for the line that the Internationale had 'collapsed' rather than being sunk by the Russian communist party for its own purposes.

As well as changing university, the other major change in my life was that I was made an assistant superior in my Legionary community of philosophy students, an *asistente de filósofos*. I know from my letters that I had been groomed for this position for some time under the guidance of Peter Coates, brother of the charming Desmond Coates who had convinced my mother to allow me to join up. The role of the assistant was to support a given number of the brothers, about ten or twelve, in their day-to-day endeavours, organising activities, distributing supplies, allocating chores around the house and suchlike. The job also meant meeting with each brother regularly for what was called 'moral orientation', not quite spiritual direction but in the same ballpark. The role was somewhere between a camp counsellor and a proper religious superior. This appointment came as a complete surprise to me and was quite counterintuitive. Here was I, struggling to contain my urges and to live a halfway decent religious life, and I was put in charge of others. I think the strategy was probably based on the belief that helping others to live this life might help me to live it as well. But alongside my exposure to new ideas and new people, the new role in the community gave me a dangerous new perspective, from the inside, into to how my superiors operated behind the scenes. The realisation of their duplicity at first hand was probably the defining element that precipitated my departure.

The Legionaries were obsessed with keeping out dangerous and risky ideas, ideas that might challenge the received wisdom of the *Constitutions* and the teaching and direction of Maciel. To help with this, one of my new jobs was to vet the English language section of the college library to check the suitability of the works for consumption by my community. As an own goal by my superiors, they didn't come much better. In the two or three days before entering the Candidacy in July 1969 I had spent hours reading *Ulysses* by James Joyce, in the certain knowledge that I would never be allowed to read it as a religious. Now, not only was I allowed to read everything I wanted to, I was actually directed to do it. It was like putting a sex addict in charge of classifying porn websites. I'm what's often called an avid reader and I did the task with relish. It's also worth saying that I had a much wider sense of what was 'suitable' than the rector and vice rector who were not 'avid readers', and whose command of English was not sufficient to contradict my ratings. I purposely left everything on the shelves. Of the books I read, three changed my life, in that they moved me significantly towards a life outside the Legion: *Animal Farm, 1984,* and *Brave New World*. In these dystopian landscapes I recognised the organisation I belonged to and the life I had been living: Doublespeak, vaporisation, and the fact that some animals were more equal than others, were all familiar to me, every day.

Another of my jobs was to censor any English language letters that the brothers sent or received. I knew that this happened, as all letters home had to be handed, open, to one's superior for vetting, but when I was directed to do it myself, I found it distasteful, and it brought home to me how it applied to my own letters. As with the job of censoring the library books, I made no comments at all, believing that what a brother wrote to his mum or what his mum wrote back was entirely their business. Knowing that letters were read, however, was important later when I wanted to write privately to someone on the outside. One day I read a mother's glowing account of a new Archbishop of Westminster, a man called Basil Hume, who had been the abbot of Ampleforth Abbey, a Benedictine monastery in Yorkshire. He sounded progressive and cultured and removed from the traditional Irish lineage of many Catholic bishops in England at the time. I filed his name away, just in case.

In a breathtaking irony for an organisation where lying, manipulation, and sexual abuse were rife, the obsessive quest for perfection continued unabated, for this was the ground on which we were supposed to act, rooting out imperfections. The schooling that had commenced in the novitiate, teaching us to constantly examine our consciences for imperfections, only got worse as we went on. Forget actual sins, the good stuff was all about perfection and imperfections. Imperfections were simply a class of things you could get wrong, they weren't sins, they weren't forbidden and there was no punishment for them. They were just things you could have done better: been kinder, concentrated harder in prayer, gone without that second cup of mint tea. It was like carrying around in your head the little voice that said: 'I'm not angry with you, I'm just disappointed'. The problem with rooting out imperfections, is that there is, by definition, no boundary to stop you trying even harder, being even kinder, praying even longer. The search to eliminate imperfections is the anorexia nervosa of the spirit; it can kill you and drive you mad, leading you into a world that no one else inhabits: *Bonum ex integra causa, malum ex quocumque defectu*[1].

The monastic practice of the 'Chapter of Faults' helped to make this soul-searching public. Every week we gathered as a community and one of us knelt before the others to receive their comments about our imperfections: *I have the impression that Brother Kevin laughed too loud in conversation... was too boisterous in soccer... took more than his fair share of eggs at breakfast...* There was no comeback, no discussion. The kneeling brother soaked it all up, taking upon himself the faults imputed to him by the speakers, even if he had no memory of committing them, or they seemed trivial or based on mistaken opinions or misunderstandings.

It really wasn't a wise idea on the part of the Legion to send me, with my periodic doubts about my vocation, to study philosophy as a postgraduate at the Gregorian. Exposure to a wider view of the world encouraged me to think new thoughts, and exposure to new people gave me a new perspective that helped me, after not many months, to see the Legion as truly bizarre. It showed me that there were credible and desirable alternatives where I could still follow my dream of being a priest and contributing to people's lives, and maybe even have fun. Besides the new style of teachers and the new adventures in thinking, the student body were also very different from the Angelicum. They were ordinary young men dressed in blue jeans and tee shirts. There were even some young nuns who were not afraid to show their knees. My fellow students laughed and chatted in breaks and seemed genuinely happy. I suddenly saw the kind of religious life I wanted to lead. Not the nit-picking, paranoid, telling-on-each-other, *Doublespeak* Legion, but whatever it was that these guys had: ordinariness and a presence in the world. I began to see new possibilities.

One sunny afternoon I was woken from siesta by a sound I had never heard before, let alone in the religious silence of a Legionary house: a man was shouting continuously at the top of his voice somewhere on the floor below me. The noise grew clearer and louder as I hurried down through the stairwell, a single word, the name *'Ignacio, Ignacio, Ignacio'* – the name of the vice rector - shouted over and over again. The noise came from a charming, gentle, funny man – let's call him Miguel - completely losing his grip on reality, shouting for several hours at the top of his voice while opening and closing his door repeatedly so that the waves of sound came and went along the corridors of the building. I can still hear him screaming the name continually, emphasising different syllables as he went in a rhythmic chant: '*Ignacio, Ignacio, Ignacio*'. Towards the end of the afternoon, he was subdued by four or five sturdy brothers and carted off to a private psychiatric hospital, whence he returned some weeks later with Mogadon-dulled eyes, before being shipped back to Mexico. I heard later that he had another breakdown while living at the junior seminary, and was returned to his family, discarded by the Legionaries as unfit. In hindsight, I think it's likely that he had been abused. He was a very sweet, gentle man, but always with some sadness in his eyes. There was no discussion of his condition or his wellbeing. When he left, as with all the others, he was vaporized in best Orwellian fashion – of no further use to the exciting and stylish mission of the Legionaries of Christ, they of the well-combed hair and shiny shoes.

Then there was the curious case of the numbers in the book. The Diocese of Rome, the Holy See, publishes a yearbook called the *Annuario Pontificio* with facts and figures about the church, the names of all bishops and cardinals, their roles in the Roman Curia, the governing ministry of the church, and details of all religious orders, where they have convents and monasteries and how many members they have. It makes for dry reading, and you can guess that it doesn't figure on the New York Times Best Seller list. I had never seen one of these volumes until 1975 when I became an assistant superior and, as you would with any book where you might get a mention, I went straight to the part about the Legionaries of Christ. To my amazement, I found that the numbers of Legionaries claimed in the yearbook far exceeded the actual numbers, and not just by a few here and there, or even a few dozen, but by hundreds! At the time the Legion had a relatively small number of establishments, I knew where they all were, and I knew approximately how many brothers and priests were in each. I checked the sums a couple of times with the same result: the numbers bore no resemblance to what I knew to be true. As the *Annuario* editors rely on each organisation or diocese to supply their own data, there could be only two conclusions: either my highly intelligent confrères couldn't count, or the congregation was supplying false numbers to the Vatican. Why would they do that, if not for some process that required the congregation to be a certain size and to garner prestige? Catholic religious orders, as they grow, must reach certain milestones to be fully approved by the Vatican, and part of the requirement is that there be a minimum number of members of the organisation: without this, no approval. It was clear to me that the Legionaries were lying to make themselves look good and secure a tick of approval, counting all who joined but few, if any, of those who left. Thus, they could present themselves as an almost miraculous phenomenon blessed by God with an abundance of vocations for the salvation of the Church. Indeed, this is how they succeeded in being seen by virtually every Pope from Pius XII to John Paul II. The cognitive dissonance filter that allowed me to accept all sorts of drivel in the first years of my religious life had well and truly disintegrated, and I was able to see the lies.

The lies and the paranoia were on display to me every day now that I was in the inner sanctum of the leadership cadre of my Legionary community. Each week this leadership team met: the rector, the vice-rector (a particularly obnoxious man), the three *asistentes* of the philosophy community, and the two *asistentes* of the theology community. The thing I found shocking about these meetings was the contemptuous way in which this elite group talked about the brothers in their care. They mocked their efforts at religious observance, their Spanish pronunciation, their intelligence, and even their appearance. In any management team this would be corrosive; in a religious community it is repellent. To preach kindness, and forgiveness, and mercy, and the boundless love of God and then to snigger at a brother's weight or mock his exam results, or his Spanish grammar, was unconscionable. As a member of the community, I had always understood that my superiors were hard taskmasters, wanting me to give to the utmost of my ability, but I never thought that they were laughing at me behind my back.

Behind the closed doors of these meetings, the valiant, heroic Legion that fought to establish the Kingdom of Christ looked very different. What I came to understand more clearly than ever was that people mattered to the organisation only in so far as they were of use to it. Once they ceased to be of use, they could be thrown away. In the Greg under the supervision of the venerable Joseph de Finance I was writing a thesis on the value of the human person in the work of the French Humanist philosopher Jacques Maritain. For Maritain, the basis of ethics is not an abstract philosophical argument, it comes with the practical knowledge that human persons have of the natural law. It is by valuing the human person's experience that we approach an understanding of the moral universe, and of how to measure goodness. In the Legion, by contrast, it was clear that people, as people, didn't matter. This confirmed the lingering discomfort I'd had in Dublin, seeing Mexican factory-owning benefactors wined and dined with Waterford crystal and fine wine, while the poor relations from the country made do with tea and plain biscuits. Not that all my fellow religious were treated like this. No, those whose families were well connected or well off, while not quite being wined and dined with the Waterford, were certainly gushed over in expectation of the good to come.

Seeing raw hypocrisy face-to-face every day tipped a wavering balance, and I began to realise that, as this behaviour went right to the top and I couldn't change it, I had to go. Ironically the sexual urges that had threatened my religious life before now seemed much less important than the corrosive culture of the organisation. Sexual struggles were understandable because I was a twenty something year old virgin with desires that don't need explaining. Much more powerful was the hypocrisy I saw around me and witnessed from the inside of the self-righteous organisation within which I had given my life to the service of God. For my Leaving Certificate examination in Dublin, I had studied *Hamlet*. One of the many lines that stayed with me was that '*a man may smile and smile and be a villain; at least I am sure it may be so in Denmark*'. I learned that it was so in the Legion.

I realised that I had lost all respect for the organisation through which I had dedicated my life to God; how was I to dig myself out of this hole? By the beginning of 1976 I had begun to formulate a plan.

ROME: THE ESCAPE PLAN

We gotta get out of this place
If it's the last thing we ever do
The Animals

During the seven years I had spent in this Legionary quest, in the belief that I was pursuing something decent and good, I had seen many of my fellow travellers leave and be vaporized with nothing: no qualifications, no work record, no assets, no plan for the future, no forwarding address, and no trace. I was determined this would not happen to me. But, as a religious, I had no access to money: I couldn't buy a bus ticket or make a telephone call without asking for money from my superior, much less buy a plane ticket to Ireland. I was completely at the mercy of whatever decision the rector, Manuel Dueñas, made about me. If I went to him too soon and said I wanted to leave, he could put me on a flight the next day, and what would I have to show for my time? What would I have that was useful for the future? A couple

169

of years of study in Madrid but no degree because the whole charade had crumbled; a bachelor's degree in Thomist philosophy that counted for little, and for which I had no certificate to show anyway - the Legionaries never received certificates. Then there were the post-graduate studies I was doing and enjoying right now; if I left part way through the year, I would lose all the credits for the work I was doing.

The other issue was that I couldn't just return to Dublin and to my family while I was full of uncertainty about what I wanted to do. I didn't want to expose my mother to the pain or embarrassment of having a 'spoiled priest' for a son in the narrow-minded Ireland of 1976. Besides, I wasn't a spoiled priest. I still wanted to be a priest, nothing else came close, so I just needed a place to stay for the summer while I worked out the future and what I would do to get to the goal.

I had to talk to someone, but for a Legionary that was easier said than done. Even to speak to a professor at the Greg required permission from the rector or vice-rector, and afterwards an account would need to be rendered of how the conversation went. Many years after I had left the Legion, my friend Trevor King once asked me what would have happened if I broke a rule? It was a great question and it made me think about the power of the internalised rule. The answer to Trevor's question was that not very much would happen. There would be no fine, no bread and water for a week, no hard labour. The most humiliating – and bizarre – punishment I had endured was to have to eat my meals kneeling on the floor as a result of some forgotten transgression, but I still got my meals. Instead of some external punishment there would be the scourge of conscience, the knowledge that I had failed an obligation I had assumed freely. Years later, when I trained in group therapy, I realised that the power of a group to effect change resides largely in its cohesion around a purpose and around emerging norms. Group rules are explicit and prescribed, but norms are not, they emerge as the intellectual and emotional property of the group members. If I transgress, I am transgressing against myself. This is the powerful trap that holds people in sects and in dysfunctional organisations like mine. It's the rear naked choke of ideology and many don't know how to tap out or don't believe that they can.

Having said that, the task of speaking to someone was a lot easier for me than for many of my brothers. I was one of a handful of Legionaries who were reading for the Licentiate in philosophy which meant there were far fewer of us attending any given lecture. This in turn meant fewer Legionary eyes to spy on any activity that was outside the rules, like speaking to a non-Legionary. It also meant that by judiciously choosing courses I could arrange to be the only Legionary in some obscure seminar, a feat I managed by choosing a course run in English. I have no idea what the course was but, in the event, I didn't attend many lectures.

Whom could I speak to safely? I chose a friendly looking young man from my metaphysics class. He was about my age, he seemed calm, with a friendly face, and he looked cool and self-possessed in his chunky-knit sweater, jeans, and sneakers. He was also fairly solitary, without an obvious group of friends, and therefore easier to approach. I observed his movements for a few days, seeing where he went at break times and when I could approach him without being seen, and I rehearsed my line a hundred times. The grand central atrium of the Greg has a balcony around the first floor with an elegant cream balustrade and grey marble columns; this was an area where no Legionary could go without permission. After several false starts, the moment came when my classmate and I were both on the first floor, unseen, far back from the balustrade and therefore out of sight from below: it was my Rubicon. Once I said the words I had rehearsed, I would have left the Legion in my head. I approached my friendly looking classmate across the polished marble *pavimento* and said simply, 'Ciao. Ho bisogno di parlare con qualcuno' – 'I need to talk to somebody'. I saw the shock in his face: Legionaries didn't speak to anyone, and they certainly didn't plead for a confidant. The shock gave way to concern, and he was wonderful in his response: warm, generous, discreet, and understanding, and asked no questions. He said his name was Milan. We didn't have much time, but I told him I was having some difficulties and I needed someone to talk things through with. We arranged that the following week I would get permission to see my thesis supervisor, Father de Finance, who had an office upstairs where there would be no students, and Milan and I could meet near his room and talk unobserved. As I write, I am aware how absurd this all sounds, all this cloak and dagger stuff in a grown man. Please trust me when I tell you I'm sane, and that this bizarre narrative is not an indication that I'm crazy, but rather an indication of what sane people may do in crazy situations.

I got permission for an interview with Father de Finance about my thesis. I think we spoke for five or ten minutes at most and then I left to find Milan. He was standing calmly at some distance from the office door, pretending to read a book. He told me he was a seminarian from what was then still Yugoslavia, and he was living at the German College in the Via San Nicola da Tolentino, a twenty-minute walk from the Greg, not far from Termini train station. He suggested that I could come and see him there, so I did. Mentally, I had well and truly left the Legion by now.

On several afternoons that term, always on a Wednesday, I took my bag and my seminar notes, received from the vice-rector my two fifty-lire coins for the bus fares, and travelled into Rome on the number 247 bus, alighting at the stop for the Gregorian, and then walking to Milan's college through the fashionable streets around the Quirinal Hill. It seemed the most daring thing in the world to walk along the street like this, but my excitement mingled with fear: what if someone saw me and word got back to the college, and I were sent away? As if a young man in a black suit would stand out on a Roman street! I told myself that in the sane world what I was doing was entirely unremarkable, it was only in the crazy world I had signed up to that anyone could see it as strange, even forbidden. When the rule makes something innocent into something bad, the rule is flawed.

Walking in the Roman heat in a full black suit is a sweaty business, and I sought the shady side on the way up along via del Quirinale and through Piazza Barberini, where the constant mist from the gushing fountain of Triton was a welcome relief. The imposing entrance of the Collegium Germanicum et Hungaricum didn't help my nervousness on my first visit. Ridiculously, I felt like a spy at a checkpoint, whose cover might be blown at any moment if their papers were found to be forged. How did I live in such a state of fear? Wasn't perfect love supposed to cast out fear?

Milan's room was plain but homely, about three or four metres square with an old-fashioned wardrobe much too big for the room, a small study table with a shelf of books, and a brass-framed bed with a padded eiderdown. I hadn't seen a padded eiderdown for seven years and it reminded me of my bedroom at home. Milan put me at my ease as we sat down to talk. Under my black jacket I was wearing a white tee shirt, my silly elasticated sleeves, and a black stock with my clerical collar. When he suggested I might like to take off my jacket, I demurred at first, saying I was just wearing a stock over my tee shirt, with some false sleeves and I would look pretty silly without the jacket. He suggested I might consider taking off the stock and sleeves as well and just be comfortable in my tee shirt. To my ears still accustomed to Legionary rules, this sounded shocking, but to Milan it was clearly just a sensible suggestion. I was moving into another world. This was the first moment in seven years when anyone had considered my comfort and ease, and when I divested myself of jacket, sleeves, and stock, it was the first moment when I was not wearing the uniform prescribed for me by my quasi military, iron-fisted organisation. It was a moment of sweet liberation, and when Milan then produced a bottle of slivovitz and two glasses, my transformation back to human being was almost complete. He only had one chair in his room, so he sat on his bed while I had the chair and we talked about everything and nothing – what a delight to talk spontaneously to another human being with no agenda! Hanging on the wall above his bed there was a framed poem that was in Greek. I couldn't translate it, but I recognised it from the single-word title: 'An'. It was Rudyard Kipling's 'If' – 'An' was a word in my small Greek vocabulary, a leftover from classical philology in Madrid. The poem had hung above my own bed at home all the years I can remember, framed in cheap *passé partout*, and the serendipity of finding it in my new friend's room was immensely reassuring: it connected me to things I had left behind and thought that I had lost. Milan's English was good, and I treated him to a recitation of several stanzas from my head full of poetry.

I told Milan about the decision I had come to and how I needed someone to talk to, and someone to help me communicate with the outside world without the censorship I knew would be imposed on any letter I sent to friends or family. Milan said he would be happy to be my postman, I could write letters with the return address of the German College, and he could pass replies to me. To exchange letters, we devised a plan straight out of a spy novel, and I feel embarrassed to describe it. The place we could both visit at university without exciting comment from my Legionary brothers was the reading room at the library. Better still, I could go there every day without arousing suspicion. When I had a letter to send, I would go to the stacks at the back of the reading room where no one would see me and put my letter into a book chosen at random, I would then wander back into the reading room, scanning the shelves as if still looking for something, and leave the book absent-mindedly on the table near to where Milan was reading. I wouldn't have to say anything, I would just forget to take the book with me when I left, he would find and post the letter for me and wait for a reply. When a reply came, I would know because there would be a book near him on his table with the precious letter slightly protruding. As before, I would wander close, this time spotting the book as if it were the very volume I was looking for, and politely ask whether I could borrow it. I would then walk back into the stacks, extract the letter, and replace the book beside him after a suitable interval with a cursory thank you. In this way I was able to let my family know that I was about to leave the Legion, and that I planned to continue my training for the priesthood by a different route. The strategy for this had yet to be figured out, but my optimism often underestimates difficulties. I suppose I thought that if I started, I would find a way. I had decided to ask my sister Margaret, then living in Ayr, in Scotland, if I could come and stay with her while I sorted out what I was going to do. She generously said I could, and the scene was set - I had a possible bolt hole. My friend Milan went on to have a stellar career and became a professor of theology.

Shortly after I had begun to visit Milan at the German College I made a second friend, out of the blue, when someone approached me one day during the morning break in lectures. I say this casually, but I want you to imagine a rabbi strolling into a café in Gaza and striking up a friendly conversation with an imam. The taboo was no less stringent, even if it was a lot less dangerous. One day at break time, rather than leave the Aula Magna, the main lecture theatre with its semicircular banks of old wooden desks, I stayed behind on my own at my desk while the other three or four Legionaries left the room. We Legionaries always left the room together at break time, otherwise people might want to talk to us; easier to run away and reassure each other of our righteousness. My behaviour in staying was strange; for a keen observer it was a minute but definite gesture of defiance never normally seen in the behaviour of a Legionary, and it drew the attention of one of my classmates, a Franciscan brother. He came up to me in the aisle between the desks and said: 'You're a Legionary, aren't you?' I looked into his face and his smiling eyes and decided in that instant to trust him. I was impressed that he had approached me, no one ever did, as they knew how standoffish we were, and that we would not, could not, chat. I looked at him steadily and answered *'Per ora, si'* ('For now, yes'). The Rubicon had already been crossed; this was just a minor tributary. His eyes widened with immediate intrigue: 'For now? How do you mean?' My eyes glanced towards the entrance to the lecture hall, and I said I couldn't really talk as the spies would soon be back from their break and I couldn't be seen talking to a stranger. He understood at once and we agreed to meet at another time, upstairs. As with Milan, I would get permission to come and see professor de Finance and we could meet upstairs near his office. The plan worked.

My new friend, Fra Umberto, threw himself energetically into helping me. Everyone disliked the Legionaries, and the prospect of helping one to escape their crazy order was delicious: he literally clapped his hands with delight on our first outing together. My liberation became Umberto's project and he invited me straight away to come and live with his community in their rambling convent on the outskirts of Rome. He had a car, so he took me there one afternoon when I was supposed to be in a philosophy seminar; whatever course the seminar was for, I'm sure I didn't pass. At the convent, we spent an hour with his friends whose minds seemed to be firmly focussed on sex - with women, rather than with each other. I'm not sure whether this was Franciscan locker room talk or reality, but I didn't care. I now knew two lots of people in Rome who understood my situation and could possibly help.

Umberto's companions in the Franciscan community were friendly and jolly, and discreet enough to know they couldn't speak to me back at the Greg. I was keen on the idea of moving in with them but how to make the move? Well, more cloak and dagger stuff obviously! How was it that I couldn't walk out the front door like an adult? My plan instead was to depart by stealth in the dead of night. Because I taught English in the college, I had access to the language-teaching lab on the ground floor at the southern end of the house. I could leave one of the windows open one evening when I locked up. Later, when everyone was asleep in the *magnum silentium,* I could come down, raise the Persian blinds and escape through the window into the grounds. I had noticed that there was a gap in the wire fence on the same southern end near the tennis court that would give me access to the road. Umberto had a car; could he arrange to meet me there one night? I could take a suitcase from the store, pack some things, and wear black clothing – I had quite a lot of that. Mercifully, Umberto thought this was a terrible idea and told me so. 'You went in there the right way and you're coming out the right way, by the book' he said, spreading his hands. 'If you sneak away, you'll regret it forever'. When I was ready, on my own terms, I should front up to the Rector and ask to apply for a dispensation from my vows. Umberto was right, of course, but being formally dispensed from your final vows is a big deal. The religious who wants to leave must apply to the Vatican Congregation for Religious and submit to a lengthy clerical bureaucratic process, that might take months, to obtain the signature of the Cardinal or his delegate on the piece of paper that frees him or her from these vows and all their obligations. The hole in the fence and a berth with these jolly friars seemed attractive, but Umberto spoke sense, especially if I wanted to continue training for the priesthood with a diocese or another order:

'So, Kevin, how did you leave the Legionaries?

'Well Bishop, I ran away one night through a hole in the tennis court fence, actually.

Not a good start.

Umberto took me out to the monastery again, this time to see his Prior, and I asked whether I could come and live with the community until the end of the academic year. The Prior was a delightful man with a slight stoop and kind eyes and his office smelt of polished wood and the special monkish, musty scent of the heavy serge of monastic habits. After listening carefully to my story, he said I would be welcome to come and live at the monastery (my heart soared!), as long as my current religious superior also approved (my heart sank!). I knew that there was no way on earth that Dueñas would give his approval to this move, but I said I would ask anyway. I had nothing to lose. My plan now had two arms: I had a possible place to stay in Rome, and my family were alerted to the fact that I might be home soon while I organised the transition to some alternative way to continue my studies. If by some miracle Dueñas would agree to me moving in with the Franciscans, I could stay and find my feet, otherwise I would ask to be sent to Scotland straight away to stay with my sister. The stage was set for the last scene.

Thanks to my mother's example, I have a horror of wasting things, so I wasn't about to waste the previous seven years and become one of those ex-Legionaries who disappeared with nothing. I was mid-way through my licentiate in philosophy, so I decided I wouldn't make a move to leave the congregation until I had accumulated enough course credits to make the academic year worthwhile and therefore make it possible to come back and finish the degree without repeating the year: they weren't going to vaporise *me*. As soon as I hit the total credits I needed, I went to see the rector, Manuel Dueñas Rojas. Others have written about Dueñas and about his part in the whole sordid, abusive mess of the Legionaries. He even gets a mention in accounts of the offshore tax evasion schemes organised by the Legion. Writing today I can happily say: not my circus, not my monkey.

The rector's office door had a bell with a little traffic light system on it: a red light for busy and a green for enter. One Friday night in May, after night prayers, I stood outside Dueñas's door and watched for the green light, clear in my mind what I wanted. For the previous two weeks I had taken advantage of one of my few privileges as an *asistente*, the fact that I was allowed to pray up on the roof terrace without asking anyone's permission. A few evenings before, I had been up there alone, walking up and down, pretending to pray during the fifteen minutes set aside for the rosary, but really just enjoying the delicious solitude; Rome and me, like the poem I had declaimed in the academia to entertain Maciel's guests three years before: *Paz al atardecer, Roma a lo lejos.* To the west the soft pink of the Roman sunset was deepening over the suburbs and the air was completely still. Over in the east the sky was darkening over the Vatican City, and no one in the world knew or cared what a twenty-four-year-old Irishman was thinking, walking up and down on the grey asphalt of this suburban roof: I was wonderfully and peacefully alone. I had decided that the moment had come for me to leave, and more importantly I had also decided that it didn't matter what Dueñas or Maciel or my mother or anyone else might say to me. Alone on the roof I had a very simple conversation with God, one-sided obviously, there was no mystical vision. I simply said: '*Look, I may be making a terrible mistake in leaving, but I'm going to take responsibility for it myself and you and I can sort it out between us, no intermediaries needed*'. It was a simple moment, a moment of looking God in the eye and speaking adult to adult, and I felt entirely confident in my plan. It was as if we had agreed on a handshake that I was acting in good faith, whether or not I was getting it right. It was all I needed to give me complete peace in my resolve, and it felt like the first truly personal decision I had taken since deciding to join up, seven years before.

Raising my eyes to the pink-grey sky I felt confident and whole, more than I ever had before. There was no anger and no complaint, just the strongest feeling that I *had* this, alone. In the classical quest narrative, there is often a moment where the protagonist realises that he or she has received a special gift, has somehow entered into the power that they came to find: that May evening was my moment. It was a sublimely liberating instant that has remained with me for almost fifty years – my break with this sect and the beginning of my departure from organised religion, the kind of religion mediated by humans who are convinced they have *the* truth, but in reality are the victims of an egregious cognitive distortion.

The green light winked on Dueñas's office door. Seated at his desk in the sparsely furnished office and lit by a single desk lamp, he looked up at me with the inscrutable public expression I knew well. When I first met him, he had seemed the epitome of serenity, his flat, round face and narrow eyes giving him an almost Buddha-like quality. He had destroyed that impression later when I saw the mocking, contemptuous, sycophantic side to him. Without preamble I told him I wanted to leave and that I had come to tell him about my decision, not to discuss it. I wanted to say that I no longer believed the Legion was a worthwhile place to be, that its hypocrisy disgusted me, that I thought that covering lies and contempt with the claim of a divine blessing on the work was nothing short of blasphemous. But I didn't say those things; I needed to stay polite so as not to cruel the remote chance he might agree to me staying in Rome with Fra Umberto and my Franciscan friends. At first, he was conciliatory, 'You seem to be under a lot of stress Brother,' and offered to relieve me of my duties as assistant superior so as to take away some pressure. I said that would make no difference and that I needed to go. He then changed to guilt and said that whereas I was of course free to go, he had to remind me I had *'put my hand to the plough'* and if I turned back, well, I was putting my eternal salvation in jeopardy. I said, calmly, that I knew I would be answerable for that. He asked me where I intended to go, and I told him I had an offer of temporary accommodation from my Franciscan friends but that their Prior wanted Dueñas to give his permission for me to stay with them. Predictably, he refused, and I said: 'Well, you need to send me home then'. I also said I wanted a proper dispensation from my vows. It wasn't a long conversation. I left his office and went to the laundry store to see what I could scavenge in the way of clothes to take with me.

How simple it seems to say, *'Well, you need to send me home then,'* and to have Dueñas accede to my request. What had all the fuss been about, if it was that easy? But the short conversation in Dueñas' office was made possible by the months of reflection, soul-searching, and planning that preceded it. I said eight short words[1] and I felt with certainty that the ties that bound me, the ties of duty and of the fear of sin, of disappointing others, of disappointing God, of disappointing my mother, began to slacken. It was like hearing the creak of a stout old wooden door as it begins to open, the massive, studded carriage door of a Roman *palazzo* perhaps. The opening is not yet wide enough to vouchsafe passage, but the process, once begun, is inexorable. The door will continue to swing, and nothing will stop the momentum. Thanks to Milan, and Umberto, and my sister, I had a realistic plan, in fact I had two realistic plans: belt *and* braces. Thanks to my dusk communing with a God who was unseen but still keenly felt and cherished, I had the assurance that I need no longer answer to these men and to this organisation that I now knew to be deeply flawed. I didn't know a fraction of the flaws that I would discover later, but the ones I knew were enough to repel me. My Legionary mentors had taught me the dictum, *'Bonum ex integra causa, malum ex quocumque defectu'.* Now I could turn and apply it to my Legionary mentors.

The next day was Saturday and, amazingly, by lunch time I had two pieces of paper in my hand: a papal dispensation from my vows and a plane ticket to Scotland. The dispensation of vows is dated May 15th, 1976, and states that I am: *'solutis a votis ceterisque obligationibus'*, freed from my vows and other obligations of my religious state. The document is grandly titled an 'Indult of Secularization' and it's signed by Basil Heiser, the former Minister General of the Conventual Franciscan Order, the 114th successor of Francis of Assisi in that role. Ironically, until a few years earlier, he had been the Superior General of the Order that Umberto belonged to and that had kindly offered to take me in but were prevented from doing so by the mean-spirited decision of my own religious superior. Heiser was Undersecretary for the Congregation for Religious and Secular Institutes, the branch of the Vatican bureaucracy that oversees religious institutions whose members take vows, like nuns, monks, and brothers of various kinds. A Legionary priest, José María Escribano, worked in the Congregation for Religious and Secular Institutes and had waved the papers through. Even in the Vatican, it's who you know and not what you know that can get you a weighty signature on a Saturday.

My departure from via Aurelia 677 was timed as departures always were – when no one was around to see. Early on Sunday morning, as I walked down the corridor towards the side door, I met just one other Legionary. Robert Meluskey, my charming, warm and friendly workmate was coming down the stairs on his early morning way to some task or other, probably to the hen house to collect eggs. He wasn't allowed to speak to me but gave me a gentle smile with his kind eyes that said something like: *'My friend, I think no less of you because you are leaving'*. Robert's smile is the only kind thing I remember about that entire day, a pivotal day in my life. There is a Georges Brassens song, *Chanson pour l'Auvergnat*, in which he thanks the simple people who helped him in small ways, with some firewood, with some bread, with a smile, when he was in need. That song is about Robert's gentle smile :

'Ce n'était rien qu'un peu de miel, mais il m'avait chauffé le corps,
et dans mon âme il brûle encore à la manière d'un grand soleil'.[2]

When we got to the airport, I was given fifteen hundred lire, enough for an over-priced coffee and a bun - just over two hundred lire (four flat-rate urban bus tickets) for each of the seven years I had spent in this crazy sect; but I was free.

AYR 1976

Dare to be honest and fear no labour
Robbie Burns

*S*ummers in the UK are notoriously patchy, to speak kindly of them, but anyone around my age, and who has lived in the British Isles, will remember *The Summer of '76*. It was the second hottest summer in the UK since Met Office records began in 1914, and therefore the perfect time to sell ice cream, so that is what I did. Within a couple of weeks of landing at Prestwick Airport I landed a job at Butlin's Holiday Camp in Ayr and for most of the summer I was woken from sleep in my little staff chalet just before seven o'clock by the gentle strains of John Williams' *Cavatina*, the theme from *The Deer Hunter*, followed by the 'pips', the six short beeps of the Greenwich Time Signal, and the plummiest of voices saying 'Here is the news from the BBC', although what he actually said was 'Hair is the ni-oos from the BBC'.

I had come to Scotland because going straight to Dublin seemed too difficult. Even though I was quite sure my decision to leave Rome was the right one, I was still uncertain how the change of plan would be received, and I wasn't yet ready to face the barrage of questions I knew would be forthcoming from family and friends. From Rome, via my Yugoslav friend Milan, I had written to my sister Margaret asking if I could come and stay for a while and she had kindly welcomed me. There is some irony here, because when Margaret got married, I was rotten to her. After a number of unpromising boyfriends, Margaret met and fell for Douglas Taylor, a Scots Presbyterian, and the wedding was to be in the Presbyterian Church in Ayr. With the angry zealotry often found in the newly enlightened, I was indignant that Margaret should consent to this, marrying outside the church, and I told her so in a most unkind letter that I wish I had never written. Reflecting on my self-righteous wrath left me embarrassed and ashamed of myself that I could have been so mean to her and so cruel about such an important event in her life, her wedding. Angry young men do flail about sometimes, so I'm grateful that during my stay with her I had a chance to redeem myself. How ironic then, that it was to Margaret that I should come to for aid, the 'little mummy' of my childhood, precisely because I knew she wouldn't judge me. With my own religious schism just a few days old by the time I got to Ayr, I was at the very beginning of a journey to learn to be slow to anger and above all things to be kind.

When I arrived in Ayr, Margaret, Douglas, and their two children, Margaret and Caroline, aged four and three, had just moved into the home of Douglas's father, a widower, to keep him company in his old age. Hunter's Avenue is a wide sleepy street, a ten-minute drive north of the town centre and a fifteen-minute stroll to the golf links at Prestwick St Nicholas. Like most of the neighbouring dwellings, Number 150 is an unremarkable two-bedroom semi-detached bungalow under a black shingled roof.

Margaret had undertaken to look after her father-in-law, shopping, cooking, cleaning, and washing for him - a kind contribution to his declining years. Unfortunately, Mr Taylor senior was one of the most obnoxious people you could wish to meet, or indeed wish not to meet. He was constantly rude and abrasive, he hated papists with a visceral hatred, and made this known to any who would listen. In 1652 Oliver Cromwell's army provided the funds for the construction of Taylor senior's church, The Auld Kirk, and he seemed to have imbibed Cromwell's hatred of Romists. As the days and weeks went by, I wondered whether my arrival in his house, in his attic to be exact, tipped him over the edge. Having one papist as his daughter-in-law was bad enough; having a second papist, straight from the Great Babylon of Rome, was too outrageous. He was at his most vocal after closing time when he would return nightly from the pub sometimes literally roaring drunk. His aggressive shouting and swearing was frightening for my sister and for the kids and many were the nights that his son had to pacify him and put him to bed.

One night Douglas wasn't at home, he was on night shift at the railway, when Taylor senior returned in his usual belligerent fashion. Perhaps because his son wasn't present to moderate his behaviour, he became particularly aggressive and threatening. I have never struck another human being in anger, but I came closer than I ever had to doing so that night. It was only the fact that, as he was a doddery old man, I might well injure him seriously, that held me back. Margaret got the kids from their beds, wrapped them in blankets, grabbed some toys, and we went across the road to a kind neighbour who took us in. The next day I went to the local council to make an application on my sister's behalf for a council flat. I sat in the pale green waiting room with its fixed rows of public office seating under caged neon lights and tried to control the anger that I felt for my sister and the kids. When my turn came, I approached the service window and perched on the plastic chair to explain that my sister wanted to apply for a home but, given the incident of the previous night, I had come in her place. The young woman behind the counter played with the pen she held loosely between her fingers as she listened, nodding. She gave a little flick of her hair, creased her face in sympathy, and said, 'I'm sorry sir, that's not possible. You see, the property will have to be in her husband's name. A married woman can't apply on her own account'. Thinking on my feet, I controlled my anger, put on a grave face, and said, 'I think you'll find that would be in breach of the Sex Discrimination Act' (somehow, I knew this had been passed the previous year). 'You'd be refusing her application because she's a woman'. With a 'Just a minute sir' she went to one of the cubicles behind to consult her manager. I waited, trying not to show my nervousness, planning the next move in case they refused. To my great relief, and to be honest, my amazement too, they conceded the point, accepted the application, and my sister, her husband and the kids soon moved into 52 Sloan Street, a block of flats not far from the Racecourse, with a permanent lease in her own name, which she kept until she died.

In those days getting a job seemed a lot more straightforward than it is today. A few days into my stay, I went to the Jobcentre in Ayr, picked a card off the notice board, called the telephone number, and went for an interview. I wish that I could remember the name of the man who became my boss for the summer, but like many details from the past six decades it has flowed down the river with the snows of yesteryear. Some memories, however, remain bright, like my first day of work. The ice cream concession in the holiday camp was held by Lyons Maid, maker of such classics as the *Strawberry Mivvi* and the *Lolly Gobble Choc Bomb*, and the ice cream company in turn hired staff locally to manage the concession. In Ayr in 1976 their choice was a family of travelling show people whose patriarch was my boss and who, besides being an entirely unflappable, *we-can-fix-that* kind of guy, was also in great demand as a Burns Night speaker. Burns Night, the anniversary of Robert Burns' birthday on the twenty fifth of January, is a night when haggis is eaten, whiskey is drunk, and the poetry of Scotland's National Bard is recited and celebrated. The first thing my new boss spoke to me about, after offering me the job, was his love of Robert Burns, whose birthplace at Alloway was about two and a half miles to the west of where we were sitting at a picnic table having lunch. I love poetry and I evinced an interest in the great man, so my boss undertook to recite a different passage of Burns to me every day at lunchtime. He kept his word and not only showed me the beauties of Burns but also, later, those of scotch whiskey.

The Lyons Maid concession boasted a large sit-in ice cream parlour for the high-end treats like banana splits and sundaes, a kiosk built into a caravan parked at the other end of the site, two mobile fridges with large wheels and handlebars to steer with, and a cold store. My second day of work consisted of checking out these several facilities to make sure they were all operational and ready to open for business. When we reached the caravan kiosk, we found that the awning that shaded the customer window wouldn't stay up. Out came the tools and I held the awning aloft while my boss hammered it into submission. It proved quite difficult and at one stage he exclaimed: 'This is a *molto cattivo* hammer!' Unsure that I had heard correctly, I asked him what he had said. 'Oh yes', he replied, '*molto cattivo*, that's Romany for very bad'. I told him, to his surprise, that it was also Italian for very bad, and in addition to sharing verses from Burns, he promised to teach me any Romany words that he had picked up from other travelling people. It was going to be an educational summer.

I was still living with my sister in these early days and one of the joys of my stay was spending time with my two little nieces. Little Margaret was four and Caroline three at the time and they were the first two small children I had ever lived with. As the youngest in my own family, all my brothers and sisters had been older than I was, so this was a new experience and, probably because I was an uncle rather than a parent, I found them adorable playmates, the perfect antidote to the prudish, buttoned up, angst-ridden life I had left behind. They were endlessly curious with unanswerable questions like: *'When will it be this afternoon?'* or, *'Is it later yet?'* They were fascinated by the contents of my suitcase and especially by the fur-lined flying jacket that lived in there (purloined from the laundry store in via Aurelia). They christened it 'Fuzzy Wuzzy' and asked for it to be brought out regularly for inspection. They had borrowed the name from a rhyme that they taught me: *'Fuzzy Wuzzy was a bear, Fuzzy Wuzzy had no hair, Fuzzy Wuzzy wasn't very fuzzy, wuzzy?'*

Another favourite that stays with me is: *'I wish I were a furry worm with fur upon my tummy, I'd crawl across a lollipop and make my tummy gummy'*. I'm not sure that Mags and Caroline know what a lasting impression they made on me, what space their games still occupy in my brain, and what fun I had being with them. They were a wonderful balm, and not of the pious Gilead variety; much more fun!

One day I was sitting with them watching one of their television programmes, *The Magic Roundabout*. This was a classic BBC show, although copied from the French original, and had an almost cult-like status. The episode typically ended with the jack-in-the-box character, Zebedee, and the words: *'Oh well, time for bed, said Zebedee'*, as the theme music played and the credits rolled. As we watched, the show drew to its close, but instead of saying *'Time for bed said Zebedee'*, the refined BBC voice said, *'Oh well, sic transit gloria mundi,*[1] *said Zebedee'*. I laughed out loud, and it struck me that, as the typical audience were two- to six-year-olds, I might possibly be the only person watching in Scotland at that moment who understood the Latin phrase and knew the early fifteenth century devotional work, the *Imitatio Christi* by Thomas à Kempis, where it is found. Coincidentally, my mother had given me a copy of the *Imitation of Christ* the day I left home to join the Legion. The glory of *that* world had certainly passed.

Perhaps the funniest moment with my adorable nieces was

occasioned by another item from my fascinating suitcase. It was a photo that I still have somewhere, of me assisting at mass in St Peter's Basilica as an acolyte. The photo was taken as I received communion from Pope Paul VI, and it shows me with open mouth at the instant when the Pope reached towards me to place the communion wafer on my tongue. Standing to the Pope's right and looking solemn is Monsignor Virgilio Noë, his courtly Master of Ceremonies, and all three of us are dressed in white. Being almost the only memento of my time in Rome, it had great sentimental value for me. For little Margaret, on the other hand, it was a puzzling photo of her uncle and two other men dressed in white. She scrutinised it for a while and then said, in the triumphant voice of one who has cracked a cod, 'Och, there's Uncle Kevin at the dentist!'

Meanwhile, back at the camp, business was booming in the heat wave, and ice creams flew out the door. Strawberry Mivvis, our best seller, cost nineteen pence, to the horror of one elderly man who accused me of grossly inflating the price for my own benefit. He threatened to tell my manager and I told him he was welcome to, but he needed to hand over the nineteen pence or leave the queue. My management potential was recognised quite quickly (in other words, I turned up on time, did my job, and cleaned up at the end of the day) and after a few weeks I was made assistant manager. Some of the other staff didn't like this, as it involved asking them to do their jobs rather than sloping off with their mobile fridges to sit and smoke in the shade where no one could see them. They complied with my exhortation to get moving, but I later discovered what was unmistakeably a blob of semen carefully deposited on the saddle of the moped I used for travel to and from work. In their defence, I was probably a bit rigid in my views. I still had a monastically inspired belief that the rule must be followed, always. Smoke breaks in the shade were simply not in the script. It took me time to learn that if I were a bit more understanding, they were more likely to come to the party and we could both win.

As Margaret and her family were moving into smaller accommodation, I moved into a staff chalet at the holiday camp. It was compact but comfortable, about ten feet square, with a bed, a table and chair, and some sort of rudimentary bathroom facilities. It was for all the world like a well-appointed cubby house with homely touches like the little red and white gingham curtains at the windows. Each morning just before seven, the strains of *The Deer Hunter* seeped into my sleeping consciousness to be followed by the pips and that cultured voice of the newsreader. Seven o'clock seemed quite a civilised time to be woken really, especially after the strictures of my religious life; plenty of time to wake up, get ready, have breakfast in the canteen with the signature pale, thin toast that comes from flavourless white, sliced, packaged bread, and be at work by nine o'clock to prepare the venue for opening at ten. The working day grew longer when I rose to the heights of assistant manager. I had to do the end of day stocktake every evening, in a little hutch between the ice cream parlour and one of the dance floors, with unpainted plywood partitions no more than half an inch thick. There were four or five dinner-dance venues in the camp, each with its own unchanging program of songs. It was cheaper to pay performance fees for a single venue than for the whole camp, and this meant you could change your musical entertainment only by changing venue. As I tallied the stocks and takings each evening, I grew accustomed to the order of the songs, rather like listening to a favourite album. It was the year of *Tie a Yellow Ribbon on the Old Oak Tree*, which was followed like clockwork by *I'm on the Top of the World (looking down on creation)*. These songs became ear-worms long before I knew the term, but mercifully they are the only two numbers I remember. After the stocktake, the evening was my own and I often spent it chatting with my boss and his wife in their chalet and having a drink to unwind. I didn't have much of a discerning taste for alcohol, but I knew that I didn't particularly like scotch. My boss's wife persuaded me to try Glenfiddich, or maybe The Famous Grouse, but with the addition of a splash of lemonade. Looking back, it seems almost a sacrilegious thing for a true Scot to suggest, but then my friends didn't stand on ceremony.

We were sometimes joined in the evenings by the boss's sister whose real name I forget, but whose performance name was Madame Astra, under which guise she told fortunes. I remember Madame Astra for her off-duty wardrobe and especially for a memorable pink cardigan with small green and red flowers embroidered in two lines down the front. The colour scheme was further enhanced with sundry unidentified stains, but she obviously loved the cardigan and wore it virtually every day unless she was draped in her colourful, sinuous, fortune-telling scarves and robes. Unlike her brother, Madame Astra did stand on ceremony, at least where her accent was concerned. In unguarded moments she had a perfectly mellifluous Scottish accent, but she was always keen to disguise this, I never understood why, and to sound 'posh'. She did this by clipping vowels and hardly opening her mouth, as if showing one's teeth were rude and would betray one's lower-class origins. This is never a good idea and is bound to end in tears. I find it difficult to convey the audio effect by the written word, so perhaps you can imagine an accent like the house-proud Hyacinth Bouquet from *Keeping up Appearances*. Madame Astra and I were working together in the ice cream parlour one day, cleaning tables, when she suddenly said in her best voice: 'Kevin, you 'member them tables what we shifted yesterday?' The effect was such a caricature of faux-posh that I burst into laughter and had to make some specious excuse so as not to offend her. Madame Astra has stayed with me as an object lesson in the perils of not being oneself.

Bedtime was around eleven, when the camp mostly fell quiet, but sometimes there was a knock on my door later in the night and a disembodied voice saying, *'Do you want it?'* I took this to mean did I want to have sex with the disembodied voice and, instead of answering no, I hid under the bedclothes until they went away. I was pretty confused as to my identity and sexuality, and I remained so for a few years to come, but I knew that I certainly didn't want to have sex with a random woman who often as not sounded a wee bit drunk. This was an unsettling experience, a bit frightening really, partly because it brought me face to face with sex, about which I was utterly clueless, and partly because I imagined that my age peers in the camp, who obviously enjoyed each other's company, would talk about the weirdo in Chalet 10 who didn't even want it when it was offered on a plate. There would be some Augean Stables to clean out before I could settle down to enjoy being me.

Despite my confusion, I did manage to go out with a woman at least for a while during that summer. I'm not sure how we met, but she worked in a clothing store in Ayr whose windows were emblazoned with the motto: *'The Best in the West for Drapery and Napery!'* – a wonderful word *Napery*, and sadly fallen into disuse. I can't say that love blossomed among the calicos and damasks, but we did become friends and we went to a dinner dance together dressed up to the nines, she in a long evening dress and me looking like a car salesman in my dependable made-to-measure suit from *El Corte Inglés* in Madrid, with my Pierre Cardin tie; well, it said Pierre Cardin on the label.

When I think back on my summer in Ayr, the transition from *Most-secretive-congregation-in-the-Catholic-Church* to *Ice-cream-salesman-with-prospects* appears crazily seamless. How had that happened in the space of a month or two? Not only was I gainfully employed and had a place to live independently, (albeit temporarily), but my lovely boss had sung my praises to the Lyons Maid Regional Manager, who took me out to dinner, bought me my first gin and tonic, and told me there was a future for me in the company. It wasn't where I saw my career, but it was great feedback and a confidence booster. I was happy. I think the soft landing from my leap out of the Legionaries was perhaps due to my congenital lack of nostalgia. Even when I'm in my cups, I spend no time lamenting *les neiges d'antan*. I can sing along to *Va Pensiero*, the *Chorus of Hebrew Slaves* from *Aida*, but I have never lamented the loss of a land, metaphorical or otherwise. When I have decided something with a clear mind, I make the jump and take what comes. The decision to leave the Legion was made with a clear mind on a handshake with God and brought immense relief. It is also the case that I was twenty-four years old, a year before, so we are told, the male brain is fully developed. Thank goodness, I say.

All in all, I was having a jolly summer. I was making and saving money, I had some friends, and I had reconnected with my generous sister Margaret. But always in the back of my mind was the counsel that a finger-wagging St Paul had given to the Hebrews: '*We have not here a lasting city!*' Where was I going? What was the plan? How could I get back to Rome to finish my studies? Could I find a diocese to send me? I knew the Scottish Bishops had a college in Rome. I was in Scotland. The Scottish church needed seminarians for the priesthood (everyone did). Ergo, why not approach the local bishop? Some quick homework told me that I was in the diocese of Galloway and that the local bishop was Joseph McGee, who had been in the seat since the year I was born, and it wasn't difficult to make an appointment.

The bishop's house in Gorsehill Road is somewhat enigmatically called the Candida Casa, which for the not classically trained, translates from the Latin as 'The White House'. Your guess is as good as mine as to the origin of the name, but the bishop who named the house was clearly in the dark about yeast infections. Bishop McGee was not an effusive man, but he was serious and substantial. If there had been a presidential connection to go with the 'White House', he was more of a Grover Cleveland than a Ronald Reagan. He was in principle pleased to have an application out of the blue from a reasonably well-qualified candidate for the priesthood, but he was understandably doubtful about the conditional nature of my request. In fact, the tacit message was, *I'll join your diocese, but you have to send me to Rome, and I have to finish my Licence in philosophy.* Now only a chosen few, very few, are sent by their home diocese to the Eternal City, given the expenses of travel, tuition, board, and lodging, let alone the temptations of living among the metaphorical fleshpots of Egypt. Galloway had no other students at Rome. Why should Bishop McGee send me? I had already dumped one organisation; would I dump his as well? Bishop McGee said he would consider my application in prayer and meditation and that he would let me know as soon as he could.

But the prayer and meditation weren't only on the side of the reverend bishop. As I considered the idea of joining the diocese should he make an offer, I reflected that I had no particular connection to Scotland, let alone to Galloway, Dumfriesshire or Ayrshire. Taking the bishop's shilling meant coming back at the end of the process to serve in one or other of these little towns, which all looked sparkling in the heat wave of 1976 but were generally cold, wet, windy, and not a little dour. I wondered if there could be a better way. I had become accustomed to living an ordinary life where I was my own boss and I quite liked it: why not just go back to Rome as me and take my chances? I let Bishop McGee know that I was making other arrangements.

BACK TO ROME

Autumn in Rome, my heart remembers
fountains where children play
Tony Bennett, *Autumn in Rome*

ho can hear the mahogany tones of Tony Bennett and not thrill to the idea of autumn in Rome? The tourist gulls have mostly left, gone to swoop on chips in warmer cities further south, and the imperial dowager reverts to a slower rhythm. Traffic moves more easily on its bumpy way through the cobbled streets, although the beeping of horns remains, of course, mandatory. The stone pines of Rome, in the Villa Borghese, on the Janiculum Hill, near the catacombs, and along the Appian Way, all look a little dusty from the wear and tear of the summer scirocco, but they know that there will be days of rain and they spread their umbrella canopies patiently providing shade despite their weariness.

Teaching for the autumn term at the Gregorian begins at the

start of October, but student registration is in the month of September and, if I didn't belong to a diocese, I needed time to find myself somewhere to live and a job to make money so that I could re-join my philosophy course. After my foray into the Candida Casa of Bishop McGee, the attraction of joining a diocese had disappeared completely - it could take me from a Legionary frying pan into a diocesan fire - so I decided to go back to Rome and take my chances as a lay student at the university. After selling my Honda moped, I had three hundred pounds in the bank. It seemed like a good sum, but to be honest I had no idea whatever how much it would cost to live, feed myself and pay tuition fees. In fact, I had no idea what I was letting myself in for, but good decisions are sometimes made by wilfully ignoring the risks and just not thinking them through: how else would many of us be born? I closed my eyes and jumped.

After a quick trip to Dublin to see my mum and sisters, I bought a one-way ticket to Rome. In my bag I had three hundred pounds worth of travellers' cheques, a few thousand lire, and the phone number of my Franciscan friend Umberto whose community had offered me sanctuary. Arriving in Fiumicino I changed a note for some coins, found a public phone box and called the one number I knew. As I stood in the booth to make the call, it dawned on me how unbelievably stupid this plan, or absence of a plan, was. I had one number and no plan B. What if I had copied the number wrongly? What if they were all at mass when the phone rang? What if my friend was no longer there? What if I couldn't make them understand who I was and what I wanted? What if they had forgotten me, the crazy Irish Legionary who disappeared without saying goodbye? As Umberto had driven me to his friary, I had no clear idea where it was, and no address to ask about. But there was no viable alternative. I had one chip and I put it on red and waited as the long continental ring tone buzzed in the distance.

To my immense relief the phone was answered, and even more miraculously my friend was found within minutes. 'Keveen! *Ma certo!* Of course, stay there, I'm coming to get you!' The castaway who sees a ship approach over the horizon was not more jubilant on his deserted beach than I was in the forty minutes or so that I waited for Umberto. I didn't know at the time that 1976 in the Chinese zodiac was a Dragon year, made for me. Umberto and his friends hugged and kissed me as heartily as ever a long-lost friend was hugged and kissed, and we crammed into the little Fiat Cinquecento for the trip that promised a bed for at least a few nights. The white-robed Prior was gracious and solemn as before and told me I was welcome to stay for as long as I needed to. I was back baby!

Keen to enrol at the university, I made the trip into the city the next day to complete enrolment forms and to see Father Filippo Selvaggi, who besides being the professor of cosmology was the chair of the bursary committee at the Greg. A bursary would take care of the tuition fees. Selvaggi was polite and solicitous for my welfare, and I think he was not a little curious: I was the first Legionary who had come back to the Gregorian as a lay person immediately after leaving the Legion. Among the (many) issues I hadn't thought about in Scotland was whether the university would accept me back as a student now that I didn't have any religious affiliation to an order or a diocese. Sitting in Selvaggi's office this question suddenly occurred to me and I asked him whether this was a problem? 'Not in the least', he said, 'you're most welcome back'. He looked at the Legionary photo on my student ID card and smilingly suggested I obtain a new card with a new photo: *'Magari co'i baffi!'* ('Maybe with the beard'). I had grown some fetching facial hair during the summer. He said my application for a bursary would have to be considered by the committee, but he was confident it would be accepted.

I left Piazza della Pilotta with a jaunty step and a beaming smile. Hopping down the marble steps in the sun I could have been a character in a musical about to burst into song: *'Oh, the Greg wants me back, my fees will be paid!'*. Now to find a job and a place to live, probably in that order. The job I had in mind was English teaching and, with no evidence whatever, I was quietly certain I would find one. Ah, the confidence of youth! Several days later I was in my little room at the friary when I was called to the phone. How bizarre! Who knew I was there? Who even knew I was in Rome? The caller introduced himself as Cormac Murphy O'Connor, Rector of the Venerable English College. He sat on the Committee that awarded bursaries to prospective students and had seen my application. Would I please come and see him? I most certainly would.

The English College is called the *Venerabile* in honour of the Venerable Bede, an eighth century monk from Jarrow in Northumbria who wrote the first history of England.[1] The College could hardly be more picturesquely situated, around the corner from the colourful, noisy Campo de' Fiori market, in a rambling *palazzo* at via di Monserrato 45. You can see the locations of all three acts of Verdi's opera *Tosca* from the roof terrace. Five minutes walk away to the east is the basilica of Sant'Andrea della Valle where Caravadossi is painting when Tosca enters and where she sings *Vissi d'arte*. A hundred metres away is the great Farnese Palace where Tosca bargains with the dastardly Scarpia for the life of her lover, and a ten-minute walk away to the north on the Lungotevere, the bank of the Tiber, is the grand Mausoleum of Hadrian, the Castel Sant'Angelo, where, in true operatic style, all three principals meet their dramatic end and Tosca throws herself from the parapet.

The college is an unassuming building from the outside, but inside it has moments of renaissance grandeur. A wide marble staircase leads to the *piano nobile* where Cormac's office was located, at the end of a high vaulted corridor that seemed all gilt frames and crimson hangings. Cormac was a charming man, friendly, open, and welcoming with a ready smile and a warm voice. His eyes always seemed merry and his face always about to crease into a slightly mischievous grin. Despite his warmth I still felt anxious in these august surroundings - like the corridor, his office seemed full of gilt and damask - but he did his best to put me at my ease in English style with a cup of tea and some cake. His Vice Rector, Peter Coughlan, was there too but Peter mostly listened to our conversation. Cormac asked me briefly about my background, my years with the Legion, my studies so far, and whether I had any plans for the future. He said that, like me, he was a Christian Brothers' boy, having gone to Prior Park in Bath, the school that my mother told me I would have attended had the family not moved during the war: I felt connected. I said that for the coming year I wanted to finish my philosophy degree and accustom myself to a life outside the confines of the Legion, and that I knew I would need to find work to support myself. Later on, the plan was to see whether an English diocese might accept me so I could begin to study theology and continue training for the priesthood. If I'm honest, I only realised that this was 'the plan' when I heard myself saying it out loud to Cormac.

After chatting for twenty minutes or so, Cormac asked me to wait briefly in the corridor while he talked to Peter. I paced up and down under the stern gaze of bishops and cardinals in their crimson and purple robes, each staring frostily at me from his gilded baroque frame; hard to imagine that the chatty, funny man who had just interviewed me was their successor. A few minutes later Cormac appeared at the door to his office and invited me back in. He said that he had only one further question for me: had I left the Legion of my own accord, or had I been asked to leave? I said that I had left of my own accord, and that far from throwing me out, my religious superior had been keen for me to stay, invoking the jeopardy to my eternal salvation if I were to leave. In that case, he said, he would like to invite me to come and live at the English College while I finished my degree and planned for the future. I was completely overwhelmed by the generosity of his offer. There is a song in the Gilbert and Sullivan opera *The Mikado* in which the comic character Koko celebrates his immense good fortune in being *'taken from a county jail'*. By being set free he not only avoids being executed, but he becomes the Lord High Executioner and reaches *'a height that few can scale, save by long and weary dances...'* I knew how Koko felt.

I pointed out to Cormac that I didn't have funds to pay for my keep and wouldn't have them until I got a job that paid well enough. I had my three hundred pounds in travellers' cheques but, for the present, that was all. Then Cormac said simply: 'I think the church should invest in people, and that's what I want to do for you'. He suggested I deposit my travellers' cheques with the bursar, Sister Mary Jo Lorello, as a kind of security, and that the college would fund my bed and board. I was welcome to move in straight away. I think I floated back out to the Grande Raccordo Anulare to tell my Franciscan friends I would be leaving them, and I returned to via di Monserrato the next day to find that I hadn't dreamed my good fortune: there was indeed a room and a bed for me and a place at the table.

The Venerable English College! Woohoo! I felt like a busker being invited to perform in Carnegie Hall. The college had started life as a hospice for English pilgrims in 1362 and became a seminary for English students in 1579. It had welcomed among its guests such eminent figures as Thomas Hobbes, William Harvey and John Milton; the initials of John Henry Newman were scratched into one of the columns by the swimming pool, and more recently the figure of Muriel Spark was often seen as a guest at lunch. The college see-sawed with the fortunes of the English church through the Reformation and emerged as a college in exile and the cradle of over forty English priests who were martyred in their home country. To this day the Venerabile celebrates Martyrs' Day on December 1st, although it has probably not been known for ascetic austerity for some time. I have never lived in an Oxbridge college, but I imagine the atmosphere is not dissimilar: ancient buildings, venerated and silly traditions, ritual and formality, a top table in the refectory, some earnest studying of arcane disciplines, and a fair amount of drinking.

My new fellow students were instantly welcoming and to be sure I was a bit of an oddity. I didn't belong to any diocese, and I had been a member of the most secretive and enigmatic of religious orders. I literally dined out on my origins for many weeks if not months, and much of that dining was done in the Caffè Ai Bancchi Vecchi, a little trattoria a few hundred metres down the street from the college, a very manageable walking distance if one overindulged in vino rosso. It was the first or second night of my new life that a number of companions invited me to join them in the Bancchi Vecchi. It was dining at its simplest: square tables with fresh butchers' paper over red and white check cloths, *un litro bianco*, *un litro rosso*, a tall glass filled with crisp *grissini*, some salt and some olive oil in little white ramekins, and some fresh crusty bread. There would be a *primo piatto* of pasta or gnocchi with a generous bowl of grated parmesan, and a *secondo piatto* of meat or fish. Dessert was a *dolce* of some kind and then a bottle of amaretto appeared on the table for use at will. The bill was ridiculously small, even for my straitened means. Just like Koko from the Mikado, I couldn't believe my luck. I had surely been '*wafted by a favouring gale as one sometimes is in trances*' into a new life of liberty and friendship and fun. At the risk of mixing the musical metaphor, we certainly weren't in Kansas anymore.

The walk from the English College to the Greg takes about twenty minutes. First you turn left through the Piazza Farnese and then into the Campo de' Fiori, an immersion in riotous colours and sounds: barrows overflowing with fruit and vegetables, a whole swordfish suspended from the beam of the fishmonger's stall, the wolf whistles of the vendors at the pretty women who pass by, men leaning in twos and threes against coffee bars nursing a ristretto or macchiato, old women in black with sceptical faces handling the merchandise critically and counting out coins and notes grudgingly, the friendly back and forth insults of the vendors, and strewn all around the detritus of the trade, ends of cabbages, stray fruit trampled underfoot that will lie there until the market has closed and the square is swept and hosed down ready to do it all again tomorrow. In the middle of the Square is a statue of Giordano Bruno, the Dominican friar and philosopher, who was burned at the stake in 1600 for the crime of heresy. The statue stands on the site of the stake and proclaims a splendid message of redemption: a man who was burned as a heretic can later be a hero. From the square, along the narrow via dei Baullari, a right turn on to the bustling Corso Vittorio Emanuele II takes you past the church of Sant'Andrea della Valle, and a left turn up the via del Gesù leads on through cobbled back streets to the Piazza della Pilotta. All of this was a revelation to me, and it was glorious. *Autumn in Rome* indeed. The last time I had walked through Roman streets, four months before, I had been a furtive figure in black, looking from side to side, worried that I might be seen and reported back to HQ. Now I was a regular guy, jeans, tee shirt, and trainers, like a million other regular guys in this smiling city where children played in the fountains.

I resumed my philosophy degree and inevitably came face-to-face with my former Legionary companions. As someone who had done the unthinkable of having put my hand to the plough and turned back, I was of course shunned by them in an obvious way. For closed religious sects who disown those who leave, 'shunning' means cutting or snubbing someone. The shunned person is not acknowledged or looked at or spoken to or spoken about: for those who remain faithful to the cause, the shunned don't exist. If we passed each other in a corridor, or were seated in the same classroom, the Legionaries would noticeably avert their eyes, studiously gazing where I was not, or looking past me. These were men with whom I had shared a religious life and its aspirations for many years. Some of us had been candidates and novices together. For some of them I had been their assistant religious superior, but now for them I was a pariah, an apostate who could no longer be acknowledged. The single exception to this ostracism was one man, Brother Ricardo, a young Spaniard whom I had not really known all that well. We met one day waiting outside a classroom for the teacher to arrive and open up. There were several Legionaries in a little group from whom I expected no acknowledgement, but to my astonishment Ricardo came forward, put out his hand, and said it was good to see me again and how was I? Did I have a good summer? Was I looking forward to this course? His gesture touched my heart: thank you Brother Ricardo. I have no doubt whatever that your colleagues dobbed you in to your 'superiors' (what an ironic term, when in kindness they were clearly your inferiors!) in via Aurelia 677, and that the rector or the vice-rector told you off for consorting with me, but I have never forgotten your guts and your kindness.

I felt no embarrassment in meeting my former brothers, only sadness for them and their constrained, brainwashed life, but I did feel some shame at having taken clothes that weren't mine from the laundry store. In the grand scheme of things, it was a minor transgression, and in any case, I had given them to a charity shop in Ayr, but it rankled with me. The shame was helped by the fact that when I was unpacking my case at my sister's house in Ayr, I found a handwritten note from the obnoxious vice-rector, Ignacio. I came across a phrase the other day that reminded me of this man. The German historian Norman Ohler in his book *The Infiltrators* refers to a Gestapo court martial prosecutor, as charming as he was vicious, as someone who was *'equally good at bowing to those above him and kicking those below him'. Mutatis mutandis*, the phrase fits. Ignacio's note began with the words: 'A *título personal me permito decirle...*' ('On a personal note, may I say...') and went on to tell me that *on a personal note* he found it deceitful that I should take things from the store without permission, and what an underhand person I must be, and it just showed how unfit I was to be a Legionary etc. Never mind that the Legion had lied to me for seven years, thrown in some unwanted sexualised behaviour, and then given me fifteen hundred lire for a coffee and a bun at the airport. Resentful? Moi? But that aside, I wanted to clear the air, so I made an appointment to see Dueñas, still the Rector in via Aurelia. I was received politely in a small reception room, and I made my apologies for taking what wasn't mine. I also made a point of telling Dueñas how very happy I was in continuing my studies for the priesthood: apparently, taking my hand off the plough had not as yet resulted in the loss of the Kingdom of Heaven. Who knew!

The contrast with my previous life could not have been greater. The Rome that I knew as a Legionary consisted of the college in via Aurelia, the classroom at the university and the occasional ceremonial outing to serve as an acolyte in a Vatican liturgy. Now I was experiencing the loud, smelly, exquisite, garish, imperial city for the first time after two years of supposedly living there. I had the freedom of the city with its architecture, its art, its music, its cuisine, and its sexiness. I found a job teaching English to student teachers at the University of Rome, with an excellent pay rate and several hours work a week. Unfortunately, it was a time of massive student unrest and I quickly got to add the word *sciopero* to my vocabulary. I'm sure I taught some classes, but more often than not there was a strike, a *sciopero*, of students or teachers I'm not altogether sure, which meant many fruitless trips to the university.

I went out to the opera or to free music performances in magnificent baroque churches. If going to the opera in Rome sounds like an elite entertainment, it is anything but that. In 1976 the cheap seats in the Teatro dell'Opera cost about a thousand lire, a few pounds, and opera played to full houses of noisy, dedicated, engaged crowds out to have a good time: no need for surtitles here! The noisy crowds were happy to let the singers know when they were having a good time and when they weren't. Bravos and cries of appreciation were not confined politely to the ends of the arias but were hurled as required, sometimes during the very bravura passage they acclaimed. The same went for boos, so that the players didn't die wondering; the verdict of the mob was quite clear. At the interval we broke out the copious picnic that we had brought, and it wasn't in Glyndebourne style with wicker hampers. We toted our food and wine in plastic carrier bags, and although the usher remonstrated with us, he didn't stop our feast of cheeses, pâtés, and generous amounts of Valpollicella.

One evening I went to a performance of Vivaldi's Gloria at the Basilica of Sant'Andrea della Valle. Arriving just a few minutes before the music began, I got one of the last remaining programs and seated myself, for want of a pew, on the enormous collection box at the back of the church. I say collection box, but the reader should imagine a huge ornate wooden chest at least a metre high, all deep carving on the corners and bas relief on the panels, the contents of which would have provided decent venture capital for an ambitious start-up. Just as the choir were coming out to sing, I was joined up on my perch by a young woman who asked me, in Italian but with a pronounced English accent, if she could borrow my program. I replied, in Italian, that of course she could. As she took the program in her hand she turned away and muttered to herself under her breath, this time in English: 'That's the last you'll see of that'. I couldn't resist. When the choir had taken their seats, I leaned over and said, very politely, in English: 'You're welcome to keep the program by the way'. I confess to enjoying the horror on her face, but we were soon both caught up in the sublime music. Towards the end of the Gloria, the choir cries out the phrase: 'Quoniam tu solus sanctus' (For you alone are holy), all on one note, like a trumpet call. The exquisite gilt coffering of the ceiling was suddenly floodlit as if to drag us upwards in some glorious rapture and into the final Amen. As we applauded, my companion and I smiled at each other, and all embarrassment was forgotten.

NO PLACE LIKE HOME

Whatever days fortune will give, count them as profit
Horace, *Odes Book 1*

*R*ome must surely pack more grandeur per square
kilometre than most other cities in the world, but in
the hotter months, especially August, its better-off inhabitants flee
the heat and humidity for the fresh breezes of the surrounding
hills. The inhabitants of the English College were no exception,
with their charming if dilapidated bolthole in the Alban Hills, high
up on the shore of Lake Albano, looking across the extinct
volcanic crater at Castelgandolfo perched on the opposite side.
Villa Palazzola, or simply 'The Villa', had been a Roman villa and
later a Cistercian monastery under the patronage of the Kings of
Portugal before becoming the property of the English College.
Nowadays the Villa is an elegant venue for fairy tale weddings
among manicured gardens and polished antiques. In the nineteen
seventies it looked unloved and run down, with ill-fitting windows

and a jumble of furniture from which clumps of rough horsehair stuffing burst out like unkempt beards. Dust was everywhere. But for many of us The Villa was a magical place, like having your own abandoned castle to play in, complete with a sort of Wind in the Willows Wild Wood affectionately called The Wiggery. For me the Villa's most striking feature was the immense terrace to the south of the main cloister building commanding a magnificent panorama of the lake and the towns beyond, stretching away to the coast and the Tyrrhenian Sea. My other favourite place was one of the toilets on the first floor which had an oval window that framed the lake and Castelgandolfo like an exquisite miniature. As I sat there in solitary contemplation, I thought how great it would be to create a coffee table book called *A Loo with a View*. I regret that I didn't write the book - the research alone would have been fascinating.

There was no heating apart from open fires that smoked, and if breakfast was required on a Thursday outing, the ingredients had to be toted up from Rome on the early bus to Rocca di Papa. The house was tended by a small band of dedicated nuns, *suore*, who fought a losing battle against architectural decay. On Thursdays there were no university lectures, so small groups of rustication-ists would take the bus, or occasionally a car, to the hills and revel in the primitive peace of the place. There was always lots to do for those who wanted to take the initiative, whether that involved clearing out cluttered rooms, tidying the library, or hacking through the overgrown ground cover in The Wiggery. I have a small watercolour that I treasure, painted for me for one of my fellow gardeners, Robert Plant, depicting the Wiggery steps that we uncovered, or more exactly, rediscovered, and restored to usefulness. Down on the shore the Villa also had a heavy old clinker-built rowboat which we sometimes took out on the lake. On one occasion as six or seven of us rowed towards Castelgan-dolfo there was an earnest discussion of where we sat theologi-cally, to the left or to the right. Cormac was in the boat with us, and he pronounced that he thought 'left of centre' was the place of his choice. Someone promptly started up a refrain to the tune of *Sing Hosanna to the King of Kings* that went:

Left of Centre!
Left of Centre!
Left of centre is the place to be
Left of centre!
Left Of Centre!
Left of Centre is for me

We belted this out in the magnificent acoustic of the lake with all the gusto of a Welsh rugby crowd singing *Bread of Heaven* in Cardiff Arms Park. Cormac, who later became Archbishop of Westminster, received a cardinal's hat, and became chair of the European Bishops' Conference, was an amazingly approachable man who was spontaneous and self-deprecating. He delighted in making fun of his own adequate but imperfect command of Italian. There was an annual lunch at the Villa in honour of the sisters who looked after us, where the seminarians prepared and served lunch and generally did the looking after. Cormac rose after lunch on the terrace to make a speech of thanks to the sisters, in Italian but with his unmistakeable Berkshire accent, expressing the appreciation of us all for their untiring work - '*Il suo lavoro instancabile*'. Some oohs and aahs greeted his use of such a long Italian word and he turned to the assembled company with a grin to say in English: 'Yes, that *was* quite impressive wasn't it!' On another occasion, the twentieth anniversary of his ordination as a priest, he told the congregation in the Martyrs' Chapel, 'When I think about my twenty years as a priest, like Edith Piaf, I can truly say '*Je ne regrette rien*', and for those of you who don't speak Spanish...' Roars of laughter greeted his quip and I said to myself, not for the first time, that studying to be a priest in the Venerabile was quite unlike the buttoned up, sanitised Legion of Christ.

Meanwhile, back at the Greg, I waded through my second year of the licence in philosophy, coming to terms with Wittgenstein and pretending to understand Kierkegaard. Among the few items I have retained from these two great thinkers is the ability to spell their names correctly. One of the most challenging seminars on my programme was with Associate Professor Garth Hallett who was, among other things, a US navy veteran. He wore enormous Western-style clip-on belt buckles and although he didn't wear a Stetson to class it wouldn't have been surprising if he had. The first challenging element of the workshop was that there were only two of us students, myself and a Liverpool lad, Peter Fleet-wood, now Monsignor Peter Fleetwood, so there was nowhere to hide. The second challenging element was that Hallett only ever asked extraordinarily sweeping questions like: *'So the middle third of the eighteenth century was characterised by ...?'* or *'So the most influential publication of the first decade of the nineteen hundreds was...?'* These were terrifying questions, and I don't recall Peter or I ever getting one right, but Hallett was an exciting teacher and an expert in linguistic philosophy. I remember only two things about Wittgenstein; the first is that he wrote part of the *Tractatus Logico-Philosophicus* in the Gresham Hotel in Dublin - an interesting piece of trivia. The second is the dictum that: 'the meaning of a word is its use in the language', and this has stood me in good stead ever since.

Philip Holroyd held the post of philosophy tutor in the College, but as I merely lodged in the College rather than being enrolled as a seminarian, it wasn't part of his job to help me with my studies. Nevertheless, he treated me as if it were, and we had long and helpful discussions and tutorials for one. I confess that I hadn't thought about him very often until last year when I bought a new laptop and the assistant asked if I would like to try out a virtual reality headset. She fitted me up with the gear and asked if I was ready for a virtual visit to Rome! I found myself flying over the city in 3D like a pro, as if a phobia of heights had never been an issue. Then she showed me how I could set myself down somewhere in the city and look around. I could see the Pantheon below me, and I zoomed down to land in the square in front of it, the Piazza della Rotonda, and walked up to the Caffe Napoletano, where Philip and I had our last tutorial over coffee on the day before my final written exam for the Licence. I don't think we talked much about philosophy - it would have been a bit late by that stage – but Philip was a calm, phlegmatic Englishman and just being with him settled my nerves.

In the days leading up to that final written exam I took *Philosophy Made Simple* up onto the roof and tried to absorb its wisdom with the early summer sunshine. It worked. From this invaluable tome I managed to recall a quotation from a philosopher called Herbert Feigl: 'Philosophy is the disease of which it should be the cure'[1], which I inserted into my long, four-hour, written paper. Even though I attributed it to Moritz Schlick, a colleague of Feigl in the Circle of Vienna, the examination markers liked my effort and gave me 9.7 out of 10, an extraordinarily generous mark. In reality, I had chosen the single essay question from the four or five questions on the paper purely on the basis that it was posed in Greek, and I wanted to show off that I understood the question. The question was: *'ti to on?'*, which means, 'What is being?' I wrote a great deal of waffle and I'm pretty sure I proved Feigl right.

The oral examination was on equally thin ice. I had chosen Kierkegaard as my author to be examined *viva voce*, God only knows why, and was asked to bring with me to the examination the three volumes I was supposed to have prepared. I sat down in front of three eminent professors and one of them asked me to open the text and read a certain paragraph. I had chosen to be examined in English and I duly read the text aloud. One of the panel members then asked me to comment on what I had just read. The text was enigmatic, juxtaposing concepts and leaving the reader with little idea of where the author was going. I couldn't provide a sensible commentary because I couldn't really make head or tail of it, so I seized on that very point of confusion. Smiling indulgently as if excusing the behaviour of a wayward but beloved child, I pointed out how very, ahem, 'Kierkegaardian' the passage was. They smiled at each other approvingly and bought it, and I came away with a degree Magna Cum Laude, not quite the top, but rather too good for the effort and the understanding.

In my new life, not only was Rome my oyster, so was the whole of Italy and, on one occasion, Switzerland. Holiday periods like Christmas and Easter were opportunities to go away for a week or two and we did so alone or in small groups of friends. Sicily was popular, as were Venice and Florence. The most exciting of my expeditions was to Lugano just across the Swiss border on the northern shore of the eponymous lake. Our next-door neighbours in Rome were a small community of Swedish Brigidine sisters who ran a guest house for pilgrims and visitors to Rome. Monsignor Bryan Chestle, who lived at the English College, served as honorary chaplain to the sisters and, as a thank you, they generously offered holiday accommodation to a small group of English College seminarians in their guest house in Lugano, entirely free of charge. Their generosity made the trip possible, because although it was cheap to get to Lugano by train, the exchange rate into Swiss francs meant that paying for accommodation, even of the cheapest type, would have been prohibitively expensive. Five of us went up by train and were greeted and fussed over by the nuns as if we were long lost family members who had escaped a war zone. Apart from being the poorest group in the house, we were also by far the youngest five guests, most of our fellow travellers being retired Swedes and Germans for whom Swiss franc exchange rates were not a problem.

The area of Lugano where the sisters have their guest house is called Paradiso and you can see why. The house is a five-minute walk to the lake and the jetty where boats for hire take the visitor to drool over the opulence that drapes the shores. In this stunning setting we were well provided for as long as we were inside the guest house. Returning to our room after an outing we would sometimes find a bottle of wine or a box of chocolates. But once outside we had to decide at what time of the day we would treat ourselves to the luxury of a single coffee or an apéritif, which exhausted the day's allowance. All this changed however when some of our fellow guests noticed that we had brought with us two guitars that we played for the hymn-singing during mass on Sunday. One of the guests proposed a little concert, to be provided by us, after dinner one evening. We were happy to oblige, mostly out of gratitude to the generous sisters, and we set about giving our best selection of English and Irish ballads to a full house. I'm sure we sang *The Leaving of Liverpool* and *Scarborough Fair* and *Barbara Allen*; I may even had done my sentimental party piece, the plaintive *Curragh of Kildare*. At some point, we noticed that one of the guests had risen and was moving among the audience with a hat into which notes of various denominations were falling. The contents of the hat were presented to us with speeches of thanks and much applause, and we high tailed it to our rooms to count the loot. We were rich! Between us we had over a thousand Swiss Francs, over two hundred francs each. After financing coffees and snacks for the remainder of the holiday, one or two of us opened Swiss bank accounts, just because we could!

On another holiday, a small group of us decided that we would eschew the regular haunts like Venice and Florence, which were all pretty hackneyed and *Room-with-a-View*. I suggested Quixotically that instead of going somewhere famous, we should 'go somewhere that's nowhere and make it somewhere'. My companions trusted me, and we settled on Spello, about ten kilometres south of Assisi. Furthermore, we would walk there, a mere two-day walk up the line of the old Via Flaminia. This was a romantic quest but a silly one to undertake, especially in the winter. Somehow, by walking and hitching rides, we made it to the vicinity of Assisi in the late afternoon of our second day. We were determined to do the last stretch on foot and we asked directions. Late afternoon became evening, then dusk, and then nightfall. We asked directions again and somehow our destination was further way than before. Had we misheard? We realised that we were climbing and had been for some time, and that it was getting colder and colder. At about ten o'clock by the light of the moon we shared our last food, an orange and some chocolate, and agreed that we should press on.

I don't know what time it was when we saw lights ahead, and not just an isolated farm, but many lights, meaning a town, that might have beds and warm fires and food. We hadn't realised that Assisi and Spello are perched on a ridge a good thousand feet above sea level, enough to be pretty chilly in winter. Somehow, we had taken an unfrequented mountain road but, to our amazement, in the first warm hostelry we entered we found a cheery group of English students from the Beda College, some of whom we knew. After a mood-lifting wine, they offered to share their quarters with us for the night, which we gratefully accepted. Later in the night it became apparent that one of the Beda students, whose room I was sharing, had a more intimate sharing plan in mind. I declined politely but firmly.

Enjoying life at the English College was all very well, but in the summer of 1977, I would finish my philosophy degree and my grace and favour stay at the college would be over, so I had to decide what to do about continuing to study. I was still sure that I wanted to be a secular priest, but in which diocese? Who would choose me? Whom would I choose? One of the plusses of being a student at the Venerabile was that we had frequent and informal access to any of the bishops of England and Wales who came to stay, and many of them did. In 1977, they were especially thick on the ground, as all fourteen of them came to make their five-yearly visit to the Pope, the so-called *ad limina* visit. Chatting in The Snug over after-dinner coffee or pre-dinner drinks, the conversation would go something like this:

Bishop - *'And which diocese are you with Kevin?'*

Kevin - *'I'm not with a diocese My Lord'* [or 'bishop', or 'John', depending on the height of ceremony he liked to stand on]

Bishop - 'Ah, how come?'

Kevin - [Brief recital of Legionary story]

Bishop - 'How interesting. So what do you plan to do next year?'

Kevin - 'Well, it depends on finding a diocese My Lord'

Bishop - 'I see. Had you considered [insert name of His Lordship's diocese]? I'm sure there would be a place for a bright committed young man.'

Kevin - 'That's very kind My Lord. I'll certainly think and pray about that [or some such pious formula, indicating I wasn't ready to decide].

It soon became clear to me that I could have my pick of dioceses in England and Wales, not because I was an outstanding candidate, but because they really needed personnel. 'Vocations' were not plentiful, so a twenty-four-year-old with a religious background and a master's degree in philosophy, and who still thought it was a desirable goal to become a priest, was a good prospect. In this vein I had interesting conversations with a number of prelates. Among these was Basil Hume at Westminster, whose name I had noticed in a letter to one of my Legionary brothers that I had read the previous year, and who represented the lure of the big smoke of London with its bustling intellectual and social life. Then there was Derek Worlock from Liverpool, an equally bustling metropolis, but a bit too old-style Irish for my liking. Cyril Restiaux was the delightful bishop of Plymouth, urbane and soft spoken, with a lisp that was unmercifully aped by some of the students, on at least one occasion in his hearing. Plymouth was a beautiful, picturesque and slow-paced option, but I felt no connection to it.

Enter Bishop Alan 'Nobby' Clark, who just the previous year had been made the first bishop of the newly-minted catholic diocese of East Anglia, covering Norfolk, Suffolk and Cambridgeshire, with his see at Norwich. Not for the first time, I felt the attraction of novelty, getting in on the ground floor, with everything to build, and a need for creativity and initiative. East

Anglia was new, with no weighty traditions, not too far from London, with an intellectual powerhouse in Cambridge, and rural idylls aplenty. I am attracted by the idea of starting from scratch; it means everything one achieves somehow counts for more, rather than rearranging the furniture in some established setting. This idea fed into my choice of the Legion, a new congregation, with everything to do, that seemed to provide such a breadth of opportunity. By the end of the summer term, I had applied to join the Diocese of East Anglia and been accepted, and I would be coming back to Rome after the summer break to start studies in theology. The Year of the Dragon had finished, but the Year of the Snake was doing me proud.

AN ENGLISH SEMINARIAN

$\mathcal{B}$y the end of May 1977 most of the Venerabile students had left Rome for colder climes: Manchester, Birmingham, Plymouth, and in the case of one wag, Kevin Firth, for the architectural splendours of what he liked to call, in a stage Yorkshire accent, the *Centro storico di Leeds*. Far from shutting down, the College was about to become busier than ever, as it transformed itself into a pilgrim hotel, or maybe just a hotel. Groups of English tourists – sorry, pilgrims – came to see the sights of Rome and beyond. Hospitality staff and tour guides were needed in the College, and I needed money, so I put up my hand. In preparation for English thirsts unaccustomed to balmy summers, I channelled my ex-publican mother and helped set up a bar in The Snug, a large common room on the first floor where in term time we had coffee after lunch or pre-dinner drinks on special occasions. Our shopping was done at the Vatican supermarket where we bought large quantities of alcohol at duty free prices: the Vatican State didn't levy excise on alcohol. Our retail pricing for spirits and fortified wines was simple: we calculated the number of standard nips per bottle and aimed to recoup the wholesale costs by selling two drinks. For beer and wine, we simply tripled the retail cost.

My tour guiding activities were a little more energetic than serving behind the bar, but they went fairly well. I had volunteered with confidence for tour guiding. After all, at the age of thirteen I'd had a minor role as a guide in the Gardens of the Bishop's Palace in Wells, a place I had never visited until the previous day, and by now I had lived in Rome for four years: how hard could it be? With a dozen *things to see* and two *interesting facts* about each, that made just twenty-four interesting facts I needed to memorise, hardly a problem. The work went well as long as I confined myself to Rome, but it was less successful when I accompanied expeditions to Umbria – thank goodness we never made it to Tuscany! I had a general acquaintance with towns like Siena and Orvieto and even Assisi but no real knowledge of their history or art that would be worth listening to. My first sortie was to Orvieto, a city that is thrown up suddenly from the Umbrian plain as the traveller rounds a bend in the A1 motorway, and drapes itself serenely over the top of an outcrop of volcanic rock like a readymade fortress. We arrived in the late afternoon as the sun was catching the western face of the escarpment and I settled my flock into the hotel, checking bags, collecting passports, and generally fussing in a way I thought a tour guide should. After an early dinner I excused myself and went to my room to cram the guidebook with special attention to the Cathedral of the Assumption and its aston-ishing frescoes by Luca Signorelli *'begun by Fra Angelico in 1447'.*

The following morning, we trooped into the hallowed space, *'My group this way!',* and I gathered my pilgrims around me in the chancel. My guidebook at the ready, I began to point out the various scenes and saints. *'So up here on our right we have St Gabriel and the Virgin...'* Except that up there it was clearly not St Gabriel and the Virgin. Hoping for better luck, I turned to the other side. *'And up here on the left you can see St Michael guarding the gates ...'* – except that St Michael was nowhere to be seen. I floundered like this for what seemed an eternity until a kind pilgrim, looking over my shoulder, pointed out that I had the illustration upside down. This embarrassment was soon overtaken by the approach of some pretty angry local gentlemen, the *ciceroni*, or official guides who worked the Cathedral. They told me in what I can only call a straightforward manner that I was to get the hell out of there as I clearly didn't have a permit to act as a guide. I blustered around a bit, protesting that we were a private party, but was secretly grateful that my idiotic attempts to fake it were being taken out of my hands. My tour group were kind to me and were indignant on my behalf, and I formed at least one friendship that lasted into my secular life and was to help my transition into the ordinary world.

The pilgrims got on well with each other until one evening we decided that we would celebrate mass as a group with the English priest who was travelling with us. I assumed this would be a reasonably simple and maybe quite a joyful task, given they were a group of like-minded pilgrims: I couldn't have been more mistaken. The division arose over nothing more complicated than which hymns we should sing in the service and the group quickly dissolved into at least two openly bickering factions who managed to be quite nasty to each other. It sometimes seems that the more trivial and irrelevant something appears to an outsider, the more staunchly it is defended and fought over by its adherents. I caught a glimpse of how people ended up killing each other over the date of Easter or how to make the sign of the cross. Thankfully, I can report that nobody was murdered on that particular trip.

When my tour guiding duties were finished, the next stop in my summer itinerary was the sleepy town of Stowmarket in Suffolk, 'St'market' to the locals, in my new diocese of East Anglia. If Orvieto scores a ten for picturesque cityscapes, Stowmarket is probably a two, and this is thanks to the parish church in the *Decorated* style, which dates from the fourteenth century. But the warmth of my welcome entirely made up for the lack of medieval and renaissance architecture, and even for the Umbrian sunshine.

My host was the parish priest, a genial man called Chris White, who made up a simple bed for me in the spare room. It was a makeshift army cot affair, but he left a posy of wildflowers in a vase on a small table beside it together with a selection of books. I came to learn that this typified Chris. He lived a simple life of making do, and he was kind, and funny, and thought that small gestures could add beauty to life. As far as I knew, I had no duties apart from hanging out with Chris for a few weeks to get to know the area and find out what it was like to live in a parish. Most of the time was spent having cups of tea with Chris and his parishioners as he drove around visiting his small flock in his huge parish – all five hundred square miles of it. In fact, to be more accurate, most of the time was spent in his beaten-up car.

Catholic charismatic renewal had reached Suffolk and the parish had a small prayer group that met weekly. I fitted in well and found myself forming the close bonds that come from being together in a small group. One of its regular members was Delia Smith, a woman I had never heard off but liked instantly. For eight years I had no exposure to English television, or to any television for that matter, and I had no idea that Delia was already a star, and about to be an even bigger star. Early on in our friendship she gave me a copy of *How to Cheat at Cooking*, which I still have. I liked the fact that someone who clearly didn't need to cheat might understand that others sometimes did, and could help them to cheat well. I think more therapists should factor this into their work.

With Chris's permission, I invited Delia and her husband Michael to dinner at the presbytery. I was serving grilled steak and my 'cheat' for the evening was a delicious mushroom sauce made with a tin of cream of mushroom soup. There was a glut of plums at the time, and someone told me that making plum jam was easy, *'just use the same weight of fruit and sugar'*. For dessert I decided on cinnamon rice pudding with a dollop of home-made plum jam, and I looked forward to surprising Delia with my culinary skill. Unfortunately, my plum jam informant didn't say anything about using water as well as fruit and sugar, so my concoction, when I managed to prise it out of the pan, had to be cut in slices with a sharp knife. Nowadays I would know to call it *artisan plum paste* and pretend that was how I intended it.

I felt at home in Stowmarket. I had never lived in a country town before and I liked the slow pace of life, the openness of the people, the way they greeted each other in the street. As a kid I had swung between feeling 'Irish' and feeling 'English'; now I thought my 'English' time had come. Above all I had a great mentor in Chris, who was just the kind of priest I thought I wanted to be, simple, straightforward, never standing on ceremony, and closely in touch with his people whom he knew well and for whom he cared deeply. Maybe I had arrived, maybe this could be home, and maybe it could be a place to bring my mother back from her exile: I would sound her out about it when I got to Dublin.

What a long way I had come in a year! Since walking out the side door of via Aurelia on May 16th 1976, I had helped manage an ice cream franchise, been invited to spend a glorious year in The English College with new companions, taught English (strikes permitting) at the University of Rome, finished my postgraduate studies in philosophy, worked as a tour guide (local ciceroni permitting), and now here I was cooking dinner for Delia Smith and her husband. My go-to lines from the Mikado came back to my head: I had been well and truly *'taken from a county jail, by a set of curious chances'.*

With my immediate future securely planned, going back to Dublin was a pleasure this time round. I had worked through my shit and could answer any and all questions, and my mother would not be embarrassed; I was safe from disappointing her and she was safe from the gossip and the sly remarks that she dreaded.

On my way to Dublin, I spent a few days with my college friend James in Southport, north of Liverpool. James was a snob and we parted company later, after I annoyed him by telling someone he lived in Birkenhead rather than Southport, not at all in keeping with James's dignity, but it is to James that I owe my introduction to Mozart opera. He had an LP of the Welsh tenor Stuart Burrows singing Mozart arias and I spent hours listening over and over again to *Dalla su pace*, and *Il mio Tesoro* from *Don Giovanni*. Burrows is seldom mentioned with the latter-day greats like Bjorling or Pavarotti or Domingo but his voice is just as magnificent - it's as if his whole body is singing – and his manner is unassuming. I owe my lifelong love of Mozart arias to a few days in Southport in August 1977.

Apart from a whistle-stop visit of a day or two the previous year, where I saw only my mum and sisters, I hadn't been home since 1969, and I was besieged with friends of the family who wanted to find out what on earth was happening to me, and who popped round at all hours for cups of tea. With my school friends, the ones who hadn't emigrated, I drank lots of Guinness – draught, never bottled – not because I especially liked it but because it seemed like an Irish home-coming sort of thing to do. My school friend Pat Shortall had moved in two doors down from my mother's house and was always happy to reminisce over a beer. In the process I acquired a taste for Guinness, and it has stayed with me ever since, along with my love of Mozart arias. I was sixteen when I left home and so I hadn't had an eighteenth birthday party or, more importantly in those days, a twenty-first birthday party, a great celebration, and traditionally the day that the young adult was given the key of the house. My mother decided that she would like to give me a twenty-fifth birthday party instead, and although I knew she couldn't easily afford it, I went along with it because I knew that it would give her pleasure. She hired a hotel venue down near the seafront in Dún Laoghaire, off Queen's Road, and invited all and sundry; best of all, she bought a grand new dress for the occasion. One of the family stories my mother told was how her oldest brother, Uncle Charles, designed and made evening clothes for her. Perhaps I was channelling Charles that evening because the only thing I remember about the whole party is her dress. It was a full-length, formal creation, an empire line gown in satin, with a bodice covered in lace appliqué. She was as pleased as punch to have an occasion to dress up, to be the hostess of a party, and to show off her son: *Yes, he's going back to Rome next month you know!* In one of those photographic moments that stay in the mind's eye, I can see her standing among her guests, a glass in her raised left hand, her face flushed, and a broad, full, smile such as I have seldom seen her show. It was the happiest I have ever seen my mother. It was important to me that I hadn't disappointed her; the spectre of our conversation at her bedside in Baggot Street Hospital had never left me.

There remained the nagging issue of whether it would be possible for Mum to move back to England. Her nostalgia for home had been a leitmotif of all my childhood and teenage years and it was clear to me that she was still unhappy in Ireland. All the wartime purpose of keeping the children safe, *'For the duration, as I thought'*, had long since evaporated. Her husband had died, the children had grown up and fled to England or Scotland or Australia. Mum felt trapped and stranded in a country that was not her own and where she didn't want to die. She had given away a life of prosperity and relative comfort, a place in her community, a church, a tribe, for a pebble-dashed council house in Sallynoggin, with few friends and still with the wrong accent. Trapped with her was my sister Bid, the only child who had not flown the coop, who would in fact never fly the coop. My youngest sister Nora was still there too, living with Bid and Mum and caring for them, and I thought there might be a chance for her to break free if I helped and if Mum were more comfortably settled. I felt sad, and a bit guilty, that Bid and Nora had borne this task of looking after Mum, and I thought that I should do something to help.

Talking to Mum it was clear that what she wanted was to move back to England, but how to make it happen was not at all clear. She had no money, she lived from pension to pension. I had no money and would be entirely dependent on a diocesan allowance of some kind for the foreseeable future and after that, a meagre stipend to cover my living expenses: no hopes there. The same went for the other siblings: none had a high-paying job, and all had families to provide for. Getting a loan was out of the question – how would we repay it? That left the English connection, my mother's two brothers Richard and John. Might they help? To approach them we needed a bit more of a plan so I took on the task of developing a scheme that might attract their kindness. They were both fervent Anglo-Catholics, so writing to them from Rome on the letterhead of The Venerable English College might strike the right note.

The summer of 1977 saw a major Charismatic Renewal Conference in Dublin at the Royal Dublin Society Showgrounds in Ballsbridge. The thousands who attended were in festive mood; we prayed, we sang, we clapped, we cheered, we healed, we ate together, and we had a rollicking good time. This was such a different religion than the one we had grown up with in the Ireland of the fifties and sixties that was all about Purgatory and Hell, and knowing which sins were *venial* and which were *mortal*. Here was joy, and fun, and hope, and openness to the unusual, and some of my Irish friends were getting involved in a new way of being Christian. One of these, Ciaran, had been all through school with me at Christian Brothers Monkstown Park. I have a fetching picture of him as one of Major General Stanley's daughters in the *Pirates of Penzance*, and another of him as my long-suffering mother in our prize-winning Irish play, *An Gadaí*. He was starting out on what was to become a stellar career in finance. Ciaran often had a hard time at school because his dad was one of our teachers, a very good teacher, but that didn't matter to the smart alecks. In the nasty, unfeeling way that some kids do, they taunted him unmercifully. Ciaran and I met up a number of times and he gave me a beautiful gift: a Waterford crystal tumbler engraved with the initials I D, standing for *Iesus Dominus*, Latin for *Jesus the Lord*. It was to be a chalice for me to eventually celebrate mass. It didn't ever get used as a chalice, or perhaps it did by one of my friends in Rome, I'm not sure, but I have it still and I treasure it.

On my way back to Rome I went via London and got to spend some days with another school friend of a different ilk, Dara Robinson. Dara needs a memoir all of his own: I hope he writes one. In 1977 he had dropped out of university, and he was working as a bus conductor for London Transport while doing his law studies at night. He met me at Victoria Station, and we set out to get something to eat and drink. Dara is a charming, articulate, and piercingly clever man: he is also very funny. As we walked down Ebury Bridge Road he was already telling jokes. 'What do you get if you mix an Irishman's brain and a bag of sugar', he asked. 'No idea', I said. 'Sweet fuck all', he replied. I put my two bags down on the pavement, threw back my head and howled with laughter. It was a good note on which to leave London and set off for another autumn in Rome.

THEOLOGY: DECLINE AND FALL

*I*f ever I had to be exiled and were compelled to live for the rest of my life in a city where I had already lived, my instant choice would be Rome. I have a very soft spot for Rome. Rome knows grandeur and decay and accommodates them side by side. I think of it as a humble city. It shrugs off its fall from grace as if to say: *'Beh! It was great fun, but it was just one of those things. Have you tried this trippa alla romana?*[1] *Deliziosa!'* I don't feel inadequate or judged In Rome as I might in Milan or Paris because my jacket is not cut à la mode, or my culinary tastes are not sufficiently refined. There is no great art museum in Rome, like the Prado or the Uffizi – Rome *is* a great art museum that wears its heritage as its everyday wardrobe, nothing is kept for Sunday best. You cannot surprise Rome or shock it. If Rome wore a tee-shirt, it could well say; 'Been there, done that'. Rome is conscious of its past, as the proud and ubiquitous letters *SPQR* (*Senatus Populusque Romanus*) attest. Out-of-towners like to interpret the letters as meaning *'Sono pazzi questi Romani'* (These Romans are mad!), but as the august letters appear most prominently on the foul-smelling garbage trucks that collect the detritus of the city, the self-depre-cating locals prefer *'Sono porchi questi Romani'* (These Roman are pigs!). So here I was back in Rome in another autumn with chil-dren still playing in fountains, but this time I was a pukka sahib, a real seminarian with a real diocese and a real bishop to pay my fees, make me an allowance, and buy my ticket back to England at the end of the year.

When I returned to the College in October 1977, I wrote to my mum that it was 'warm sunny weather' and that I was looking forward to a change of subject and to studying theology. I was no longer an orphan: I belonged, and I was still enthused about pursuing my path of becoming a priest: nothing else came close. The Legionary religious life had gone, and good riddance, but my zeal was undiminished. My letters were now less frequent and less gushy, but I was still writing to my mother to say, 'Thanks again for all your prayers – they really worked'.

Rooms in college were not allocated but chosen on a first come first served basis. In the previous year, arriving late, I had a long thin room on the second floor overlooking via di Monserrato, a room with curious angles as if two parts of the building met there and didn't quite match. It faced southwest and was often shaded by the buildings across the narrow street. I remember it being dark and full of nocturnal creaks from its ancient woodwork. The creaks were loudest in the night as the timber cooled down, and they were especially loud the night that I read, in one sitting, *The Exorcist*. I finished at about three o'clock in the morning and I don't think I have ever been more frightened in my life. For this new academic year, I was able to move instead to a quiet room on the third floor at the back of the building, above the garden, filled in my memory with a buttery yellow light and well away from Roman traffic noise. Gone were the exhaust fumes of the incessant high-pitched *motorini* dodging and revving through the streets, and the straining engines of the little three wheeled Piaggio delivery vans. The vans look like scooters with a freight tray on the back and they're called *Api* or bees, because they're the little worker bees that deliver everything from a wardrobe to a sack of *fagiolini* into the narrow, cobbled backstreets where no other vehicles will fit.

There was a spirit of generosity about the College and people gave each other odds and ends of furniture or paintings that didn't fit into their rooms or that they no longer wanted. I acquired easy chairs, a desk, some wall hangings, some cushions. Junk shops abounded and a trip to the markets in Trastevere would normally yield some cheap treasure, a bookcase that had seen better days, or a terrible print that was worth buying for the frame. If things needed fixing, one of our number, Dave Plummer, was a self-proclaimed expert in 'bodging', and could nail, screw, or glue anything to anything. For the first time in my life, I had a cosy room of my own that I could trick out to my taste. I went to the Vatican supermarket and stocked up on Martini, Campari, and Punt e Mes for when people came to my room for 'drinks before'. Many of us in the student body needed little incentive to have a drink, and inviting companions to 'drinks before' (before lunch or dinner) was a common custom, a sort of informal marker of one's status and sociability in the College. There's no doubt that a number of us drank a great deal too much and carried that habit into later life whether as priests or not.

Apart from getting into my theology studies, the most pressing task was to sort out a house in England for Mum to live in. I had come back acutely aware of how unhappy she was in Dublin and how trapped Bid and Nora felt there with her. My sister Eileen and brother Derry already lived in England, in Didcot and Oxford respectively, and my sister Margaret was in Scotland. I suppose I hoped that once Mum was a car trip away, rather than a flight or a mail-boat trip, that relations with them could become closer and they could help out a bit in what sooner or later would be her declining years. What I realised later was that if you want someone in your life you have to let them in, and my mother turned out to be choosy about who was to look after her. In any event I was headed for East Anglia, and I knew and liked the little town of Stowmarket. In fact, I already had some friends there, Chris, Delia, and Michael, and various other parishioners who I knew would make Mum and Bid welcome. I just needed some financial backing.

I wrote to Mum's two brothers, my uncles Richard and John. They were both retired and, while they weren't rich, they were certainly comfortably off. Richard had ended his career as the Chief Children's Officer for the County of Berkshire and his wife Betty, who trained as a social worker at the London School of Economics, was a Children's Stipendiary Magistrate when she and Richard met. Betty had an income from her family's business and her father, a prosperous grain merchant, had been Mayor of Shrewsbury. Uncle John had a long career as an accountant, much of it with General Electric, including in the development of credit card technology. Some early advertisements for the new credit cards show a mocked-up card with the name *John England* as the cardholder, and family tradition has it that this was in fact John. Neither brother had any children nor any onerous financial obligations: could they pitch in? Could they help me move their sister back home? When my father died, they had offered to take care of some of us eight children, could they help now? I would find a place, I could help Mum pay rent, all I needed was to know that they would back me up if I needed it. A few weeks later their joint reply reached me at the English College. They had talked about my proposal and my appeal for help, and they commended me for my kindness in wanting to help, but '*Miss Otis regrets...*' - they were unable to assist. I was disappointed by their response and a bit angry with them, but I wasn't about to give up.

One of the friends I had made in Rome was Andrew Williams,

who belonged to a charismatic prayer group that I attended at the Greg. In addition to charismatic spirituality, Andrew was one of a number of young catholic seminarians very taken with the Russian Orthodox liturgy, so much so that they had each arranged for a variety of cassocks and hats to be tailored for themselves in brilliant colours, blues, reds and maroons, to wear when they were attending services in the orthodox communities in Rome. One of them had acquired a large silver samovar with which he made scented teas that he sweetened with jam. There was more than a touch of Wildean flamboyance about the group and they were good fun to be with. I was chatting to Andrew one day in my room and I told him about my plan for my mum, which had just been stymied by my uncles' refusal to help. I jokingly said something like, 'You don't know anyone with a spare five thousand pounds they could lend me?' To my astonishment Andrew said immediately: 'I could do that'.

Andrew said simply that his family were rich and that his dad, a baronet and Oxfordshire landowner, had vested part of the family assets in Andrew, who could use his share as he wished. Andrew thought it was pretty straightforward: he would simply give me the money. When he enquired into the mechanics of doing this, he found that the reality was not quite so straightforward. The funds were held in trust and the trustees were obliged to use them in such a way as to benefit the beneficiary, who was Andrew. Andrew saw this as no obstacle and instead of simply giving me the money, he arranged for his father's agent to fund the purchase of a house in Stowmarket, a place where I would have every chance of visiting Mum and Bid fairly regularly. The house was to be owned by Andrew's trust, which would grant a 'licence to occupy' to my mum. Eventually the asset would appreciate, thereby benefiting the trust, but that was in the future and not to be considered now. It was an act of pure generosity on Andrew's part; the following summer he bought a house for my mother to live in.

The prayer group where I had met Andrew was one for English

speakers that convened in the psychology department building on Piazza della Pilotta on a Sunday afternoon. During my first year at the College, I had encountered the Catholic Charismatic Renewal movement and it blew my mind. These prayer meetings were unlike anything I had experienced before: there was minimal hierarchical leadership and participants spoke spontaneously, sharing a prayer or a bible verse or talking about their insights or their struggles as they wished to do. A hymn was sung because someone, anyone, started it and others joined in. Often, we sang with no words at all, vocalising and harmonising in cadences that rose and fell until they were somehow spent. If someone wanted to speak, they simply got to their feet and told the group they wished to share. People asked for prayers, for healing, for the laying on of hands, for help with the resolution of distress. The rationale of the movement argues that as the gifts of the Holy Spirit like healing and prophecy and speaking in tongues were present in the early church, why shouldn't they be present today? In the modern Catholic church, the movement dates from 1967 at Duquesne University in Pittsburgh and it later spread to Notre Dame and other universities in the Midwest. The group in the Greg attracted a mixture of men and women, religious and lay, old and young. Having said the group wasn't hierarchical, there was a leadership group who tended to sit in the front circle and who opened the meeting and closed it. Andrew was in this group as was a charming and colourful Englishman who styled himself, entirely spuriously, the Baron de Breffny, and had a business in Rome tracing genealogical lineages. The Baron was by this time living in Ireland and restoring what was to become his stately home, Castletown Cox in County Kilkenny. The family had just moved in, and the hired servants and maids were uncertain as to the provenance of this handsome man and his stunningly beautiful wife. Preparing for their first formal dinner, the maid who was to serve in the dining room asked: *'Are ye' gentry or do ye' stack?'* The answer was that they were most definitely gentry.

My favourite member of the inner circle was an extraordinary Englishwoman called Sister Margaret, a member of the Sisters of Sion, an organisation unique in the Catholic Church in that it exists as an order of nuns solely to foster friendship and understanding between Jewish and Catholic people. Another two Englishwomen sat in the circle too, Ginny and Gina, as well as an Italian woman, Maria, who worked for the UN Food and Agriculture Organisation in Rome. It was a heady time as we explored new ways of seeing faith, spirituality, God, religion, scripture, and moral behaviour. The time held a sense of urgency and a sense of importance, as if we were shaping, as if we *could* shape, what a renewed church would look like. I suspect I was a more serious proposition than I had been as a freewheeling layman in the previous year, but I still managed to have fun and seek the kingdom of heaven as well.

I made visits to the beloved Villa as often as I could make them. The very decay of the place gave it a quality of wildness, of wilderness almost, that brought the soul up short and disconnected me from the concerns of the world. On walks in the surrounding hills with my friend Vincent Stokes from the Beda College, I learned to look at nature differently. Vincent had been at Art School and showed me how to look at a nondescript patch of ground at my feet until it became a teeming mass of insect life and a universe of colours, shapes and textures. Behind us, the heavy, dark waters of Lago Albano concealed who knew what in their stillness, and seemed unruffled even in high winds, as if they clung to their volcanic depths with too much power to be moved.

In the college I put myself forward for the job of Bishops' Agent, a task that attracted a small stipend, always welcome. Bishops, priests, and laity often approach the Vatican for various purposes: a couple might seek a Papal Blessing for their twenty-fifth wedding anniversary, or they might seek an annulment of their marriage that would allow them to marry again. A bishop might seek advice from the Curia about a regulation to be implemented, or a priest to be disciplined. For all of these things it was helpful to have a man on the spot – *Our man in Rome* – and in 1977-78 that was me. The bread-and-butter work consisted of the requests for Papal Blessings of one sort or another, which were available in a range of finishes, large, medium, small, fancy, plain, framed, unframed, in Latin, in English, at a range of prices, which weren't called *'Prices'* but rather *'Offerings for the good works of the Holy See'*. A practical role for the Bishops' Agent was to check that English names were spelled correctly by the Italian printers. You didn't want to spend twenty quid plus postage on a beautifully illuminated parchment only to have your blessing conferred on *Our Beloved John and Marjorie Smeth.*

Without a doubt, the main joy of my new life was connecting with others and making friendships. After seven years of not touching another human being for fear of *amistades particulares*, those pesky 'special friendships', I revelled in being able to let myself like someone and be spontaneous, but I had a lot of catching up to do. For seven years I had lived in closed communities where, paradoxically, I was isolated entirely from my fellows. Of course, we saw each other every day, we knew each other's names, we played soccer or basketball together, we did chores and tasks together, we hiked together, we prayed together. But we did all of this without sharing anything other than the game or the chore or the hike. We were expressly forbidden to communicate any of our concerns to each other. In group theory, groups can be described as working autonomously or allonomously. In the autonomous group all the members relate to each other equally in pursuing the purpose of the group. A diagram of the autonomous connections looks like a busy star with as many points as there are members. In an allonomous group everything goes through the leader and the diagram looks like an open fan with all the spokes leading into one focus – the leader. The Legionaries were an entirely allonomous group. At the top, Maciel exercised unques-tioned power and judgement: you were in or out – no discussion or disagreement. Further down the food chain his minions enforced the same ideology – you accept everything, or you go. Besides my major paper on Jacques Maritain for the licence in philosophy, I had also written a minor paper on Machiavelli and the autocratic methodology of *The Prince*. I'm quite sure Maciel had never read *The Prince*, but he embodied perfectly the character who is a law unto himself.

All of this meant that I had no idea how to connect meaningfully with another person; I was completely out of practice. Early on I struck up a friendship with a lad called Billy from the Irish College. He was funny and we laughed a lot together. On one occasion we convinced Tim, a friend from the English College, that we could speak Irish fluently and we demonstrated this by reciting the Our Father, a prayer that every Irish schoolchild has to learn. We broke up the phrases and said them to each other as if we were having a conversation, and when we came to end of the prayer we just started again, and Tim was none the wiser. I couldn't keep up the pretence and I revealed our trick to Tim the next day.

At some point Billy sat me down and asked me if everything was okay between us.

'Fine!' I said. 'Why wouldn't it be?'

'Well', said Billy, 'It's just that I seem to be doing all the running'.

'To be honest, I don't know what you mean by that'.

'I mean that I'm always the one suggesting things, I have to arrange everything we do. You never invite me, it's always me inviting you'.

Reflecting on our friendship I saw that he was right, and this was nothing short of a revelation to me. It seems bizarre, but I had lost any sense of the reciprocity that nourishes relationships. Billy's honesty had done me a favour: I began to be more attentive to my friends in college and outside. Luckily, I was surrounded by people who understood this and helped me to open up and to connect, and the person who helped me most was Martin Higgins, a tousle-haired, bespectacled, ever-smiling student from Manchester. Even before I had spoken to Milan and begun to make my plan to leave the Legion, Martin was one of the seminarians I had noticed at the Greg, simply because he always looked so happy. I spoke to Milan rather than to Martin because Milan was more solitary, and I could run into him alone. Martin became one of the important men in my life, men I have met along the way who have taught me and shown me something about being a man. Martin was kind, and compassionate, and funny, with an infectious laugh. Some of our companions could be acerbic and critical in a nasty-witty way about their fellow students. Martin was never this: he simply didn't judge others. We became fast friends, and we were both part of a College prayer group that met in the Lady Chapel, a small oratory at the end of the ground floor corridor. Looking back, this is the group where I learned most about intimacy and reciprocity.

There were perhaps six to ten people who attended, and the group was mostly a quiet affair, with much less of the ecstatic singing of the large Sunday group in the Greg. We sat silently together unless someone wanted to share an experience, a prayer, a challenge they were facing, or to offer some encouraging feedback to another member. The directness, the simplicity, and the honesty of these interactions was something I had never experienced, in fact I think it's something that many people never experience. The process has many of the characteristics of a process therapy group where the focus is on the interactions between the members as the mechanism that brings about helpful change. Sharing in this way involves taking a risk, that others will judge you, that you'll sound silly, that no one will be interested, but the relationships that form in these kinds of groups are deep and lasting and often generate sincere love between individuals. That's what I felt about the group of people who prayed with me: that they loved me. When I thought back on my seven years as a religious, I had no sense of being loved for me, or indeed of loving others. Human love was deemed inconsequential, it was all about the love of God. To love another person was portrayed as a weakness, a 'special friendship' that couldn't co-exist with the love of God. No wonder that this translated into a utilitarian, manipulative view of people. If you were useful to the cause, welcome! If not, you were of no account.

Through one of the prayer groups Martin and I became friends with a young Italian priest, Father Adriano, from Ancona, on the Adriatic Coast. A few of us, Martin, Margaret, Maria, Ginny, and Gina, visited Adriano in Ancona in his ancient crumbling monastery in which two or three rooms only were usable. We made food together and laughed a lot as we ate, we read, went for walks, rested, and sang; and we prayed. One evening as we did the washing up together, we sang improvised madrigals. Someone would lead with a phrase like 'These forks go in the middle drawer' and others joined in at will, threading the trivial phrases into beautifully woven harmonic textures, some efforts more successful than others. Over a distance of forty-four years and ten thousand miles I can hear us singing in the kitchen and I smile with pleasure.

As we sat in our small circle to pray, I was wrestling with what to do about the future. Just as life in the Legion had eventually seemed to me barren, hypocritical and unchristian, the priestly caste of the Catholic Church was looking increasingly out of touch with the struggles of ordinary people trying to live a Christian life in an ordinary world, alone, in families, in couples, at work, at play. It seemed to me that many of my companions, accustomed to breathing the rarefied air of the spiritual heights they inhabited, had no idea what it was like for the hoi polloi down in the vale of tears.

Through Sister Margaret I had become friends with an English Dominican friar living in Rome, a man in his eighties, full of life and wisdom, who radiated warmth and kindness in his person. On his eighty-fifth birthday we celebrated with afternoon tea in English style. During tea the conversation came around to what we saw as the future for our faith. I'm not sure what point was being discussed, when another Dominican friar at the table, a young go-getter who had just published a book on spirituality, turned to me and said: 'Well, it all depends on whether or not you believe in the church as an institution'. In that moment I realised that I didn't. The *church as an institution* seemed to me like a huge supermarket chain with branches all over the world staffed by more or less efficient, and more or less committed managers. They were selling something I was no longer interested in buying: dogma, and arcane ritual, with gold and silver ware, and churches that looked like palaces, and robes and forms of address that separated the priests from their people, and focussed everything on sin and eternal life rather than loving kindness here below. It was a moment of clarity and of choice.

Despite this, I wasn't confident that I could make a decision about the future from where I was sitting. Having joined the Legion at the age of sixteen, a far less sophisticated person than I thought I was, I really wasn't clear about who I was or what I wanted. I had never had a relationship, I had never fallen in love or even been infatuated, I had never known tragedy, I had done little paid work, and I hadn't tested out my ideas in any other forum than the Literary and Debating Society of Monkstown Park College or a tutorial group at the Venerabile. I was frighteningly unprepared for the future.

As we sat quietly in our prayer circle in Ancona, someone said, 'I have some words that I think are for you Kevin: be yourself'. I began to cry silently, touched to my core by the simplicity, the directness, and the accuracy of the words. I realised that I was frightened to be me, uncertain of who that was and whether I would like what I found if I let this self emerge. Maria was sitting beside me on my right. She reached out and gently caressed my cheek with the back of her left hand: I find it impossible to describe the intensity of feeling that came to me with her gesture. All of the love of the world was around me, there were people here who loved me. They would love me whatever happened. I would be okay.

Emboldened by the sense that people supported and loved me, I began to make a plan that would enable me to become a priest but to do so while living in a world of ordinary people. What if I were to finish the bachelor's degree in theology at the Greg and then move to complete my studies in London, living in digs like an ordinary student? I could study theology at Heythrop College, a college of the University of London that was run by the Jesuits. It was a bold idea and I didn't know anyone else who had done it, but it was worth putting to my bishop, Alan Clark, so I wrote and told him, somewhat cryptically, that I had a proposal to make about my studies that would take far too long to explain in a letter and could I meet up and discuss it all with him in England at the end of term? Alan wasn't impressed, and he wrote and told me so. His response was simple: *If you have a proposal for me, write it down so that I can see you've thought it through.*

At the end of spring term 1978, a few days before I left Rome, our small College prayer group met for the last time in the term. We sat in silence, and I thought about how I would miss this group with whom I felt such an intimate bond. I told them I would miss them and asked them to remember me and pray for me. One by one my friends began to speak, telling me in turn simply how much they loved me, that they wished me well and that they would miss me and not forget me. In response I could say nothing; tears trickled down my cheeks. I sensed a powerful feeling of being loved that took my breath away, a feeling that came as a choking pain in my chest, almost overwhelming me. I felt I was being given the most precious of gifts. It even made me wonder whether I was making a terrible mistake by leaving. If I was in a place where I was so loved, why on earth would I think of leaving? I had a moment of panic that I was missing a boat because I had decided to stay on the quay, watching while the gangplank was drawn up, not realising that the boat contained most of the people I loved and who loved me. If I had felt like this before, it might have weakened my resolve. I am not prone to nostalgia: I knew what I had to do.

GOODBYE TO ALL THAT

*I*n response to my cryptic letter telling the Bishop I wanted to talk to him 'at length', Alan did me a great favour: he asked me to explain in writing exactly what I was thinking about. I have his letter, and mine in reply, and there seems no better way of telling the story of how the year ended than by placing them here as they were written. If the soul-searching that follows is too intense, the last paragraph of the chapter will serve to continue the narrative.

Rt. Rev. Alan C. Clark D.D.
20th of May 1978

MY DEAR KEVIN

You're not in the right league if you cannot put down on paper matters of serious import in your judgement which require you to talk 'at length'. Only yesterday I received a letter from Canon [ ]... to express certain hesitancies about the direction of the ecumenical movement at this present time and of his involvement in it. This was accompanied by a 6-page typed well-reasoned backup paper.

So accept the self-discipline, please, of putting your thoughts on paper. You ask too much without a wee thought for the engagements of yours truly. I'm completely committed to meeting my students, the future priests of the diocese: in fact I met some last night. But I do have a scheduled programme, O noble Roman! ...

Do I detect that 'my' Kevin is becoming restless with ideas? That he is joining the school of minor prophets? Please tread the path of the spirit on tip-toe. You have joined a diocese where we all have to accept the cross of the limitations of people (and of ourselves) as we strive to give shape and form to the future. ... The diocese keenly awaits your own contribution - you must be a man of mission and maintenance. It's a double 'incarico'.

Have I over-interpreted you or have I discerned something of your spirit? If you want to meet me in London... I'm sure I could arrange a time and place. If here, Tuesday or Wednesday the 27th / 28th. Most welcome

> *Blessings on the brethren,*
> *Dev.mo et aff.mo,*
> *Alan*

In response, at the end of May and the beginning of June, I sat down to write out my thoughts, seven closely-typed pages of them, a sort of manifesto; it was the end of the Roman Spring in more ways than one. Rome the city, I still loved, but Rome the English College lifestyle, and Rome the institutional church, I did not. The style of my letter is formal, even a little pompous, with sections and sub-sections, echoes of my Thomist philosophy perhaps, but I am relieved to find that the voice is both coherent and cogent, and that I can read without cringing, or at least not too much. The Literary and Debating Society had trained me reasonably well.

BISHOP ALAN CLARK
Poringland

DEAR FATHER

Point taken. Thanks very much for your letter – I'm in fact glad you wrote even though I said not to. In retrospect I should apologise if my note was abrupt; the phrase *"...I shall come straight to Poringland..."* certainly sounds peremptory, it wasn't supposed to. Your request is entirely justified, so here goes.

MY PERSONAL SITUATION

In this first part I want to set before [you] as nearly as I can where I'm at. As with any personal situation there is an amount of emotion and feeling, in the sense of intuition, involved. There is also, I would like to believe, an amount of clear thinking. I will begin with a short lead-up and then describe how I think now:

Antecedents

One of the key ideas in my mind had already come to me as a strong conviction when I left the Legion in 1976 – that is, that it is totally unreal for students for the priesthood (as indeed for anything else) to spend all their time in institutions. That they should at least for a significant period of their training live out a simply Christian commitment not being 'of the world' but certainly being fairly and squarely 'in the world'. I thought of this both in general and as a necessity for me. When I returned to Rome in October '76, as you know, I had every intention of implementing this and only a shortage of money (combined with Cormac's great kindness and the good Lord's providence), led me to the Venerabile. I have already told you how the experience of human friendship and the renewing grace of God helped to remake my life.

When I came to the end of that first year and decided to stay, what tipped the balance were the words of Saint Benedict recommending that no monk should go on his own (to be a hermit), until he had been prepared to do so by life in the community; this you also know. Servatis servandis, that applied to me then, I do not think it applies to me now.

When we spoke at Christmas I told you that I had found the prospect of doing a licence here in Rome hard to take. Another five years in the same place seemed excessive. You weren't dazzled by the idea then and you made that perfectly clear, saying that you felt obliged to have me do an STL[1] here - we left it at that.

About six weeks ago I had an interview with George Hay[2] about things in general and candidacy in particular. One of the things I mentioned was leaving Rome after the STB[3]. George invited me to reflect to what extent this was really a considered desire and how much of it was due to the normal taedium [sic] of seminary life. I accepted his invitation to reflect and came, (very hesitantly at first), to the conclusion that not only did I want to go after another two years, rather, I wanted to go straight away.

At Present

I must preface all these remarks by saying that they are not intended as a criticism of George's leadership of the House or of anybody else's for that matter. I live here in a system which cherishes fondly certain values and a certain style of life with which I can no longer identify. I live in a community (although this name is questionable) which in my opinion lives turned in upon itself, more preoccupied with 'doing the liturgy' well, living comfortably, and not having to work too much, than in giving one of our many, many coats to him who has none. Your point about taking people as they are, (as we are with all our limitations included), is very valid, but this must not become a euphemism for compromise: "Will you also go away...?" He let them go. He didn't say: "Oh I'm sure we can find a solution to suit everyone..." Are we interested in preaching the gospel in season and out of season or in keeping a fairly coherent system ticking over? Granted, the choice shouldn't have to face any of us, but when it does, I know which I must choose.

This way of life, which I don't for a moment believe I have oversimplified, makes people outside (and inside) our church despise us who are called Christians. if we are to suffer for doing good – hurray! But if we are to suffer mockery and scorn for betraying Jesus Christ, then we deserve it all and more. Dear Father, I can truthfully say nothing else in the whole world matters a fig to me than to give men the message of the good news of salvation in Jesus Christ. For this reason I love the church with all my heart, and it is this love - shown in the only, however poor, way I can show it by offering my life in service - that gives me, dare I say, the right to be sad and be angry when I see something that is not the message of Christ passed off as being so. A tiny example: we have just read in the liturgy the letter of Saint James. On the stone seat at the corner of Palazzo Farnese there sits day after day an old beggar - perhaps you know old Massimo. Isn't it strange that a rather large chunk of Church - the College - preparing men to be 'other Christs' will have nothing to do with this least of His brothers. Do people matter or not? Comes college feast day we all don our best clothes and entertain twenty or so well-mannered, well-spoken people (against whom I have nothing since they too are children of God) then we go into the celebration of the Eucharist and listen in pious recollection as the reader says: 'If a well-dressed man comes into your synagogue...'. How can a set-up like this possibly prepare us to share in the Christian life, let alone in the priesthood of Christ?

Against this background I feel very deeply a personal need (i) to come into close contact now with people who think differently from myself and (ii) to share the day-to-day life and problems of the people to whom I so earnestly desire to minister. The need for contact with people who think differently comes especially from a combination in my life so far of a very closed religious community where everyone had to think the same, and five years in the Greg where only the most occasional breeze from the outside penetrates. Does this really equip me to dialogue with people of vastly different value sets and outlooks? Yes, I know one must have a solid foundation but houses are not just built with foundation stones. As for sharing the day-to-day life and problems of lay people, I think the point is clear: I would feel a complete fraud if after continuing here, (or in any other seminary), for a couple of years - which I could do quite easily with a bit of teeth-gritting - I were to get up as an ordained deacon or priest and preach to people, instruct them in the way of Christian life without ever having had to live it as they do. Father, it is because of the great seriousness with which I take priestly ministry that I feel convinced I must not simply stay in the groove until I reach the centre.

This contact and this openness I consider it is impossible to achieve in the set-up in which I now live of the Venerabile and the Gregorian. This should be clear from what I've said before so I won't elaborate on it. I just add here that I am at the end of my ninth consecutive year, (since I left school), of living in religious institutions. This is more time than most priests ever spend in a seminary!

This leads me to an assertion which on the face of it can seem arrogant - it's not intended to be, nor is it any criticism on a personal level of any member of staff. It is simply that the College has nothing to offer me at this moment that I could not get as well in the life-situation I will propose later on. What does the College propose to offer anyway? Spiritual formation? To my way of seeing it, very little goes on; certainly in my personal case I must make the rather harsh statement that it doesn't do anything at all for me. Assessment of the candidate's suitability? In theory yes – here, in practice, it's questionable. The plain fact is that the staff know very little about me. Many of my companions and friends outside college know me much better, and I am by no means the only student who would say that! Control and discipline of the student's life? I think after nine years, even if only one of them was spent in commitment to the diocese, it's fair to ask the question: 'Do you trust me?' If you do then you are confident that I'm not going to mess around with your time and money, but I'm going to take the thing seriously wherever I go. If you don't trust me that much then it's also fair to ask: 'Why not?' I have the distinct impression that if I stay here I will shrivel up and die of alienation from reality.

I think it's also necessary to say that my 'position' as I'm trying to explain it is not intended as a global criticism of the system or a protest

244

against everything. I began by reflecting on what was right for me here and now. It was my conversation with the Rector and other staff members that brought out the implications of some of the things I was saying for seminary training as a whole and indeed the church in general. When I began to reflect I did so with no illusions whatsoever of pioneering new methods of priestly training or of prophetism in one form or another. If I mention them now it's because all the staff seem to hit on them immediately!

The moment has come to say that in all this my commitment to the diocese remain substantially unchanged. By 'substantially' I mean that it is still my desire, as it was when I first spoke to you, to be a priest in East Anglia. It may change accidentally as regards the means by which to reach the day, it may put that day off a year or two: painful for you, necessary for me. The staff, and particularly the Vice Rector, seemed to question and make a problem out of this continued commitment to (i) priesthood and (ii) in East Anglia, which surprised me initially since I had simply not thought in terms of leaving this commitment. In linea di principio I agree with the Vice Rector - of course it is possible for me (as it is for you, him, or any priest, seminarian or Christian), to imagine that there could come a time when he might have to make pretty radical changes in his life's direction which could involve leaving ministry, the Church or the Bishophood (there are precedents). But surely, as I pointed out to Peter, this is to deal in hypothetical questions in which it's very easy to drown in possibilities. In cambio, what I'm talking about is what I believe I need here and now to follow the path along which God calls me. So what do I need, and what am I proposing?

My initial proposal was that you allow me to go in October to London, to attend Heythrop and to live out in digs. The staff suggest a modification of that: they don't want to recommend that you send me to Heythrop as a 'Church student' but that I should go as a layman (as far as financial considerations go I will limit myself to saying that it should be viable even if difficult). They also think in the circs. that a year out altogether might not be unwise. Formerly I had dismissed this idea out of hand on the principle of 'melius hodie quam cras', but I do accept now that it has a lot in its favour. It would allow a certain period of sorting-out time - which considering the amount going on right now in my head and my heart, might not be a bad idea.

THE STAFF

This second half of my letter was to be a summary of what the staff thought individually and collectively but since George told me this morning that he would like to write to you I'll limit myself to the briefest of comments. I spoke to each member of staff individually and found a great deal of understanding and support. So much in fact that I was a little surprised to find they hesitated to recommend that you send me to Heythrop, although as I said above I can see the advantages of a year out. The conversations I had with George have been among the most enriching I've ever had - they helped clarify a lot of ideas. John Short was particularly positive, as was also Phillip. Keith was a little reticent at first. Peter I found rather daunting and not terribly positive but it was at least useful to see another approach to the matter; I'm afraid we're worlds apart. For the rest I'll let George (who incidentally will have read this letter) tell you more about their opinions and conclusions.

Some final personal reflections stimulated by your letter. 'Restless with ideas?' Yes, thank God, I am; but tell me if any of them are not inspired in the Gospel and the love of the church? 'Joining the school of minor prophets?' As I pointed out, the prophetism in my desire and opinions was picked out only by others - it was not intended by me. But what if it is true upon reflection that 'zelus domus tuae comedit me?' Our Blessed Lord and Saviour didn't exactly end up in favour with the Establishment. If a priest of the new covenant cannot be a prophet, and a major one, then who can? If 'treading the path of the Spirit on tiptoe' means avoiding everyone's toes and not making any noise then it seems a pretty poor show. 'Fides ex auditu': if they can't even hear our footsteps they'll never realise we're here!

Dear father I'm sure my attempt at soul-seeking on paper wasn't as good as Canon [ ]'s paper on ecumenism but for the moment it's the best I can do. Could we pray for one another. Particularly ask the Lord to give me a great gift of humility and an ever listening heart.

Affectionately

PS. I too will be in London on the 22nd and 23rd so just name the time and place. Perhaps we could talk once then and if necessary meet again on the 27th or 28th in Poringland. If you have no objections, I would like to spend the intervening days in Stowmarket seeing about a house for my mother. Would you mind if I stayed with Chris?

A FEW DAYS after my letter, George Hay, who had succeeded Cormac as rector of the English College, wrote to Bishop Clark.

June 8, 1978

My Lord

I hope you are keeping well and not too overworked

Kevin O'Sullivan has shown me his letter to you and we have had two or three talks and I thought I should write to you to let you know how I feel about what he has said. It is not easy to strike the right balance. We have discussed his position amongst the staff and are in substantial agreement, but what I say must be my own comment.

Certainly the staff are unanimous in their respect for Kevin. He is a man of many gifts, personal and intellectual; he appears to be a man of prayer and is involved in the charismatic renewal; he has been a good influence in the house. We feel he has the potential to make an excellent priest. We had no hesitation about recommending him for candidacy.

With hindsight one or two of the staff feel he has been less part of the house, less involved, in the last few months. Before he spoke to us questions were raised about whether his mind was really on his work. We knew already that he wanted to do a diaconate year in England and not to stay on for a licentiate in theology.

He has now revealed to me all that he has said to you in his letter and this has left me with at least some question marks.

I respect his integrity and honesty. I find he is a person who talks openly and to whom I can talk. There is great sincerity in his ideals of living a truly Christian life and his desire within this to serve others, especially the poor. I met some such ideals among some students in Exeter. I do not take them lightly and hope that they can be expressed within the church. But I have also talked to him about tolerance and encouraged him to accept within the church those who may have many virtues and many weaknesses and feel this particular form of service is not practical for them. His letter has left me wondering how he would fit into the diocesan priesthood and whether he could have the patience to persevere in it, if he did not see his ideals accepted. His personal vocation may be elsewhere although he is still convinced at present that he would like to be a diocesan priest.

I accept his desire to get away from a clerical institution and I feel that this would be the right thing for him to do at present. Unless he changes during the summer I cannot see him settling here next year. He has suggested that he should go to Heythrop to continue his theology and continue as a student for the diocese although no longer living in the seminary. This could be an experiment in training for the priesthood. I have hesitations about it however. I think without support it will be more difficult for him to persevere and I think also that there is some uncertainty as to where his ideals are leading him. I feel, and I cannot put it stronger than this, but it might be wiser to have a year or two off with a job and let the question of priesthood rest for the time being. He perhaps needs to give himself time and experience before coming to a decision.

I have therefore some doubt about his future. We have recommended him for candidacy and with respect to his personal qualities I had no hesitation in doing so. I am now less sure whether it would be right for him to be accepted as a candidate at this stage. This is something that I hope you and he can decide later.

Finally, I should like to say, that if you and he decide it is right for him to continue here we should be very pleased to have him back; but this would of course mean that he had worked through his present disillusion and I think that would be difficult for him in the course of the summer. My hopes are that he might return after some time away. We are of course not without faults and the challenge he has presented us with can *help to keep us from complacency, but I do not think in his case that it is merely the failure of the College to inspire adequately.*

I feel it right to show him this letter before I send it to you as it might help him in his discussions with you to know what I have said and I would rather be open with him.

With all respects to your Lordship and all good wishes,

Your sincerely,

George Hay

I MET with the bishop in London for our 'chat'. I have no recollection of the meeting itself, but the outcome was that he offered me time out of the seminary, with a twist: if I wanted to be in the world rather than being in a seminary, I could spend a year working in a parish in Liverpool. The surprising thing was that the parish in question was the Anglican parish of St Peter in Everton, Liverpool, where the vicar was a friend and colleague of Alan's, whom he had met through their work together in ARCIC, the Anglican-Roman Catholic International Commission that was examining the possibilities of unity between the Church of Rome and the Anglican Communion. I would get to live in the parish, help out with community work, youth groups, prayer groups, pastoral care. It must have attracted me because I said yes. Or perhaps that was my only option. Who knows? It was arranged that at the end of the summer, instead to going back to Rome, I would present myself for service to the good people of Everton.

NOT KNOWN BECAUSE NOT LOOKED FOR

And the end of all our exploring
Will be to arrive where we started
And know the place for the first time.
T.S.Eliot, *Little Gidding*

There were no rumblings, no hints of unravelling, as I boarded the train at Liverpool Street Station in London for the trip to my adoptive East Anglian home in Stowmarket. Alan's plan for my year in Everton was not unreasonable, I hadn't achieved exactly what I wanted but he had listened to my point of view, and I would have a year in the world with ordinary people, trying to answer my questions about how to put faith into practice in the real world. Chris White was his usual welcoming self, the spare bed was ready, the posy of wildflowers again on the bedside table. He was ready with support and counsel too, and we spent many hours talking about the church and the priesthood and how to walk the path I wanted. I renewed my friendship with Delia and

Michael and told them all that my mum and sister would be coming to live in the town. Delia said her mum would be coming too and it was comforting for me to know that there would be a few friendly faces already when Mum and Bid arrived. Visits to estate agents took up most of my time; this was long before the internet would allow us to search for a house while sitting on the sofa with a cup of tea. I traipsed around town on foot, because anywhere I found would have to be in walking distance of the shops, or more likely in pushing distance, as Mum looked like she would need a wheelchair more and more

Eventually I found number 56 Stowupland Street, a tiny two-storey two-bedroom house on the end of a terrace of four. The back garden was south facing and sunny and the red brick garden wall ran along the west bank of the little River Gipping, all of ten feet wide as it flows south through the town on its way to Ipswich. It was a ten-minute walk into the town for shopping and a level two-minute walk to the train station around the corner. There was a real prospect that Mum might get out and about. It was a much smaller house than the one she was leaving in Dún Laoghaire, but it was hers for as long as she needed it and it was in England! I look back and I think how crazy she was to trust me with moving her from her home of several decades, a settled place, with a garden she had planted and was proud of, and with her things around her. I was backing myself with inexplicable confidence, but she and Bid were the ones taking the risk. I wrote to Sir David Williams, Andrew's dad, and the trust purchased the house, as promised by Andrew, and prepared a 'licence to occupy' for Mum. We were relying on the kindness of strangers.

I went to Dublin for Mum's seventieth birthday in July. We celebrated with dinner at a restaurant in Dún Laoghaire, and a photo from the night reminds me that for the first and only time in my life I had my hair permed. The Art Garfunkel curly look was popular, and I had masses of tiny, crimped curls around my head. When you have a perm, they should show you a photo of what it will look like when it grows out – it might make people think twice and could save them a lot in hairdressing bills. I have the after photo too, where, with the addition of a shaggy beard, I look like a fully paid-up backwoodsman. Now, of course, I would be a hipster, but at the time the term was strictly reserved for low-cut jeans.

The clock was ticking on two plans in tandem: Mum and Bid's move to Stowmarket, and my move to Everton. In practice, the time was taken up with making arrangements for Mum and Bid; for my year in Everton, I just had to turn up, so I put it to the back of my mind. By 1978, some public housing in Ireland was being sold to long-term tenants. My mother had paid a pound a week for twenty years and qualified to buy the property at 16 O'Rourke Park. The problem was that none of us had or could obtain the few thousand pounds it would have cost at the time. Having found out somehow that my mother was moving, more than one person came forward with an offer of cash so that she could buy the house and then sell it to the lender straight away, receiving a modest premium in consideration of the deal. I remember one offer of a thousand pounds – a princely sum in those days, half a year's income for some people. But Mum was naturally conservative and cautious, with the generational fear of 'getting into trouble', even though the arrangement would have been perfectly legal. The usual packing and sorting ensued, with a certain fraying of tempers. My youngest sister Nora, still living at home, was not going to make the move to Stowmarket. After many years of worry and care for the wellbeing of Bid and Mum, she was trying for a clean break, heading to the South of France with a friend to make a new life.

I went on ahead, to see to the house and be there to welcome Mum and Bid when they arrived. As the mail boat left Dún Laoghaire Harbour, I threw my house key into the water in a gesture of finality. There was indeed *a tide in the affairs of men*, and I was taking it at the flood. The war-time exile of thirty-eight years was coming to an end. The new plan might go well, or it might not, but Mum and Bid would both be back in the land where they were born, and closer to their tribe than in a country where they had never really felt accepted.

It's all a bit of a blur, but somehow it worked, and they moved into 56 Stowupland Street, with as much of their furniture as they could accommodate. We celebrated with lunch in The Pickerel, a lovely old Tolly Cobbold pub conveniently situated across the road, complete with polished oak bar, tapestry seat covers, and shining horse brasses hanging on black leather straps. The menu staples were the *Ploughman's Lunch* with crusty bread, cheddar cheese, and pickles, *Scampi in a Basket*, and *Cottage Pie*, which I think is a euphemism for *undefined-ingredients-in-a-thick-gravy*, hidden under mashed potato to prevent too close an inspection. Chris, Delia, and Michael were true to their word and fussed over the new arrivals, inviting us to tea and to dinner. Things started well and I had some satisfaction in having pulled off the move despite the lack of help from my uncles. I had a sense of relief that Mum was now where she had longed to be since I could remember, and I would be a train ride away if help was needed. I felt I could now go and face whatever awaited me in Liverpool. I had a suitcase, a second-hand duffel coat, a perm that was growing out, and a one-way ticket from Euston to Liverpool's Lime Street Station, destination Everton.

When I was a child growing up in Sallynoggin, one of the rituals that punctuated the week was the visit of the insurance man to collect the premiums for the life insurance policies. I'm not sure whose life was covered, possibly my mother's, possibly all of us. The insurance papers lived in small cardboard sleeves each with an illustration of the grand Royal Liver Building on the banks of the Mersey in Liverpool. Atop its two towers, a hundred metres tall, stand the two giant Liver Birds with heads erect and vigilant and wings spread as if to dry. The policies lived in the top drawer of the sideboard and were initialled by the insurance man when the funds, shillings and pence rather than pounds, were handed over. Sometimes there weren't enough shillings, and the insurance man would carry over the debt with an assurance that Mum would make it up the next week, after pension day. In this way I learned at a young age about the possibility of death, not in a morbid way, but as something that was there and should be provided for.

Now, at the age of twenty-five, I was standing less than two miles from the Liver Birds on their towers, in Langrove Street near Everton Park, and I didn't like what I saw. To my eyes it was grim, rundown, decaying, grey, desolate. I had grown up on a council estate in Dublin, surrounded for the most part by families who lived week to week, who scrimped and mended, and made do, but this was different. It seemed barren and sad, and none, not a single one, of the gardens around had a flower or a flowering bush growing in them. I thought despondently of Pádraic Colum's poem about learning, where he laments that,

> *'...east there lies*
> *A city with its men and books;*
> *With treasures open to the wise,*
> *Heart-words from equals, comrade-looks'.*

I thought of my companions walking down sunny streets, past Renaissance *palazzi*, past men and women dressed with the casual elegance of good taste, enticed on corners by the smell of coffee and *pasticcini*, walking into classrooms at the Greg to hear clever people discourse about the world, sitting down to convivial dinners in the *Banchi Vecchi*, and I knew for sure that I had made a mistake. I had heard people say *'Beware what you wish for'*: now I knew what they meant. I knew nothing about the place I had arrived at, other than that it was an 'inner-city parish' in Everton, with all the connotations that this phrase held of being 'run-down' and 'poor' and 'deprived'. I didn't know that this ugly sprawl of buildings in Langrove Street held a fascinating piece of history, social as well as religious.

When St Peter's church was rebuilt in 1974, having been

bombed in 1941, it was built as part of a community centre, youth club, and hostel affectionately called 'The Shewsy'. 'The Shewsy' had started life in 1903 as the Shrewsbury School Mission, an outreach project devised by the masters of the prestigious Shrewsbury School in the broader tradition of the Settlement Movement of the late nineteenth century. 'Settlements' were communities that brought together rich and poor so that they could learn from each other by living, working, playing, and studying together. The first, founded by Church of England minister Samuel Barnett, opened in Toynbee Hall in the East End of London in 1884, with students from Balliol College Oxford and local East Enders. The idea spread fast, and settlements soon opened in other English cities as well as in the United States and Australia. In the late nineteen twenties, my beloved Uncle Richard had lived in a Settlement called Roland House, belonging to the Scouting movement, in Stepney Green, in East London.

When I arrived for my stay in Everton in 1978, the project, now called Shrewsbury House, was already seventy-five years old and had moved into new digs in the rebuilt parish complex in 1974. It was a ground-breaking and still enduring experiment in pastoral and social action, but I knew nothing whatever about its ancestry. To me it simply looked bleak and unwelcoming. It sat in the shadow of three tall tower blocks nicknamed *The Ugly Sisters*, a post-war urban density mistake, and already scheduled for demolition in 1978, although two of them are still there. It's a bit harsh to say that the architect's brief was to make the new church complex fit in as much as possible with its ugly surroundings, but to my jaundiced eyes this seemed to be the outcome. Rather than a building that might inspire, a thing of beauty, 'as *in wild earth a Grecian vase*'[1], or just something pleasant to look at, the visitor is confronted with red brick and more red brick; solid grubby brick walls, two stories high, unrelieved by decoration other than the words 'St Peter's' on the right-hand side, a plain white cross in the middle, and a plaque with times of service on the left. The positioning of these signs suggests they have been purposely put too high up to be vandalised. The church building, which is attached to the rest of the complex, is a hexagon, and from the road you can see three of the angled sides, the rest is hidden from view behind yet more red brick.

The person who was the vicar of St Peter's was also the Warden of Shrewsbury House. 'Warden' was a title I had only ever seen in the Barchester novels of Anthony Trollope, but unlike Hiram's Hospital, the wardenship of the Shewsy was no sinecure. The dozen aged wool-carders in Mr Harding's alms-house were no match for the several hundred rambunctious scouse youth that came to the Shewsy to play, and flirt, and learn, and pray, and occasionally to fight. Julian Charley, the Warden from 1974 to 1987, was a remarkable man, *'A much loved Christian gentleman'* is how his Church Times obituary describes him[2]. Alan had told me nothing about him apart from the fact that he was a keen ecumenist and a member of the Anglican Roman Catholic International Commission, which is presumably why he was happy to have a Roman Catholic seminarian in his Anglican parish. In the previous year we had two Anglican ordinands from Cambridge staying at the English College who, apart from lively theological discussions, provided us with hours of entertainment with their all too accurate mimicry of various Anglican clergy of their acquaintance. In the same year the College accommodated the ecumenically-minded Archbishop of Canterbury, Donald Coggan, on his ground-breaking visit to the Pope. It was a time when the possibility of union seemed real, and Julian Charley played a major role in the movement for change. He was also a member of the Anglican Church's Advisory Council for the Church's Ministry, which had a voice on all aspects of the preparation of men and women for ministry in the church. In short, he would have been the perfect mentor for me to spend a year with - but that wasn't going to happen.

If I had better understood the opportunity that was being

offered to me, would I have stayed? And if I had stayed, would it have been better? I don't know the answer to the first question, but I do know the answer to the second, and it's a 'no'. Whatever has happened in my life has led me to be here, and here I am happy. No hypotheticals are needed.

My stay was short and not altogether sweet. Julian greeted me and welcomed me with the courtesy and openness that was his hallmark, but after a few hours he handed me over to the care of two lads from the Shewsy. I'm not sure what their role was in connection with the church, I think they may have been staying in the youth hostel attached, but I have sometimes wondered whether they were tasked with testing my staying power. Like me, they were in their early twenties and, unlike me, all of their conversation and most of their energy seemed to be focussed on finding girls to have sex with; it puzzled them no end that I didn't share their interest. We spent the afternoon and evening together and my sole recollection of their conversation is about having sex; they talked about nothing else. Even when they told me that the tower blocks at the end of the road were due for demolition, they peppered the story with accounts of their exploits with 'girls from the flats'. Explanations that I was a catholic seminarian, and I was preparing for a life of celibacy, didn't impress them at all. They sort of understood that in the future I might have a vow of celibacy, they knew about Roman Catholic priests, but it just didn't compute for them that I would not at least *want* to have sex with a pretty girl I saw.

In this, and completely unbeknown to themselves, they did me a huge favour. I believe that afternoon was the moment when I first truly acknowledged to myself that my sexuality was a major issue that needed to be faced and resolved. There was nothing these young men were saying that I could relate to or even wanted to try to relate to. What did that say about me? I began to agree with them, in my head, that my explanations didn't wash. I wasn't celibate because I had a blissfully strong sense of vocation that helped me sublimate my desires and removed my interest in women. I was celibate because I had no interest in women, at least as far as sex went.

Previously, as a teenager and as a young man, I knew that I sometimes had erotic thoughts about men, but I also knew that making those thoughts a reality was simply not an option. It was sinful, mortally sinful, wrong, taboo, dirty. The words in my head for men who were attracted to men were all insults: Nancy-boy, poofter, queer, pansy, fairy. I knew no one, or at least I wasn't aware of knowing anyone, who was homosexual and who looked like someone I wanted to be like. Danny la Rue and Liberace both came into our living room once we hired a television when I was eleven years old, but they were sniggered at with the flapping of a wrist and tolerated because of their talent, unlike the young man in the barber shop who had a scrubbed face and was rumoured to wear eyeliner. Even before the vow of chastity or the prospect of priestly celibacy took the matter out of my hands, I knew that I if I were to have a relationship, I would want it to be with a woman. Apart from being sinful, the idea of a relationship with a man seemed strange and somehow pointless. Why would anyone do that? Surely it would be much better to try and have a relationship with a woman, to have a family, a future? I somehow thought that I just had to try a bit harder.

Then came the Legion with its strict prohibition of physical touch, its focus on sin and imperfection, and its obsession with banning 'particular friendships'. All of these prescriptions heightened our sensitivity and for some of us, certainly not just me, they increased the natural desire for emotional contact and the touch of another.

Next came the experience of the English College, relaxed, friendly, open, where connecting and bonding with other males could happen without sexual overtones. In College I had experienced being loved, being valued, being held as dear. The broader Italian culture in which we lived also had much more space for physical contact, handshakes, kisses on the cheek, hugs of greeting and goodbye. Young men regularly walked arm in arm or with a hand draped over a male friend's shoulder. All of this allowed for some expression of my craving for contact and allowed it to the point where my affection found sufficient outlets so as not to need to go further. But now all of that was stripped away. I was in a church hostel in a bleak part of a strange city, where I knew no one except the Warden and these two sex-obsessed young men.

When Rosencrantz and Guildenstern finally left me and went to the pub to find someone to have sex with, I was left alone in my graceless room. It was nine feet by twelve, painted off-white, a single bed with a foam mattress, a desk and chair, a view of the car park through a thinly-curtained window: it held nothing to relieve my sickening sense of failure. Gone was the buttery, sunny light, gone were the easy chairs, the pleasant, framed prints handed on to me that I might in turn hand on to another; gone were the sounds and smells of the *Campo de' Fiori* and the interminable tolling of ancient bells. I could expect no friendly knock on the door to invite me to impromptu and convivial *drinks before*. And the crazy thing was that I hadn't been banished from Paradise; I had run away in a huff.

How quickly it all unravelled, like Mike's bankruptcy in Hemingway's crisp phrase, '*gradually, and then suddenly*'. The endgame would have made a decent Greek tragedy, with the three classical unities of action, place and time all intact, unfolding in twenty-four hours and in one place. I was miserable, lonely, and unreasonably angry at Alan who I felt had dumped me in this forsaken place, whereas all he had done was to try and accommo-date my desire to be in the world. I sat on the side of my bed with my head in my hands and owned up to having made a huge mistake, and not only that, to having fooled myself for too many years about who I was. Sometimes, one train of thought that shows us in a good light prevents us from thinking other thoughts that are less flattering. All the clichés about the past catching up, and the arrival of the day of reckoning, and *The higher they fly the further they fall*, mocked me without pity: *Ha! You said you were saving others. Try saving yourself!* I was tired of explaining myself and my sins, and my almost sins, to older men who I allowed to be the arbiters of my worth - to Izquierdo, to Arumí, to Acevedo, to Dueñas, to Maciel, flawed men all, and then to George Hay and Alan Clark, much better men, but still sitting in judgement. I didn't want to add Julian Charley to the list, and I did want to be answerable to myself for my own decisions. My one-sided conversation with God on the roof at via Aurelia was with me still: I *had* this. I could trust myself, and if I made a mess, it was my mess.

I've never been one to hang around when it's clear to me I've made a mistake and I'm in the wrong place, so I did something I had sometimes done before and have never done since: I took out my Bible and opened it at random for guidance. For the uninitiated, this is where you open the Holy Book and trust that whatever verse your eye sees will contain some kind of useful advice about your predicament. Holy Moly if the verse I saw wasn't Mark 5:17: 'And they began to beg him to leave their city'. I needed no further prompting. I got some sleep, and early the next morning I packed, left a note for Julian, went to Lime Street, and a matter of hours later I pitched up once again in London.

On the train ride I remembered a day in the summer of 1963, I was eleven years old, sitting at the red Formica table in the kitchen in O'Rourke Park with my sisters Nora and Margaret, having our toast and marmalade and tea and corn flakes. My mother came into the kitchen in her long pink candlewick dressing gown, with her hair unbrushed and her face streaked with tears. She held a crumpled note in her right hand. She looked unsteady and leaned against the wooden draining board behind her. 'She's gone', she said. 'Mary's gone', and her face puckered into sadness and betrayal and failure. My sister Mary had left a note on her pillow the night before, and by breakfast time, as we sat at the kitchen table, she was probably on the same train that I was on now. It was sad, but it was swift, and surgical, and quickly accomplished: no rows, no shouting matches. Better like that than the frightening raised voices when my oldest brother had rebelled and come to blows with my mother. Far better. Mary had become Heidi and was now the happy mother of two gorgeous kids in faraway Melbourne. Things could work out.

The train line from Liverpool to London is practical rather than picturesque. The surveyors of the terrain traced the straightest line possible between the two great cities, and the only points of any charm are Nuneaton, the birthplace of George Eliot, and Rugby, home of the eponymous school. Otherwise, the train simply gets you as fast as it can to Euston station. From about Watford Junction, you know that you're approaching London, and by Harrow and Willesden you're surrounded by endless sprawl. Nearer in, the two-storey suburbs give way to higher and higher buildings that eventually tower over the railway as it snakes into the maze. Here is a place you can get lost, be anonymous, reinvent yourself. Walking out into the blank cityscape, no one knows you're there; you're unnoticed amid the rush of a million others.

The train glided to a halt under the practised hand of the driver. I gathered my things and prepared for whatever was next. I knew that the train ride to Euston was most definitely the end of something. I guessed that it must also be the beginning of something, but of what, I had no idea. All I knew was that Brutus's words, that I had thought applied to my mother and her move back to England, now applied to me:

> On such a full sea are we now afloat,
> And we must take the current when it serves,
> Or lose our ventures.

I knew what I had to do: I walked out into Euston Road to take the current and pursue new ventures.

AFTERWORD

EQUAL HOPE AND HAZARD IN THE
GLORIOUS ENTERPRISE

I am aware that I have left the reader abruptly, standing, somewhat perplexed perhaps, in the Euston Road, wondering what has happened and what is about to happen to the well-behaved young man they had accompanied for twenty-five years. He seems to walk away and not look back, going perhaps to find a cup of tea and a cheese sandwich and consider what to do. There is a lot to take in, and Milton's brave phrase from *Paradise Lost* is not quite accurate, not yet. Just now the hopes are vague and the hazards appear in a sharper light. If we could see into the future, we might find the young man, for the next fifteen years, shovel in hand, working through the detritus of his own Augean Stables before emerging into some further clarity about life, the universe, and everything. But that is another story and for another day.

As to the Legionaries of Christ, in March 2022, when I had drafted the last chapter of this book, I wrote to John Lane Connor, the current Director General of the Legion of Christ, to formally report Guillermo Izquierdo's behaviour: a gesture of closure for me. In addition to writing to Connor in Rome, I sent the report, via the website 0abusos.org, to the Designated Liaison Person, Ireland, whose role is to receive reports of abuse committed in the Legion of Christ.

In his courteous reply, the Liaison Person thanked me for bringing this to his attention and gave me the name and address in Dublin of an officer in the Garda Siochána, the Irish Police, to whom I could report the abuse. I did so.

John Connor also replied, offering me *'an unreserved apology for the unacceptable situation'* and telling me that the Legion would be happy to provide me with the professional aid that I considered necessary to address any issues that continued to affect me *'from this most unfortunate experience'.*

I accepted his response in good faith, but I worry that there may still be those who cannot believe the extent of the wrong-doing perpetrated by Maciel and by other Legionary priests, like Izquierdo.

In the meticulously researched 2013 documentary *Scandal at the Vatican* (https://www.youtube.com/watch?v=QcBx0TMMIfE) there is a chilling moment when the film makers attend an Open Day at an Apostolic School run by the Legion in Mèry-sur-Marne, an hour east of Paris. They carry a hidden camera. As they chat to the Legionary who has shown them around, the film-maker asks him how he accounts for the fall of Maciel. The Legionary replies:

*'The fact that Maciel had this life really saddens me. This man who was destined to become a saint, and today the founder is reduced to nothing. That makes me very sad for him. But I think that history will do justice to this man. How could such a man as twisted and evil **as they say he was**,*[emphasis added] *have created a community such as this?'*

Cognitive dissonance may be alive and well.

It is no surprise then that two Legionaries teaching at the school at Mèry-sur-Marne were convicted of child molestation in 2013 and were each sentenced to two years in prison, although one of the convicted men fled to Mexico.

There are now a number of groups that offer moral support to ex-Legionaries, principally the ReGAIN network (https://regain-network.org) available in English and Spanish, and the International Cultic Studies Association (https://www.icsahome.com). Those who have been hurt by their contact with the Legion or with Regnum Christi can now contact these groups and they can also report abuse via the 0abusos.org website.

There are several books that describe life inside the Legion, and all are available online, although not all are in English.

Memoirs

Our Father Maciel Who Art in Bed - My life in the Legion of Christ, by J. Paul Lennon

Driving Straight on Crooked Lines, by Jack Keogh

Yo Acuso al Padre Maciel y a la Legión de Cristo, by Francisco González Parga

Moi, Ancien Légionnaire du Christ, by Xavier Léger

History / Critique

Vows of Silence - The abuse of power in the papacy of John Paul II, by Jason Berry and Gerald Renner

Marcial Maciel - Los Legionarios de Cristo: testimonios y documentos inéditos, by Fernando M. González

El imperio financiero de los Legionarios de Cristo, by Raúl Olmos

NOTES

10. THE NOVITIATE

1. Investigators concluded that he abused minors under his charge as novice director in Cheshire, Connecticut, 1982-1993. https://legionar-iesofchrist.org/members-of-the-religious-congregation-of-the-legionaries-of-christ-who-were-active-in-ministry-in-the-united-states-with-substanti-ated-sexual-abuse-allegations/
2. Raúl Olmos, *El Imperio Financiero del los Legionarios de Cristo*
3. https://pedrojuarezmauss.com/2014/07/11/obediencia-perfecta-en-isla-mujeres/
4. One of the best is *Vows of Silence* by Jason Berry and Gerald Renner

12. MADRID

1. A wonderfully formal way of saying *'the ashphalting of the road system'*
2. *'Hey, careful where you put your biro!'*

13. MONTICCHIO

1. *'Excuse me Madame, we're on the train to Italy. It's just about to leave. We need...'*
2. *'A peaceful evening, Rome in the distance'*

14. ROME 1974-1976

1. Francisco Gonzalez Parga (2010). *Yo Acuso al Padre Maciel y a la Legion de Cristo.* ISBN 97814564411336

15. THINGS FALL APART: ROME 1975-1976

1. *A thing is good if it entirely good. If it has any defect, it is bad.* Attributed to Diony-sius the Areopagite, 1st century CE.

16. ROME: THE ESCAPE PLAN

1. *Entonces por favor, que me mande a casa*
2. *'It was only a little honey, but it warmed my body, and in my heart it still burns like a great sun'*

17. AYR 1976

1. *'Thus passes the glory of the world'*

18. BACK TO ROME

1. His name is celebrated twice in Rome, with another college called The Pontifical Beda College that caters for English-speaking men who are so-called 'late vocations', men who have come to training after the age of thirty. In the nineteen seventies, in comparison to the Venerabile, the Beda was an altogether more staid affair.

19. NO PLACE LIKE HOME

1. When I checked this quotation I found that it is attributed to Bruce Lee (!). I'm pretty sure he didn't have an entry in *Philosophy Made Simple*, nor did he belong to the Circle of Vienna

21. THEOLOGY: DECLINE AND FALL

1. *Trippa alla romana* is a delicious dish with thin strips of tripe in spicy sauce. I once had three helpings in one sitting – one for each course.

22. GOODBYE TO ALL THAT

1. STL – *Sacrae Theologiae Licentia*, a post graduate degree in theology
2. Rector of the English College, successor to Cormac Murphy O'Connor
3. STB – A bachelor's degree in theology

23. NOT KNOWN BECAUSE NOT LOOKED FOR

1. Padraic Colum *A Poor Scholar of the Forties*
2. The Church Times 22 September 2017, Obituary by The Rt Revd Dr Colin Buchanan

Made in United States
North Haven, CT
10 July 2022

21175479R00152